TIBERIUS
The Resentful Caesar

By GREGORIO MARAÑÓN

With a Foreword by
RONALD SYME
CAMDEN PROFESSOR OF ANCIENT HISTORY
IN THE UNIVERSITY OF OXFORD

DUELL, SLOAN AND PEARCE
New York

COPYRIGHT, 1956, BY DUELL, SLOAN & PEARCE, INC.

All rights reserved. No part of this book in excess of five hundred words may be reproduced in any form without permission in writing from the publisher.

First Edition

This translation from the original Spanish, *Tiberio: Historia de un resentimiento* (Espasa-Calpe, Madrid), was made by Warre Bradley Wells.

MANUFACTURED IN THE UNITED STATES OF AMERICA

VAN REES PRESS • NEW YORK

FOREWORD

by

RONALD SYME

Camden Professor of Ancient History in the University of Oxford

HISTORIANS have a lot to answer for. It has become almost impossible to think of Tiberius apart from Tacitus. Hence a problem. How far does the Tacitian Tiberius correspond to fact and equity, how far is he a literary creation—the crafty and rancorous tyrant? The rehabilitation of Tiberius has been practised for more than a century, most assiduously. Scholarly research has demonstrated (and it is clear enough) that many features were admirable in that ruler's administration of the Empire. That is not all. Bad men can be good emperors. What manner of man was Tiberius Cæsar? Perhaps the restorers, sober and diligent, have washed most of the colour off the picture.

Tiberius belonged to no ordinary family. The patrician Claudii left their stamp on many epochs in the long history of the Roman Republic. They tended to be ruthless and innovatory. Tiberius, however, with all the Claudian arrogance, was conservative and old-fashioned, as he showed in his tastes and his vocabulary: he preferred archaic words, and he had no liking for the new literary glories of Augustan Rome. An anachronism in more ways than one (and proud of it), Tiberius Cæsar was in his fifty-fifth year when he came to power. He then told his Roman Senate that his nature was set and would never change—so long as he retained control of his faculties.

To understand the man and his predicament, it is necessary to go back a long way. Tiberius was of the opposition: doubly so, personal and political. His parents had been on the side of the Republic in the contest against the military despotism of the triumvirs. After certain vicissitudes, the boy's mother, Livia Drusilla, was annexed by one of the triumvirs, the upstart Octavian, who was to become Cæsar Augustus and stage a 'Restoration of the Republic.' Tiberius owed honour and advancement to Augustus, but his younger brother, Drusus, enjoyed greater favour and affection from the stepfather (and some believed that Drusus was the son of Augustus). Drusus died, but there were the grandsons of Augustus, the princes Caius and Lucius, whom he adopted and marked out as the heirs to his monarchic station.

Tiberius quarrelled with Augustus and went away angrily to Rhodes, there to sojourn in the company of classical scholars and astrologers, in exile self-imposed. He might never have returned. It was only the deaths of the young princes that compelled Augustus to choose Tiberius as his successor.

Tiberius could never forget the humiliations he had endured. Reminded of the past when as emperor he was delivering a speech to the Senate, he broke out into a savage attack on one of his enemies, a certain Marcus Lollius, dead twenty years before. (The historian Tacitus was careful to register the incident.)

A grim and morose person, *tristissimus hominum* so the elder Pliny styled him, Tiberius was ill at ease under the heavy inheritance of Cæsar Augustus, resentful towards the smooth, perfidious men who profited from the monarchy, and suspicious (with good reasons) of his entourage. To one man alone he surrendered his confidence (it is reported), to Sejanus, the Prefect of the Guard, and that to the point of infatuation. Deceived at last, or fancying himself deceived, he had to plot the ruin of the minister whom he had raised so high. Sejanus, when expecting a full association in the imperial power, was circumvented by arts the equal of his own, and the famous despatch from Capri, *verbosa et grandis epistola*, consigned him to destruction. After that exhibition of virtuosity, who could fail to regard Tiberius Cæsar as a master of dissimulation?

Tiberius is a proper subject for a psychologist, and, perhaps, for a doctor. Gregorio Marañón happens to be both, and it is no accident that his other field of historical investigation should be the court of Philip II—and precisely the favourite Antonio Pérez, who captured the trust of that pedantic and suspicious ruler. Like other politicians in that age, the minister of Philip read Tacitus as his author of predilection: on his own avowal he saw himself in the rôle of Sejanus, and he was a Sejanus who escaped the toils and survived to compose his memoirs.

The record of Rome and the Cæsars has been worked upon with minute study. It is too much to expect that everybody will follow Dr. Marañón all the way (details or interpretation). None the less, his testimony must be heard with respect. He offers something new and much-needed—the resentments of Tiberius as the principal clue to an enigmatic emperor and to a reign that began with fine prospects and terminated in despotism.

CONTENTS

FOREWORD v

PROLOGUE

I. LIFE AND HISTORY 3
   Truth and legend, p. 3; The truth and the legend about Tiberius, p. 5.

II. THE THEORY OF RESENTMENT 9
   Definitions, p. 9; Resentment, generosity and affection, p. 10; Intelligence and resentment, p. 11; Envy, hatred and resentment, p. 11; Timidity, gratitude and hypocrisy in relation to resentment, p. 12; Social success and resentment, p. 13; Age, sex, æsthetics and resentment, p. 14; False virtue in the resentful man, p. 17; Appearance and resentment, p. 17; Humour and resentment, p. 18; Success and the resentful man, p. 18.

PART I: THE ROOTS OF RESENTMENT

I. CHILDHOOD IN EXILE 23
   The crucial date, p. 23; Tiberius's parents, p. 23; The omen, p. 25; The flight, p. 26.

II. DOMESTIC TRAGEDY 28
   Livia's divorce, p. 28; Who was Drusus's father? p. 30; The resignation of Tiberius Claudius Nero, p. 35.

III. TIBERIUS'S LOVE-LIFE 36
   Tiberius's marriage to Vipsania, Atticus's granddaughter, p. 36; Divorce from Vipsania, p. 37; History repeats itself, p. 38; Asinius Gallus, the implacable rival, p. 40; The vengeance of Tiberius, p. 42.

IV. TIBERIUS'S LOVE-LIFE (*continued*) 43
   Julia the Mad, p. 43; Julia's husbands and lovers, p. 46; Tiberius's sexual timidity, p. 49; Tiberius's left-handedness, p. 50; Julia's scorn, p. 51; Tiberius's flight through timidity, p. 53; The legend of Capri, p. 54; Julia's exile, p. 57; Punishment of the lover, p. 58; The populace and Julia, p. 59; Portrait of Julia, p. 59.

CONTENTS

PART II: THE CLASH OF CLANS

I. JULIANS VERSUS CLAUDIANS 63

Warring passions, p. 63; Tiberius's triumphs, p. 64; Genealogical memorandum, p. 66; Outline of the clash of families, p. 67; A stepfather's antipathy, p. 67; Marcellus versus Tiberius. Agrippa's anger, p. 69; The new Cæsars, p. 72; Lucius and Caius versus Tiberius, p. 74; Death of the two Cæsars, p. 76; Augustus adopts Tiberius, p. 78; The elimination of Agrippa Postumus, p. 78; Germanicus versus Tiberius, p. 79; Augustus's death. Tiberius's embittered triumph, p. 80.

II. CLAUDIANS VERSUS JULIANS 83

Livia, virtue incarnate, p. 83; The strength of sexual austerity, p. 84; The tragedy of Scribonia, p. 85; Livia's ambition, p. 87; Augustus's cleverness. Torment in the night, p. 90; Psychology of the last phase in the struggle, p. 91; Death and resurrection of Agrippa Postumus, p. 92; Germanicus, the popular hero, p. 96; Relations between Tiberius and Germanicus. The old debt, p. 97; Germanicus's journey to the East. The legend of poisoning, p. 99; Rupture between Livia and Tiberius, p. 102.

III. AGRIPPINA THE MANNISH 105

Agrippina's exploits and qualities, p. 105; Germanicus's conjugal patience and final farewell, p. 107; Tiberius versus Agrippina, p. 108; Agrippina's attempt to re-marry, p. 111; End of Agrippina and her sons, p. 112; Agrippina's guilt, p. 114; The death of Agrippina, p. 114.

IV. TIBERIUS'S SONS 116

Drusus II, the sportsman, p. 116; Marriage of Drusus and Livilla, p. 118; Livilla's belated beauty, p. 119; Mamercus Scaurus. Eudemus the Doctor, p. 120; The legend of Drusus's poisoning, p. 121; The 'vendetta', p. 125.

V. THE DRAMA OF SEJANUS 127

Sejanus's life and ambition, p. 127; Sejanus's intrigues, p. 132; Trials of Silius and Sabinus, p. 133; Persecution of Caligula and Antonia's intervention, p. 135; Downfall and death of Sejanus, p. 136; The guilt of Tiberius and Sejanus, p. 138; Why Caligula was saved, p. 140; Sejanus's character, p. 142; The monstrous law, p. 143.

PART III: OTHER CHARACTERS

I. TERENTIUS 147

An exemplary speech, p. 147; The eternal voice, p. 149.

II. Antonia, or Rectitude 150
The happy pair, p. 150; Drusus's death, p. 152; The exemplary widow, p. 152; The weak-minded son, p. 153; Antonia and Tiberius, p. 154; The final bitterness, p. 155.

III. Tiberius's Friends 157
Unfaithful friends. Agrippa the Jew, p. 157; Faithful friends. Lucilius Longus, p. 158; Nerva's suicide, p. 159; Messalinus Cotta's jests, p. 161.

PART IV: THE PROTAGONIST

I. Tiberius's Person, Health and Death . . . 165
Portrait of Tiberius, p. 165; His strength. His short-sightedness, p. 166; His fetid ulcers, p. 167; Tiberius's busts, p. 168; The baldness of the emperors, p. 170; Psychology and appearance, p. 171; The 'colum', p. 172; His sobriety, p. 172; Tiberius and the doctors, p. 173; The emperor's death, p. 174.

II. The Ogre's Virtues 176
Tiberius's governmental tradition, p. 176; His military qualities, p. 176; Tiberius's culture, p. 177; His political mistakes, p. 178; His concern for discipline, p. 179; Philanthropy and charity, p. 180; Tiberius's austerity, p. 181.

III. Timidity and Scepticism 183
Tiberius's timidity, p. 183; His mother and his favourites, p. 184; Crises of will-power, p. 185; The timid sceptic, p. 186; Persecution of religion, p. 187; Tiberius and omens, p. 188; Consolation in the stars, p. 189.

IV. Antipathy 191
Two kinds of antipathy, p. 191; The displeasing gesture, p. 192; Tiberius's unpopularity, p. 192; Strictness without warmth, p. 194; From unpopularity to hatred, p. 196.

V. Resentment and Informing 199
Tiberius's ambivalence, p. 199; The cycle of resentment, p. 199; Informing, p. 201.

VI. Solitude and Anguish 204
Tiberius's resentment and his humour, p. 204; 'Island' psychology, p. 205; The flight to Rhodes, p. 207; 'Callipide', p. 209; The flight to Capri, p. 210; Abnormality and madness, p. 211; The tragic round, p. 214.

EPILOGUE
Death of the Phœnix 219

APPENDICES
Genealogical Tables of the Imperial Families . 224
Chronological Summary of Tiberius's Life . 227
Bibliography 231

Prologue

I
LIFE AND HISTORY

Truth and Legend

ALL we know about the public and private life of Tiberius comes from four main sources: the *Annals* of Tacitus; Suetonius's book, *The Twelve Cæsars*; and the Histories of Rome by Dion Cassius and Velleius Paterculus. We also find some interesting, but purely incidental, references in Josephus's *Jewish Antiquities*, and in the works of Philo, Juvenal, Ovid, the Plinys, and the Spaniard Seneca. But for a few details, mostly of a chronological kind, modern research, archæological and epigraphic, has been able to add scarcely anything to what has been handed down to us by these historians and authors.

History, however, is made up not only of data, but also of interpretations. The same facts as seen by the historians of the Middle Ages, the Renaissance, the seventeenth and eighteenth centuries, or the liberal decades that followed the French Revolution, appear to the present-day observer in quite a different light. Fresh knowledge in the various branches of human learning, or simply greater experience in history, enables us to explain many things which once seemed obscure, or to give a new interpretation to something already known. Above all, this progress has been influenced by the application, nowadays quite common (though not always very successful), of the science of biology to the study of classical history.

Classical history used to be almost exclusively chronological and archæological. Often it was sheer scenography. Reading not only ancient historical tomes, but even ambitious treatises of modern times, the reader feels as though he were present at some vast theatrical spectacle, in which, thanks to patient research, the environment, the clothing, the doings and the sayings of a dead and gone character are faithfully reconstructed. As though on the stage, expert actors solemnly reproduce the great tragi-comedy of the past.

But, if we compare the life thus resuscitated with the life which every one of us is living, we realize how ingenuous is this artifice. The personages who represent before our eyes the great rôles of heroes or heroines are, in fact, simply symbolical types: one is the good king, another the gallant knight, the invincible general, the traitor, the martyr, the spurned wife, the *femme fatale*.

If one thing is certain, however, it is that in this life every human being plays several different parts: the rôles imposed upon him by the secret forces which germinate in his soul combined, in inexorable variation, with his reaction to his environment, to other people, and to cosmic influences. We are, whether we know it or not, blind instruments of the contradictory working of fate, whose secret significance God alone knows.

The effort to which modern writers devote themselves is to transform all this stylized representation of history into real life. Life and history are one and the same thing: the pompous history of the past is our own humble, daily lives. The life of today will be history tomorrow, just as it is today, without passing through the professors' paraphernalia of humbug.

Experts in classical history used to strive, above all, to winnow exact data from legend in the legacy of antiquity. The naturalist of today knows that legend makes up a part of the life that is gone, and that, in order to understand this life, legend is just as important, just as essential, as formal history itself. Together with any given fact which history records springs legend too, from its very source. It represents the reaction of his environment to the personality of the character concerned, or to the overriding nature of the event. Accordingly it teaches us much about the environment and much about the character, and, accordingly again, part of the real truth about what happened.

It is both from fact and legend, therefore, that we should try to reconstruct history, interpreting them in accordance with the criterion of the naturalist. I stress this word 'naturalist,' so wide in its scope, in order to offset any suspicion that I am concerned here to defend any purely psychological interpretation—so much in vogue in present-day literature—of historical characters and their doings. On the contrary, it seems to me that most of these interpretations, set forth in a strict and arbitrary terminology, are inevitably doomed to disappear.

Life, which is wider than history, is much wider than psychiatry, that non-existent science, and, above all, wider than certain schools of psychiatry. Life is doubtless largely a matter of psychology, in the broadest, almost the empirical sense of that term; but it is never a matter of pathology, as understood by neuropaths in the latest fashion.

The Truth and the Legend about Tiberius

These considerations apply, in a singularly exact way, to the life of Tiberius. The ancient historians, some of them close contemporaries of the emperor, others living very little later,[1] have handed down to us a picture of his reign made up of the usual mixture of history and legend; but Tiberius happened to be one of the great historical characters in whose cases it is very hard to place the point at which history ends and legend begins.

The apologia for him written by his contemporary Velleius Paterculus is pure legend, but based upon the emperor's unquestionable virtues. Suetonius's diatribe is legend too, but similarly based upon the emperor's undeniable vices. We find legend even in his marble statues, which present his features to us as impeccable, whereas their pristine beauty was disfigured by repulsive ulcers and scars.

[1] Tacitus and Suetonius wrote roughly a century after Tiberius's death. As for their sources—documents of the period and narratives by old people who had lived through it—one may agree with Fabia that they were almost contemporary with Tiberius (Fabia, 25, p. 342). (In my bibliographical references, figures in italic relate to the bibliography at the end of the book.) Dion Cassius came later: he was born about the year A.D. 170. Velleius Paterculus was a close contemporary: he probably died before the end of Tiberius's reign. Philo Judæus's lifetime also covered much of that of Tiberius: 20 B.C. to sometime after A.D. 54. Flavius Josephus, again, was almost a contemporary: he was born in Jerusalem about the year A.D. 37 and spent part of his life in Rome, where he died when the first century was drawing to a close. Ovid, Seneca, and Pliny the Elder were also contemporaries. Pliny the Younger lived at the same time as Tacitus. Concerning all these historians and writers and the value of their testimony about Tiberius, see my book (66). The first draft of that book, entitled *The Avatar of Tiberius Cæsar*, was in fact a broad introduction to the present biography.

On the basis of these two facets of the truth, the historical and the legendary, modern commentators, in accordance with the temper of the time, have gone on making interpretations of Tiberius which are not merely different, but diametrically opposed. All of them are equally history, for they represent what every phase of human thought has kept on adding to his personality, in a process which did not end with his death, but perpetuated itself afterwards in his reputation, in endless evolution.

For many centuries Tiberius was regarded by humanity as a monster, almost comparable with Nero or Caligula in his iniquity. It has been said that his ill repute was influenced by the Christian culture which filled the Middle Ages and the beginning of modern times: not for nothing was Tiberius the emperor of Pontius Pilate, who let Christ be crucified through cowardice.

But it is unquestionable that all the evil we know about him was recorded by two historians who never achieved real understanding of the new doctrine: Suetonius and Tacitus. Tacitus, moreover, shared the hatred or contempt for Christians which was felt by the Roman society of his time. Christian reaction, accordingly, may have helped towards establishing the idea of Tiberius's infamy; but it did not create it.

On the other hand, it is undeniable that the emperor's rehabilitation was influenced by the rationalist, and sometimes the decidedly anti-Christian, spirit of modern historical writing, from the end of the eighteenth century onwards. Let us not forget that one of Tiberius's first defenders, and therefore one of those who had the most influence in creating an atmosphere favourable to him, was Voltaire.[1] Other revolutionary writers, such as Linguet, served him as chorus. One of the legends against which Voltaire rose in rebellion was precisely the legend that Tiberius contemplated becoming a Christian.

Then came the apologetic revisions of Tiberius's character by French, German and English historians, many of them infused with Protestant puritanism, for in many aspects, in fact, this Cæsar

---

[1] In my book already mentioned (66), I carefully studied Voltaire's attitude towards Tiberius and Tacitus, together with his motives, which were of political rather than historical interest.

presents himself as a predecessor of Calvin. Finally came more historians, Italian this time, whom the prevalent nationalism of their own country made favourable towards such vindication of the great figures of ancient Rome.

But it would be incorrect to say that the rehabilitation, and indeed the glorification, of Tiberius were the result solely of sectarian or nationalist prejudice. It is obvious that these views were readily grafted upon the fact of the undeniable political virtues possessed by the hated Cæsar, already definitely set on record in the works of his contemporaries, which were much less biased than is commonly supposed. It is true that they told us all about his bad qualities; but who, if not they, would have enlightened us about his good ones?

In these alternations of historical thought about Tiberius we find, above all, that prejudice, to which I have already referred, in favour of the myth of the representative personage: in other words, preoccupation with a character who is an archetype, made all of a piece. In the eyes of some people, Tiberius was a human being thoroughly wicked, from the beginning of his life to its end; and, as he was despotic and cruel, it followed that he was a bad ruler, responsible for all the calamities of his time. In the eyes of others, he was a model of bureaucratic perfection; in the words of Mommsen,[1] the *pontifex maximus* of the history (though not of the life) of Roman civilization, 'the most capable emperor Rome ever had'; and, as he administered his empire beautifully, it followed that he was also a faultless man, a loving son, a person of just mind and kindly nature.

But the truth is that, if ever there was a man whose life was an example of alternations of mind and changes in conduct, an example of a personality made up, not of uniform material, but of diverse and contrasting bits and pieces, that man was Tiberius.

Tacitus, who saw him close enough and through the eyes of genius, has given the best definition of his character. 'His behaviour,' says Tacitus, 'varied in accordance with his age.' He was 'a mixture of good and bad until his mother's death.'[2] Dion calls him 'a prince of good and bad qualities at one and the same time.'[3]

[1] Mommsen, 72, XIX.   [2] Tacitus, *107*, VI, 51.   [3] Dion, 22, LVII, 23.

So he is depicted by Pliny the elder: 'the saddest of men'; 'a ruler at once austere and sociable,' who 'in his later years turned stern and cruel.'[1] Similarly Seneca, when he refers to his good government, does so exclusively in connection with the early years of his emperorship.[2]

To all this, which happens to be the truth, which happens to be life, historians, fascinated by the myth of the character made all of a piece, reply that there is some humbug here, and that, if Tiberius was good at the beginning, he must have been good at the end. As for his vices during his later years in Capri—probably an invention—they are refuted with the one argument which is quite worthless: namely, that a man who was chaste until he was seventy could not possibly launch out into licence from that age onwards.

In fact, every age in a man's life may mean quite a different life, and not only any age, but also, on occasion, any year or even any hour in it, may, given some overruling cause, entitle us to assume a fresh phase within the vast scope of human personality.

This occurs, above all, in the case of men like Tiberius, whose life, despite appearances to the contrary, is almost exclusively an inner life; because in their cases the impact of environment, especially when it is so great as the impact which Tiberius endured, produces a fermentation of feeling that breaks out, when it is least expected, in some arbitrary form of conduct. This fermentation is what we call resentment.

Tiberius was, in fact, an authentic example of the resentful man. It is for this reason that I have chosen him as the subject of this study, begun many years ago now, at the time of my juvenile reading of Tacitus.

So I make no claim to write yet another biography of Tiberius, but rather a study of his resentment.

---

[1] Pliny, 79.

[2] Seneca, 101, I. Some authors have quoted this passage as favourable to Tiberius, but the great Spanish writer speaks expressly of the merciful reign of the divine Augustus and 'of the earlier years of Tiberius Cæsar': in other words, later his mercifulness came to an end. See also Seneca's passage about informing (100, III, 26), which is a violent attack on the later years of Tiberius's reign. I shall comment on this further in Chapter V of Part IV.

II

THE THEORY OF RESENTMENT

Definitions

'AMONG the deadly sins,' once wrote Don Miguel de Unamuno, 'resentment does not figure, and yet it is the gravest of all: worse than anger, worse than pride.' In fact, resentment is not a sin, but a passion, a passion of the mind; though, to be sure, it may lead to sin, and sometimes to madness or crime.

It is hard to define the passion of resentment. Some impact upon us of another person—or simply of life, in that imponderable and varying form which we are accustomed to term 'bad luck' —produces in us a sense, fleeting or lasting, of pain, of failure, or of one form or another of inferiority. Then we say that we are 'hurt' or 'sore.'

In normal conditions, the wonderful aptitude of the human mind for getting rid of disagreeable components of our consciousness makes this feeling of pain disappear after a certain lapse of time. In any case, if it persists, it is transformed into ordinary resignation.

But, in abnormal conditions, the impact remains present in the depths of our consciousness, perhaps unknown to us. Down there, the resulting bitterness incubates and ferments. It infiltrates throughout our whole being; and it ends by becoming the director of our behaviour, of our slightest reactions. This feeling, which has not been eliminated, but on the contrary has been retained and incorporated in our very soul, is resentment.

Whether an affective impact produces the passing reaction which we call 'being hurt,' or whether it produces 'resentment,' does not depend upon the nature of the impact, but upon the make-up of the person who receives it. A similar reverse of fortune, a similar failure in some undertaking, a similar slight from some snob, may be suffered by a number of people at the same time and with the same intensity. But, in the case of some, it will cause simply a fleeting feeling of depression or pain. In the case of others, it will be felt for ever.

Accordingly, the first problem which our study of resentment suggests is to find out which characters are susceptible to its attack and which are immune from it.

Resentment, Generosity and Affection

If we review the human material at our disposal—in other words, the resentful people we have known in the course of our lives, and also those who, because they suffered a similar impact, might have been so, but nevertheless were not—one conclusion emerges clearly.

The resentful person is always a person lacking in generosity. To be sure, the passion opposed to resentment is generosity; but this is not to be confused with capacity for forgiveness. Forgiveness, which is a virtue and not a passion, may be imposed by a moral imperative upon an ungenerous nature. A generous nature has, as a rule, no occasion for forgiveness, because it is always disposed to understand everything; and, accordingly, it is impervious to the offence which presupposes forgiveness.

The deepest root of generosity, I repeat, is understanding. But the only man who is capable of understanding everything is the man who is capable of loving everything. On this plane of profound causes, in short, the resentful man is a human being poorly endowed with the capacity for affection; and, accordingly, a human being of mediocre moral quality.

I stress the word 'mediocre,' because the amount of wickedness required for the complete incubation of resentment is never excessive. The bad man, strictly speaking, is simply an evil-doer; and his potential causes of resentment are drowned in the darkness of his misdeeds. But the resentful man is not necessarily a bad man. He may even be a good man, if life treats him kindly.

Only in the presence of adversity and injustice does he become resentful: in other words, in the presence of circumstances which purify the man of high moral quality. Solely when resentment accumulates and poisons the soul completely may it find expression in a criminal act; and this criminal act is distinguished by its specific relation with the origin of the resentment concerned.

The resentful man has a stubborn memory, impervious to time. When it does occur, the aggressive explosion of resentment is usually very belated: there is always a very long period of incubation between the offence and its revenge. Very often the aggressive response of the resentful man does not come at all, and he may end his days in the odour of sanctity.

All this—its nature, its slow evolution in the consciousness, its close dependence upon environment—differentiates the wickedness of the resentful man from that of the common evildoer.

Intelligence and Resentment

Many other features mark the resentful man. Usually his intelligence is of a high order. Almost all outstanding cases of resentful men have been those of men well endowed with brains. The man poorly endowed with them accepts adversity without this type of bitter reaction. It is the intelligent man who, in the presence of any adverse circumstance, draws a contrast between it and what he thinks he deserves.

But we are concerned, as a rule, with an order of intelligence which, though high, is not the very highest. The successful man of talent is, in fact, distinguished by his aptitude for adaptation rather than anything else, and, accordingly, he never feels himself cheated by life. There have been, it is true, many cases of men of extraordinary intelligence, and even of genius, who were typically resentful men. The largest contingent of this type, however, is drawn from men endowed with a talent which falls short of realizing that, if they fail to reach a higher category than they have attained, this is not the fault of other people's hostility, as they suppose, but the fault of their own failings.

Envy, Hatred and Resentment

I should add that resentment, though it looks very much like envy and hatred, differs from both. Envy and hatred are sins of a strictly individual cast. They always presuppose a duel between the hater and the hated, or the envier and the envied. Resentment is a passion which has about it much that is impersonal, much that is social. What causes it may be not this or that person, but life, 'fate.' The reaction of the resentful man is directed not so much against another man who may have done him an injustice, or profited by injustice, as against destiny. In this respect it possesses a certain quality of grandeur.

Resentment filters throughout the soul, and betrays itself in every action. Envy or hatred, on the other hand, has a place of its own within the soul, and, if it is extirpated, may leave the soul intact.

Moreover, hatred almost always has a swift response to offence, whereas resentment, as we have already seen, is a passion with a belated reaction and a long period of incubation between its cause and its social consequences.

Timidity, Gratitude and Hypocrisy in relation to Resentment

Very often resentment goes hand in hand with timidity. The strong man reacts directly and energetically to attack, and so automatically expels affront from his mind, as though it were some foreign body. This saving elasticity does not exist in the resentful man. Many a man who turns the other cheek after a buffet does so, not from virtue, but to cover up his cowardice; and his enforced humility afterwards turns into resentment.

But, if he should later happen to become strong, with that adventitious strength which is conferred by political power, his resentment, hitherto disguised as resignation, bursts forth in revenge. It is for this reason that weak men—and resentful men—when chance places them in a position of power, as often happens in time of revolution, are so much to be feared. Here, too, we find the reason why so many resentful men respond to revolutionary confusion and play so large a part in its development. The most cruel of leaders often have antecedents which betray their former timidity and show unequivocal symptoms of their present resentment.

Similarly, what is very typical of such men is not merely their incapacity for gratitude, but also the facility with which they transform the favours conferred upon them by others into fuel for their resentment. There is a sentence of Robespierre's, that tragic example of a resentful man, which one cannot read without a shudder, so stark is the light which it sheds on the psychology of the French Revolution: 'I experienced, from a very early age, the painful slavery of gratitude.'

Once he has done a favour to the resentful man, the benefactor remains inscribed on the black list of his dislike. As though moved by some obscure impulse, the resentful man hovers around the powerful man, who attracts and irritates him at one and the same time. This twofold feeling creates a bitter bond which makes him one of the leader's retinue. It is for this reason that we so often find the resentful man at the courts of the mighty. Woe betide the mighty if they do not realize that within their shadow, infinitely more dangerous than envy, inevitably grows the resentment of the very men who live by their favour!

Almost always the resentful man is wary and hypocritical. Scarcely ever does he manifest his inner bitterness to those around him. But, beneath all his dissimulation, in the long run his resentment becomes patent. Every one of his acts, every one of his thoughts, ends by being permeated by an indefinable bitterness. Above all, no passsion shows itself so clearly as resentment in a man's looks, which are much less amenable to the discipline of caution than his words and his actions.

Closely allied with the resentful man's hypocrisy is his addiction to anonymous letters. Almost all such letters are written, not in hatred or envy, or in a spirit of revenge, but by the trembling hand of resentment. A tireless writer of anonymous letters, who happened to be found out—an intelligent and very resentful man—declared that, with every one he wrote, he 'got rid of a weight inside him.' I knew just what he meant. But, in his turn, the resentful man, sensitive to the hurt of his own chosen weapon, is usually very much upset by anonymous letters from other people.

Social Success and Resentment

All those causes which make social success difficult are the very causes that have the greatest efficacy in creating resentment.

For resentment is, for the most part, a passion that belongs to great cities. The resentful man whom we often find seeking refuge in the solitude of a village or wasting his time in fruitless travelling is always a migrant from some city, and it was there that he fell sick. On this account, too, in proportion as civilization advances and the struggle for success becomes more embittered, so the social significance of resentment increases.

Let me repeat that the essential condition for the genesis of resentment is lack of understanding, which creates in the man doomed to become resentful a disharmony between his real capacity for success and what he imagines to be his capacity. The normal man accepts failure with equanimity. He always manages to understand it, and, accordingly, is able afterwards to dismiss it from his mind and overcome it.

But the mind of the resentful man, after its first inoculation, becomes more and more sensitive to fresh impacts. Henceforth all that is needed to fan the flame of his passion is not some definite disappointment, but simply some vaguely derogatory word or act, or perhaps mere absence of mind, on someone else's part. Everything, in his eyes, is equivalent to an affront or comes into the category of an injustice. Indeed, the resentful man reaches the point of experiencing a morbid need for the causes which serve to keep his passion alive: a condition of masochistic thirst that makes him seek them out or invent them, if they do not come his way.

Age, Sex, Æsthetics and Resentment

As a rule, this passion strikes root in minds predisposed to it during the period of adolescence; for it is then that the sense of competence or the sense of incompetence, the source of resentment, originates, either at school or college, or during those first free steps in life that possess a clearly marked social significance. From this point resentment, in the mind conscious of incompetence, takes the place of envy—a more elementary feeling, proper to the child while he spends his earlier years at home.

People who live side by side with the young usually have no idea of the significance of many things, trivial in the eyes of adults, yet capable, in adolescents, of being transformed into moulds of future conduct. A prize, regarded as deserved, which is not bestowed, or something similar which we consider childish, often lies at the root of a future passion of resentment. So may mere preference in affection on the part of parents or superiors, when it is interpreted as unjustified.

On the other hand, punishment, even though it be unjust, rarely originates resentment. Unjust punishment arouses humiliation, fleeting hatred or equally fleeting desire for revenge, but scarcely ever resentment, unless it be frequently repeated and thus betrays a personal passion charged with specific injustice.

In the creation of resentment, an important rôle, side by side with causes of social significance, is played by causes of a sexual kind, above all in the case of the man; and this is precisely because of the profound social repercussion which, in his case, is exerted by the sexual instinct.

Sexual failure, in whatever form, exercises a depressing influence so great as to make essential its immediate concealment in the consciousness. Hence it transforms itself readily into resentment. For this reason, it may be affirmed that a large number of resentful men are sexually weak: they suffer from timidity, they are husbands unfortunate in their marriages, they are people affected by abnormal or repressed tendencies. In the case of every resentful man we must be on the lookout for some frustration or abnormality in his sexual instinct. At the same time, we must not overlook the fact that there are—as I know from my own experience—some men sexually frustrated or abnormal who are nevertheless full of heroic fortitude, and accordingly impervious to resentment.

With all this is bound up another important aspect of the problem: the relation between resentment and æsthetics. Many resentful men are so thanks to a condition of inferiority—social or sexual, or both together—created by some physical imperfection, especially some illness, difficult to conceal, which is offensive to the senses, or some defect, which people lacking in consideration are accustomed to regard as a matter for joking, such as a hump-back or a limp.

On the other hand, as a rule mere ugliness, even in a high degree, does not originate resentment, even where a woman is concerned. This is doubtless because, if it is not actually repulsive, ugliness is instinctively and progressively offset by the cultivation of friendliness, which the ugly person exerts himself to achieve from childhood, in order not to compare unfavourably with anyone who is not ugly. For the opposite reason, the possessor of physical beauty is very often lacking in charm or definitely disagreeable.

A woman defends herself better than a man against resentment. Other things being equal, resentment is a definitely male passion. The reason is obvious if we consider the sense of social failure which belongs to the fundamental causes of resentment, for women, even those women who devote themselves to the same occupations as men, are almost deficient in any sense of social competence.

All those who have made a close study of students of both sexes, treated in identically the same way in classes and in examinations, have had, I am sure, the same experience as myself as to the much smaller and much more fleeting effect which is produced upon young women by scholastic failure, in comparison with young men. Scarcely ever is such a failure, in the case of a young woman, the origin of that incurable resentment which we find in so many male students. No doubt this is so because the woman's instinct tells her that, despite it, her essentially feminine rearguard, which is maternity, remains intact.

Even though she lacks beauty, as I have already noted, the woman usually defends herself against the danger of resentment. This is because, in her case, the compensating factor, namely charm, reaches a much higher potentiality than in the case of the man. For a plain woman charm suffices to enable her to avoid that specifically feminine failure which consists in lack of sexual attraction; and at the same time it saves her from resentment.

Most resentful women are so in consequence of their specifically sexual failure: sterility or enforced celibacy. But even in these cases they defend themselves better than frustrated men, because they keep more alive their capacity for generosity, and readily channel their inactive sexual instinct towards sublimated objectives.

False Virtue in the Resentful Man

Physical or moral inferiority, not offset by generosity, imposes upon the resentful man a certain number of limitations which look like virtues. For this reason, and for the reason of his hypocrisy, to which I have already referred, the resentful man often presents to inexpert eyes the semblance of respectability.

This false virtue of the resentful man is generally affected and pedantic, and on occasion it achieves the rigid magnitude of puritanism. Many puritans are simply resentful men, incapable of affection or understanding; sometimes they are men who have made a name for themselves in history, like Robespierre, that monster of odious rectitude; like Calvin, at once perverse and upright, or like Tiberius.

Their sense of powerlessness—unjustified, as they believe—to attain complete success in life makes them renounce any possible greatness, so they present themselves as unselfish and humble. In the same way, their sexual failure becomes transformed into ostentatious chastity.

Sometimes this sense, as I have already noted, makes them shun the world. They seek refuge in flight, which people find it hard to explain. Yet it is only natural because they are fleeing from their very selves, unhappily in vain.

Appearance and Resentment

All the circumstances which favour resentment often coincide with a definite physical and mental type. Resentful men are frequently asthenic people, tall and thin, given to introspection and to that affective frigidity which marks schizophrenics.

Be it noted that this tendency to introspection is compatible with complete lack of knowledge of their own aptitudes, which, as we have already seen, is one of the sources of the sense of resentment. Indeed, the 'introvert' is the very man who knows least about himself. We learn our own personality from outside ourselves, in the mirror of other people's reaction to it. We never contemplate ourselves.

The corpulent, plethoric man, extroverted and expansive in

disposition and bursting with outlets for it, may be a bad man, an amoral man, but he is rarely a resentful man.

This explains, too, why the resentful man is so often uncongenial. The thin, reserved and egoistic man almost always is; or, at least, he is much more likely to be so than the plump, generous and sociable man. The ultimate root of uncongeniality is lack of generosity, which is also the root of resentment. Uncongeniality increases in proportion as the person concerned outwardly exudes the repressed bitterness of resentment.

Humour and Resentment

Lastly, let me touch upon the relationship between resentment and humour. True humour is very difficult to define, since it is almost impossible to distinguish it from the different varieties of good humour. Good humour is the aptitude for giving expression, in an unrestrained, noisy form, to those aspects of life which are obviously comic. Humour is the art of extracting the comic sediment which is to be found in the serious side of life, and giving expression to it with dignity.

Good humour may make us weep with laughter. Humour makes us smile at sadness. The charm of good humour is to be found on the surface of trivial things. That of humour is to be found in the depths of serious things. The charm of good humour expresses itself riotously; that of humour, dryly.

Humour may be an inborn aptitude of individuals or races. But sometimes it is an occasional reaction, typical of resentment; for it is our warrant for tormenting, with a smile on our lips, people, things or symbols which have done us harm, or which we believe to have done us harm. It is obvious that the origin of humour is often an affront which, instead of being forgotten or avenged, has rankled in the mind and transformed itself into resentment. It is true, at the same time, that many resentful men have made their passion inoffensive thanks to the compensating factor of humour.

Success and the Resentful Man

Resentment is incurable. The sole antidote to it is generosity. But this noblest of the passions is born with the soul, it may therefore increase or diminish, but cannot be created in one who does not already possess it. Generosity cannot be lent or administered like some external medicine.

Since the resentful man is always an unsuccessful man—unsuccessful in relation to his ambition—it would seem at first sight as though success ought to cure him. Success may, if it comes, calm the resentful man; but it never cures him. On the contrary, it very often happens that success, far from curing him, makes him worse. This is because he regards success as a solemn consecration of the fact that his resentment was justifiable; and this justification intensifies his long-standing bitterness.

This is another of the reasons for the vindictive violence of resentful men when they attain power, and so for the enormous importance this passion has held in history.

Nothing demonstrates this better than the life of Tiberius.

PART I

The Roots of Resentment

I

CHILDHOOD IN EXILE

The Crucial Date

TIBERIUS was born in Rome in the year 42 B.C. He died, at the age of seventy-eight, in A.D. 37.

In other words, his life was divided into two by the most memorable happening in human history: the space of time intervening between the birth and the death of Christ.

It gives us, in itself, much to think about if we bear in mind that this happening took place without any realizing on the part of Rome, then the capital of the civilized world, that all its wars, its triumphs, its successions, its orgies and its executions, which seem to fill the chronicles with their grandeur or their horror, were no more than fleeting anecdotes in comparison with the humble events in distant Judæa that gave birth to a new humanity.

Apart from the innumerable cares of his government and the passions that made up his life, Tiberius, without being fully conscious of the fact—though he may have had a painful presentiment of it—fulfilled a truly transcendental destiny: he presided over a world which was taking its last steps in antiquity and crossing the threshold into the life of our own era.

We see him, as the representative man of his time, passing over the highest peak of history; a single day, the day of the drama of Calvary, that seemed just like any other day, but was to become the nucleus of his history and his legend. The stars, which predicted so many things to him, could not tell him that.

Tiberius's Parents

His father was Tiberius Claudius Nero, whose nobility, intelligence, and high moral qualities the historians extol.[1] He was, so

---

[1] See Velleius, *114*, II, 15.

it seems, an 'exemplary Roman.' Nevertheless, into this model personage entered certain ethical elements which would strike us today as simply those of a scoundrel. Suetonius tells us that he had some ancestors of pure Claudian blood who sated themselves with misdeeds;[1] and perhaps, if this was so, some drops of impure blood found their way into his veins.

What is certain is that his conduct does not seem to me so irreproachable as it did to ancient and modern apologists for the Cæsars. We need only recall that, having served Julius Cæsar as admiral of his fleet and received substantial commissions and honours at his hands, he hastened to rally to the side of his assassins, and with more fervour than most. Then he fought against Octavian (the future Augustus); but, a few years later, he meekly handed his own wife, then six months pregnant, over to Octavian, and proceeded to live side by side with the usurper of his bridal bed, perhaps deeply hurt, but with every appearance of the most cordial friendship.

Morality in those golden days, even Roman morality, was very much a matter of circumstances. It was to be a few years yet before there were laid down those eternal rules of good and evil which to this very day, twenty centuries later, humanity, we must admit, delights in forgetting.

Tiberius's mother, Livia, also belonged to the proud stock of the Claudians. She was the daughter of 'the illustrious and noble Livius Drusus Claudianus; and, by her birth, her virtue and her beauty was pre-eminent among the Romans.'[2] We shall come to her virtue in a moment. Her beauty, if we may judge by the Pompeii statue of her (which presents her in the bloom of her youth), was indeed much to be admired for the grace and perfection of her features. What strikes us especially in this piece of sculpture is the suggestion of a smile on the perfect lips, and the large, ecstatic eyes of this precocious girl. In later statues, such as that in the Louvre, in which she appears clad as the goddess Ceres, the grace is gone and there remains a matronly face with grave though still perfect features, doubtless accentuated by the flattering sculptor. The face and the whole figure are

[1] Suetonius, *106, Tib.*, 2.   [2] Velleius, *114*, II, 75.

stamped with the adaptable but inflexible energy which marked all the empress's maturity.

Tiberius Claudius Nero was much older than Livia, who was only fifteen when she married him. It is very probable that their marriage, celebrated in the year 45 B.C., was arranged thanks to the ambition of the adolescent bride, for ambition was a passion which she demonstrated to the full throughout her life, and to which her beauty and her puritan virtue served her as instruments. Tiberius Claudius Nero was her cousin and a man of great influence in Rome. This latter fact heavily outweighed, in Livia's calculating eyes, the lack of youth on his side and, on her side, the lack of love.

The Omen

Soon after the marriage Livia became pregnant. It suited the designs of her ambition that her child should be a boy. Impatient to make sure, she warmed a hen's egg between her breasts and those of her wet nurse[1] for many days until the shell broke and there appeared a chicken with a fine crest and the rudiments of spurs. This made Livia certain that her desire would be fulfilled.

The omen came true. The child was indeed a boy: the Tiberius with whom we are concerned. Soon after his birth, Livia hastened to consult the famous astrologer Scribonius about the child's future. As is the way of soothsayers, Scribonius slavishly lent himself to the wishes of young and beautiful Livia, and assured her that beyond doubt her boy would become emperor. What his mother was seeking, without knowing it, was not Tiberius's horoscope, but that of her own ambition: a man who, hatched by the heat of her desire, should become the instrument of her passion to rule the world.

---

[1] Pliny, *79*, XI, 76. According to Suetonius's version (*106*, *Tib.*, 14), Livia and her servants warmed the egg between their hands, but it is more logical that she should have warmed it between her breasts, both by way of a symbol and as a matter of convenience. This was not Livia's sole omen. Another, and a very curious one, was as follows: while she was betrothed to Augustus a young eaglet, white as snow, fell from the sky into her lap, with a sprig of laurel in its beak. This laurel was planted in the garden of Cæsar's villa beside the Tiber. It struck root and became a large tree, and Augustus carried one of its branches in his hand on days of triumph (Pliny, *79*, XV, 40).

The Flight

During the civil war which followed the assassination of Julius Cæsar, Tiberius Claudius Nero had to flee from Italy with his wife and Tiberius, still an infant. Pursued by the troops of Octavian—later to become Livia's submissive spouse—the fugitives reached Naples, where they took ship in secret, amid so many dangers that old Velleius Paterculus, grandfather of the historian, who accompanied them, nobly committed suicide in order to lessen the number of the party and give the married couple a better chance of escape.[1] The infant Tiberius, torn from the breast of his wet nurse and then from the arms of his mother in order to enable the two of them to jump on board, started crying, thus threatening the party with discovery and death.

Exile lasted two years. It was prodigal for Tiberius's father in those disappointments proper to the unhappy hours of expatriation, which never fail, have so much to teach, and are so rarely understood and turned to advantage.

From Sicily the family went on to Achaia and other Greek provinces.[2] One night, when they were travelling through a wood in the province of Corinth, a fire broke out which caught hold of Livia's clothes and hair, and was on the point of burning Tiberius.[3] Thus for the second time, in his earliest years, he tried out the leading rôle in the great family tragedy which was to make up his life.

At length the family returned to Rome; for exile, though it seems endless, scarcely ever is so. A little later, in the year 38 B.C., Livia, once more pregnant, divorced her husband and united herself for ever with the future Augustus, at that time a triumvir full of ambition.

With that silent skill with which children absorb and estimate whatever happens around them, Tiberius, in the depths of his four-year-old soul, must have realized that an essential change had

---

[1] Velleius, *114*, II, 76.

[2] It is a fact typical of Augustus's conciliatory, generous and intelligent character that, when he became emperor, he ceded Cythera to the Lacedemonians in remembrance and recompense for the protection which they extended to his wife at this time when she was his enemy during her youthful exile.

[3] Suetonius, *106, Tib.*, 6.

come to pass in his life. Gone was the life of exile with its ups and downs, and a new life was beginning, full of glory, of material well-being, and of potential greatness. His mother's desertion of her husband, his father's pain, perhaps he did not understand as yet. But in his mind must have remained the dreary dregs of wanderings and dangers away from his country, and before his eyes the vision, inexplicable but indelible, of his father in his deserted home, silent and solitary.

Almost all the men I have met who spent their childhood, even their earliest childhood, in exile were grave, melancholy men. Perhaps this is through the influence of their parents, saddened by their sundering from their native land. Perhaps it is because nostalgia for one's native land is so subtle a thing that it takes root in the mind even before full consciousness comes to birth.

A woman is less sensitive to exile. As the poet puts it, her home is always in the piece of sand in which she sets foot: for a woman fatherland means, above all else, her home. But for a man his home means his fatherland. For a man exile is a suffering so great that we may find it hard to understand how those who have endured it sometimes contrive afterwards to discharge their burden of it upon others.

Old Tiberius Claudius Nero was a prudent and a proud man; and during his years of expatriation and persecution he may have consoled himself, like Seneca, by reflecting that the distance which separates us from Heaven is exactly the same in our fatherland as in the land of exile. But consolation, though it may alleviate, does not overcome sadness; and his exile's sadness was undoubtedly one of the sources of that passion which tormented his son—that 'saddest of men,' as Pliny put it—and lasted till the day of his death.

II

DOMESTIC TRAGEDY

Livia's Divorce

LIVIA, Tiberius's mother, was the daughter of Aufidia, doubtless a woman of much beauty, since, though she was not of noble birth,[1] she married that great nobleman Livius Drusus Claudianus, renowned for his harsh character, who committed suicide at the battle of Philippi when he saw that all was lost. Some authorities assume that he was the Drusus 'avaricious and vile of spirit' to whom Cicero refers in one of his letters, but this is not certain.

This stern Roman was the uncle of Tiberius Claudius Nero, with whom we have already made acquaintance as Livia's first husband; and both of them, uncle and nephew, permeated with the patrician spirit, held the same republican and anti-dictatorial ideas. Livia's childhood and youth were, therefore, nurtured by views opposed to those represented by Augustus, with whom she spent the rest of her life.

At that time, much more than at any other period in history, women were used as a means of uniting, through the bond of marriage, families which were politically estranged. But this does not prevent us from assuming that Livia, who, like many women, was very responsive to political ideas, preserved her sympathy for those views which were sacrosanct in the home of her forebears. Later we shall see that the fidelity with which she clung to the Claudian family and the tenacity with which she favoured them demonstrate that this was the case.

What, then, was the motive for Livia's separation from her

---

[1] Aufidia's father was a man of note, but not a noble. His name was Aufidius Lurcus, and he held public offices in Rome. Years afterwards, Caligula disowned Livia 'on account of her plebeian origin,' basing himself on the fact that Aufidius was a humble decurion of Fondi (Suetonius, *106, Calig.* 23).

first husband and her marriage with Octavian the triumvir? This kind of conjugal quadrille was quite a common thing among the upper classes in Rome. But in this case what gave cause for scandal even among the most sophisticated—and what strikes us as repugnant to this very day—was that her divorce and her fresh marriage took place at a time when she was far gone in pregnancy.

Octavian consulted the pontiffs on the question whether the marriage would be lawful in these circumstances; and the reply of these solemn functionaries was in the affirmative, 'on condition that the conception was certain.' It was certain enough in this case in view of Livia's obvious state of deformity as a woman six months pregnant. For this reason, Tacitus reasonably stamps Octavian's consultation of the pontiffs as ridiculous.[1] Pontiffs in the service of a powerful person naturally tended towards such an accommodation, dangerous though it might be for their prestige. The moral question involved was not the fact of Livia's pregnancy, but quite a different one, to which the pontiffs did not refer, though the man in the street did. It was this: who was the father of the child soon to be born?

Various reasons were given at the time, and have been given ever since, to explain this unusual marriage. Tacitus says that Octavian, 'enamoured of Livia's beauty, took her away from her husband—whether with her consent or not is not known—and in his impatience made her his wife without waiting until she gave birth.'[2] In other words, Tacitus adduces the supremely noble reason of love, and gallantly allows it to be understood that Livia may have resisted Octavian, at least until her child was born.

But it is possible that there was another reason, 'less absolute and more Roman,' as Ferrero puts it:[3] the advantage to Octavian of allying himself with a patrician family in order to offset the patricians' opposition to him, which hindered his imperialist plans; or, to put it more simply, the fact so often attested by history that the chief concern of a man recently raised to power by a revolution is to turn himself into an aristocrat.

Since all hypotheses about human actions are admissible, it is pertinent to point out that these suppositions leave out of account

---

[1] Tacitus, *107*, I, 10.   [2] Tacitus, *107*, V, 7.   [3] Ferrero, *27*.

a factor which may have been the decisive one: Livia's own will Her life-story shows us to what a point ambition was her ruling passion: we may say that it was the very soul of her. So it is possible that, when she was courted by the future Augustus, who possessed all the amorous impetus of twenty-four and, above all, the halo of political triumph—an irresistible magnet to some women—she saw in this ailing but lucky young man the path proper to her dreams of grandeur. It was through ambition that she married her first husband: the same impulse threw her into the arms of her second.

Who was Drusus's Father?

All these reasonings, however, do not explain the most enthralling question in connection with this historical love-affair: the haste with which the marriage was undertaken.

A woman six months pregnant, however beautiful she may be, is in no position to excite a violent passion. There are, indeed, sound biological reasons which explain why, above all during the second half of pregnancy, disappearance of the instinct which in ordinary conditions mutually attracts the two sexes is a normal phenomenon.[1] At this time a different and more lofty order of emotion takes the place of the purely sensual link between the future parents, though it enables the sacred fire of passion to be kept alight, or at least to be fed with different fuel. Even in the case of a man not responsible for the conception, it is exceptional, we may almost say it is unnatural, for love to flare up at this moment; and, above all, a love so strong, so directly carnal, as that which apparently would not let Octavian wait even the three months required to enable Livia to recover her graceful form and allow her beautiful face to become cleansed of the blemishes and defacements proper to her pregnancy.

In my view, the sole explanation of the haste of this love-affair is that it began much sooner than would seem, and that though the problem of paternity is insoluble, the child whom Livia awaited may very well have been that of Octavian, young and triumphant, and not that of her valetudinarian husband.

[1] See my books 62 and 64.

I should not venture to say something which might besmirch the memory of two people who have enjoyed eternal peace for so many centuries were it not for the fact that everyone said it at the time. Suetonius, as much of an enthusiast for Augustus as all his contemporaries, tells us that this little couplet passed from mouth to mouth through Rome:

> 'They are the lucky ones,
> Who in three months have their sons.'

The innuendo was obvious: that Augustus was responsible for Livia's pregnancy, and so was the father of Drusus I, Tiberius's younger brother.

It is much easier to suppose that Livia and Octavian fell in love, and that in the rapture of their adulterous passion they made the slip necessary to bring about conception, than it is to suppose that, without previous love and purely as a matter of convenience (or in a moment of unbridled lust), they let loose the scandal of the divorce, with no consideration either for the venerable grey hair of the husband, or even for that delicate condition of the wife by which the life of humanity perpetuates itself and which is respected by even the most depraved of men.

The effect of this marriage in Rome was bound to be disastrous. Groups gossiped about the details of such a remarkable love-affair with that sour satisfaction always aroused by a dubious sexual relationship between prominent people. But it was not solely the whispering mouths of the malicious that spat upon the patrician pair. Mark Antony, in his attacks on Augustus, reproached him as one of his gravest misdeeds with this sudden marriage, which he regarded as the most scandalous of all Augustus's adulteries, already amounting to quite a long list.

By way of excusing Augustus, Suetonius tells us that the real object of his amorous adventures was not so much libertinage as politics, since he sought out the wives of his enemies, from whom, in the transports of passion, it was easy for him to worm out the secrets of their betrayed husbands. This explanation is extremely ingenuous.

The truth is that Augustus, like many another man as small in stature as himself, was very much of a womanizer. He had all the impudence bestowed upon him by the state of morality at that time, together with the abusive prestige of power, an effective help at all times to many a conqueror of feminine virtue. The story goes that, during a banquet, Augustus paid court to the wife of a consul with such shamelessness that, before the very eyes of her shocked husband, he and she withdrew from the table, to which they returned some minutes later, he with an air of triumph and fatigue, she with her hair in disorder and cheeks disgracefully flushed.[1]

It may have been, at the beginning, just one more of these sudden passions that made Augustus fall in love with Livia. But she, incapable of scandalous adventures, and possessing that superiority which frigidity confers on some women, caught the headlong conqueror in the trap of paternity and marriage.

The child was named after Livia's father, Drusus Claudianus (let us call him, for short, Drusus I), and Augustus, 'to quiet evil-speaking,' sent him to his grandfather's home. Anything else, however, would have proclaimed the scandal of adultery in a way which neither the future emperor nor this puritan spouse could face. But, despite this precaution, the haste of the marriage remained strongly suggestive.

There are several other factors which support the hypothesis of adultery. Whereas Tiberius presents himself to us from the beginning of his life as a taciturn and harsh person, just like his father, the old and unfortunate Tiberius Claudius Nero, Drusus was jovial, receptive and full of geniality. Such were the qualities of Augustus, inherited in his turn from Julius Cæsar, whose affability and courtesy to everyone were the source of his popularity.[2]

Velleius eulogizes Drusus I for 'the kindliness and agreeableness of his manner,'[3] and Horace[4] sings his praises in similar terms. The populace made Drusus I a popular hero; and, according to Henting, this was precisely because people believed him to be Augustus's son. Such was this popular enthusiasm for him

---

[1] Suetonius, *106, Aug.*, 69.
[2] See Plutarch, *81, Cæsar*, 4.
[3] Velleius, *114*, II, 97.
[4] Horace, *45*, IV, 2.

that when he died in Elba, at the age of thirty, his son Germanicus inherited the love of the people which, as we shall see later, bordered on fanaticism, and all the popularity (misplaced though it was) which fell to the lot of his nephew Caligula when he came to the throne was equally his inheritance from Drusus I, upon whom from his birth seems to have shone the bright but ill-fated star of the love-child.

Another interesting fact is that Drusus I suffered from fantastic and obsessing dreams, such as that of a woman of supernatural stature who appeared to him in Germany and ordered him to stop his conquests.[1] Dreams of this kind were typical of the family of Augustus, his presumptive father. We are familiar with the dreams of Julius Cæsar, one of which, based upon what was later to be known as the Œdipus complex,[2] together with other visions, was undoubtedly of an epileptic character. Augustus's mother, Atia, niece of Julius Cæsar, suffered from similar dreams, sometimes erotic. In one, for example, a snake—that priapic symbol—wound itself around her body so softly that, when she awakened, she purified herself as though she had just left her husband's arms.[3] Her son inherited such dreams. Many of Augustus's plans and undertakings were dictated by these dreams or apparitions, 'which he never despised, either his own or those of other people which related to him.'[4] Drusus I's son, Germanicus, had fits suspiciously like epilepsy; and Germanicus's son, Caligula, was an undoubted epileptic.[5]

All these phenomena betray a line of epileptoid inheritance common to the Julian family, which separates them sharply from the Claudian family. One characteristic of Drusus I's temperament was the same as that of the great Julius Cæsar, 'the impetuosity which led him to run great risks':[6] very different from the caution which marked the political and military activity of his brother Tiberius.

Finally, let us note the suspicious preference which Augustus always showed for Drusus I over his brother: a preference noted

---

[1] Suetonius, *106*, *Claud.*, I; Dion, *22*, LV, 1.
[2] Suetonius, *106*, *Cæsar*, 8 and 33.
[3] Suetonius, *106*, *Aug.*, 94.
[4] Suetonius, *106*, *Aug.*, 91.
[5] Suetonius, *106*, *Calig.*, 50.
[6] Suetonius, *106*, *Claud.*, I.

by ancient and admitted by modern historians.[1] This preference Augustus transferred to Drusus's son Germanicus, whom he would doubtless have liked to succeed him as emperor.

In the long struggle between the Julians and the Claudians, Drusus I and his sons were the most definite representatives of the Julian branch; and, though this may be explained on the maternal side by the fact that Antonia, Drusus's wife, had Julian blood, Augustus's ardour and the clear classification of popular instinct give ground for the assumption that into it entered also the common certainty that Drusus was Augustus's son.

Against this assumption of adulterous paternity some authorities set the resemblance which is to be found in statues between Drusus I and Tiberius. Baring-Gould makes much of this.[2] But there is no gainsaying that it is a poor argument; for even if Drusus was Augustus's son he might look much like his brother through their common mother. Nor must we fail to take account of the margin of doubt which we must always allow for such iconographic attributions in classical times.

Against the hypothesis of adultery, other authorities adduce the fact that, though she became pregnant by Tiberius Nero, Livia never became so again by Augustus. Pliny regards her subsequent infecundity as a deciding factor in this much discussed marriage, and presents it as an example of sterility 'through bodily aversion':[3] an odd commentary which does not accord with the passion which (according to other testimony) Augustus felt for the woman he had once persecuted. The argument is inadmissible, since there are many explanations for the fact that, in marital relations, there is one child and then no more: especially if the woman changes her husband.

Moreover, Suetonius[4] tells us that, soon after her marriage to Augustus, Livia became pregnant again, but that she had a miscarriage. So she was fecundated by Augustus too. At the same time it is quite likely that, as often happens, her miscarriage left her

---

[1] Suetonius, *106, Claud.*, 1. Among modern historians see Homo, *44*, p. 97, and Ciaceri, *17*, p. 97.
[2] Baring-Gould, *10*, p. 170.
[3] Pliny, *79*, VII, 11.
[4] Suetonius, *106, Aug.*, 63.

with some lesion that made her incapable of any further childbearing.

The Resignation of Tiberius Claudius Nero

I have made these reflections on the circumstances surrounding this marriage, one of the strangest that history records, because I regard them as essential to our subject. What is harder to explain is the resigned attitude of the husband, once at enmity with Augustus, but now making him a friendly offer of his own wife. We might suppose that his suspicion or his certainty of her adultery was one of the reasons for this unusual indifference, and that, feeling himself to be old and already vanquished, he withdrew in favour of his young supplanter.

But even so we can hardly explain the humiliating compliance of this proud aristocrat, who not only gave his wife a dowry for her new marriage, but even occupied a place of honour at the bridal feast. Velleius,[1] who was closely linked with the imperial family, goes so far as to say that it was the husband himself who offered his wife to Augustus. It is true, of course, that in the morality of those days there was much more apparent strictness than real ethical substance: at least, in the morality of Augustus's time, about which Seneca[2] said that 'its vices maintained themselves thanks to the virtues of the ancients.'

The unquestionable fact is that Livia's marriage was scandalous; and that all these questions which still arouse our curiosity, twenty centuries later, must have been an insufferable torment in the mind of young Tiberius, as his awakening consciousness and the voice of calumny kept on informing him about the details of this phase of his childhood, and kept on filtering fresh drops of bitterness into his soul.

That this is no gratuitous hypothesis is demonstrated by Tiberius's later relations with his mother and his stepfather, with which I shall deal in due course.

[1] Velleius, *114*, II, 94.   [2] Seneca, *99*, X.

III

TIBERIUS'S LOVE-LIFE

Tiberius's Marriage to Vipsania, Atticus's Granddaughter

OUT of his saddened childhood Tiberius grew to the age for love. His sexual life, too, was profoundly unhappy, and it was undoubtedly one of the most abundant sources of his misanthropy and his resentment.

Thanks partly to his reserved, sceptical and frigid temperament, partly to his puritanism, Tiberius was a man suited to find the solution of the problem of his love-life in the placid, unadventurous existence of the monogamic pair; and at the outset he found it in his marriage to Vipsania, daughter of Agrippa and his first wife Pomponia.

Pomponia, in her turn, was the daughter of Pomponius Atticus, 'Cicero's great friend,' as all the authorities have it; but in fact the friend of everyone, since in those days of civil war and inflamed faction he was a wonderful balancer in the most difficult task of sitting on the fence.

I quote these antecedents of Vipsania because they unquestionably explain, by the law of heredity, the passive placidity with which we find her Tiberius's loving wife until the very day of their separation, and, from the very next day, the equally exemplary wife of Asinius Gallus, one of her first husband's worst enemies. Atticus's granddaughter adapted herself to anything without the least effort.

We do not know the exact date of Tiberius's marriage to Vipsania, but it must have been about the year 19 B.C., when Tiberius was twenty-three.[1] It is said that his mother, Livia,

---

[1] Tarver (*108*) assumes that this marriage took place some years later than the date I have mentioned, about the year 10 B.C. But this is an untenable hypothesis, since in the year 12 B.C. Tiberius married Julia I as his second wife. Tarver bases

wanted him to marry Augustus's daughter, Julia, but failed in this desire because the emperor preferred to wed her (she was now the widow of Marcellus) to his general Agrippa. This attitude on the part of Augustus is to be explained by his dislike for Tiberius, and also, perhaps, by the deep regard in which he held his great general. With eugenic intuition, from Julia's marriage to Agrippa the emperor hoped for robust boys who in turn would make heroic commanders in the field. It was only much later, when Agrippa was dead, having indeed fulfilled his paternal duty in quantity, if not in quality, that Augustus agreed to satisfy Livia's desire and allowed his daughter to marry Tiberius as her third husband.

Tiberius, with his peculiar character, managed to make a success of marriage with Vipsania, with her inherited adaptability. Suetonius tells us that they lived in perfect harmony.[1] They had a son, Drusus II, who was born about the year 11 B.C., and so, according to my calculation, several years after their marriage. But this belated fecundity was offset by the speed with which it repeated itself, since, a year after giving birth to Drusus, Vipsania, was once more pregnant. Later on we shall see how popular calumny called in question Tiberius's responsibility for this paternity.

Divorce from Vipsania

It was now that took place one of the deepest tragedies in the private life of the future emperor: perhaps the greatest of all. The year was 12 B.C. Agrippa had just died, leaving Julia a widow.

---

his calculation upon the fact that Tiberius's and Vipsania's son, Drusus II, was born about the year 11 B.C., from which he infers that they must have married a year earlier. But it is clear that such rapid reproduction, though frequent, is by no means obligatory, since very often the first child is born several years after marriage. It is more logical to date this marriage about the year 20 or 19 B.C., the date which Baker (8) also defends. From what contemporaries vaguely indicate, it also follows that the divorce between Tiberius and Vipsania took place after several years of married life. For example, Suetonius tells us that their separation was a great grief to Tiberius, 'because habit had united him to his wife' (Suetonius, 106, Tib., 7). 'Habit' presupposes several years of living together; and this would have been impossible on Tarver's assumption that the marriage took place much later.

[1] Suetonius, 106, Tib., 7.

Augustus decided to marry his daughter to Tiberius. This meant the thunderbolt of Tiberius's divorce from Vipsania.

From the standpoint of the psychology and the morality of our time, it is hard to understand the justification which then existed for such matrimonial puzzles. It seems clear that Tiberius was living happily with his wife, now pregnant for the second time. It is obvious, too, that Julia, before she became a widow, had produced sufficient masculine progeny to have assured the continuity of the imperial line in accordance with Augustus's desire, if death, which is beyond the will of emperors, had not swept away all these sons in the flower of their youth.

The logical thing, therefore, would have been to leave Tiberius at peace in his home, and to leave Julia a widow. So far as her scandalously gay mode of life was concerned, it was all the same to her whether she had a husband or not. Or, if the laws which governed matrimony required her to marry, she might have been married to any other husband better suited to her than taciturn Tiberius. Indeed, at one point this appears to have been what Augustus intended, when, before Tiberius, he contemplated marrying her to one of two simple knights, G. Proculeius or Cotesus.

Augustus's failure to carry out this intention and his final choice of Tiberius were certainly due to the satisfaction which, by this choice, he gave to Livia's long-standing wishes. It may have been influenced also by the intrigues of Julia herself, for, even while Agrippa was still alive, this insatiable woman, not content with her numerous lovers, tried to seduce Tiberius in so marked a way that all Rome was scandalized by her behaviour.[1] It seems that at this time Julia had a great influence over her father, so she may well have helped in his ordaining Tiberius's divorce and his new marriage.

History repeats Itself

There is no record that Tiberius tried to resist the imperial will. Doubtless he was much too weak a character to do so. But in any case, where marriage for reasons of state was concerned, to oppose the orders of a ruler, especially when that ruler happened

[1] Suetonius, *106, Tib.*, 7.

to be Augustus, was a heroic undertaking. The historians of the period refer, for example, to Julius Cæsar's opposition to Sulla's matrimonial intentions for him with almost as much admiration as that with which they describe his conquest of the Gauls.

Tiberius was certainly no Julius Cæsar, and he let himself be divorced from his wife while she was pregnant, just as his mother was when Augustus took her away from Claudius's home in order to marry her. His mentality, so attuned to horoscopes, may have sought in the stars an explanation of this humiliating fate of the males of his family. From the psychological point of view, we may perhaps find cause to interpret it as the work, not of chance, but of Livia's subconscious design. When she made her daughter-in-law in her turn undergo divorce in the middle of her pregnancy, Livia was justifying that divorce of her own, when she too was pregnant, which had set the evil-speakers of Rome talking so much, and, at the same time, she was teaching resentful Tiberius, by way of a practical though painful lesson, that men subject to public duty have to endure trials such as his father had suffered and were now being repeated in his own person.

After her divorce, Vipsania was no sooner recovered from her childbirth than she married Asinius Gallus. It was not long before the suspicion was bruited abroad that this important personage, who was a senator, well-known for his impetuous character and his eloquence, had had previous relations with Tiberius's wife, and it was said that he was responsible, not only for her second pregnancy, which ended in miscarriage, but even for her first, which gave birth to Drusus II.

Against this charge Baring-Gould adduces the resemblance which exists between the busts of Drusus II and those of Tiberius.[1]

[1] See Baring-Gould, 10. If the bust in the Tortonia Museum is, in fact, that of Drusus II, the likeness is so great as to be striking. As for the two presumed statues of Drusus II in the Louvre, their authenticity is doubtful. But if they really represent Drusus, in these two heads the resemblance to Tiberius is negative. They lack even the characteristic common to all the Claudians: the growth of hair very low down on the neck. On the other hand, in these two heads a surprising feature is the unmistakable resemblance, especially in the retraction of the lower jaw and the somewhat foolish expression of the mouth, between this presumed Drusus II and the statues of Antonia II, the mother of Germanicus, which are to be found in the same gallery. In other words, these two heads of Drusus II have an unquestionably Julian air about them.

There is, in fact, no difficulty in admitting that we are concerned here with yet another calumny; or, as it was also said at the time, with a deliberate invention on the part of Livia and Augustus, in order to ease the pain of Tiberius's separation from his wife by giving him the grudge of feeling that he was already conquered in her affection.

But this precaution, if in fact it was taken, served no purpose. Tiberius never consoled himself for the divorce imposed upon him by the will of Augustus. After his marriage to Julia, when he happened to see Vipsania passing in the distance, he was so much moved that tears came to his eyes and he swore to keep out of her way in future.[1] His resentment at the idea that she was living in the arms of another man—and a man who was one of his worst enemies—kept on growing, and played no small part in the mental tragedy of his life.

Asinius Gallus, the Implacable Rival

His successful rival, Asinius Gallus, was implacable towards Tiberius. He was a celebrated personage, the son of Pollio, consul in Augustus's time, to whom Virgil dedicated his Fourth Eclogue. His son wrote a work drawing a parallel between him and Cicero: a work which was doubtless one of the favourite readings of Pliny the Younger.[2] It is said that Asinius Gallus, whose vanity and ambition knew no bounds, supposed himself to be 'the youth who should enjoy the life of the gods,' of whom Virgil speaks in the Eclogue in question, but the probability is that the poet was referring to Marcellus II, Augustus's presumptive heir at the time.

What is beyond doubt is that, whether Virgil's prophecy applied to him or not, Asinius Gallus aspired to the throne of Rome. Tacitus tells us expressly that Augustus 'in his last conversations, sought among the Romans those who had both the ambition and the talent to reign as his possible successor,' and that the three candidates were Lepidus, who had capacity, but no ambition; Gallus, who had ambition, but no capacity; and Arruntius, who combined both conditions.[3] This important passage informs us once again about Augustus's efforts to eliminate

---

[1] Suetonius, *106, Tib.*, 7. [2] Pliny the Younger, *80*, VII, 4.
[3] Tacitus, *107*, I, 13.

Tiberius from the succession, and also about another of the deepest sources of Tiberius's resentment against Gallus, who dared to dispute the throne with him.

We find constant reference in the historians to the rancorous state of tension which always divided Tiberius and Gallus. From his lower position Gallus drew himself up in a bold and somewhat petulant attitude, rather symbolical of his name, in front of his eminent rival. I shall refer later to the angry intervention of the impetuous senator when Tiberius could not make up his mind to accept the throne. There were many other signs of their spiteful disagreement.

In A.D. 15 there was a great flood in Rome. The Tiber suddenly rose, sweeping away the debris of shattered houses and many corpses. Asinius Gallus proposed that, in order to avert any such disaster in the future, the Sibylline books should be consulted; but his proposal immediately met with opposition from Tiberius, 'as mysterious in religion as in politics.'[1] In the following year, Haterius and Fronto presented to the Senate a complaint about the luxury of Rome and a proposal for combating it. Gallus opposed the whole proceedings, presumably with the intention of annoying Tiberius, that paladin of puritan standards.[2] On another occasion, when Tiberius, now emperor, had to be away from Rome, Piso, in agreement with him, proposed that the Senate, precisely because of the emperor's absence, should redouble its activity. Once more Gallus opposed this, alleging hypocritically that the emperor's presence was essential to the Senate's deliberations.[3] Again, over a question of nominating magistrates there was a direct and embittered clash between the two rivals.[4]

But the struggle reached its greatest violence during the closing period of Tiberius's reign, when he, in alliance with and dominated by Sejanus, was fighting against Agrippina I, Germanicus's widow. I shall refer in more detail later to this violent battle. Agrippina needed on her side an influential man, full of enthusiasm, who would counteract Sejanus's influence. Asinius Gallus, now a widower, lent himself to this alliance, and, though

---

[1] Tacitus, *107*, I, 76.   [2] Tacitus, *107*, II, 33.
[3] Tacitus, *107*, II, 35.   [4] Tacitus, *107*, II, 36.

it was purely political, proposed to marry Agrippina in order to make it more effective. So the two rivals once more found themselves face to face. Tiberius, as we shall see, refused permission for the marriage, and perfidiously spread the rumour that Asinius Gallus and Agrippina were united by scandalous ties.[1]

It may be taken that this was not true. Asinius Gallus was by this time rather elderly, and Agrippina was incapable of compromising her strength, which consisted precisely in her virtue, in a senseless intrigue. What united them was solely their common hatred of Tiberius.

The Vengeance of Tiberius

But Tiberius knew how to wait. When a suitable time came, he denounced Gallus in a letter to the Senate. Dion tells us that he carried his perfidy to the point of inviting Gallus to dine with him on the same day, and drank a cup of friendship with him at the very moment when the accusation was being read in the Senate (A.D. 30). Gallus was imprisoned in conditions of extreme severity. He had no one to attend upon him in his cell. He saw no one but a slave who compelled him to eat in order to stop him committing suicide by starvation, and his food was so chosen 'that it prevented him from dying, but gave him no pleasure.' Not until three years later did Tiberius, according to Dion, taking pity on his victim, allow him to die of his own will. Other authorities say that he was executed. A certain Sinacus also died about this time at the hands of the executioner, solely because he was Gallus's friend.[2]

Life would have it that even Tiberius's love for Vipsania, the purest sentiment to which his soul gave shelter, should convert itself into a source of implacable resentment. By this time it was thirteen years since his beloved Vipsania had died; but his memory of her still lived on, and, with that memory, his grudge against the man who had spoilt his sole chance of love.

[1] Tacitus, *107*, VI, 25.
[2] Dion, 22, LVIII, 3 and 23. Tacitus (*107*, VI, 23) tells us that when Tiberius heard of Gallus's death, he said he was sorry that he should have died before coming up for judgement, thus allowing it to be understood that Gallus might have been acquitted: a fine piece of hypocrisy, since Gallus's trial seems to have been delayed through Tiberius's own fault.

IV

TIBERIUS'S LOVE-LIFE
(continued)

Julia the Mad

A CONTEMPORARY author[1] has remarked that it is incomprehensible to what an extent writers, eagerly seeking subjects in the classical world, should have overlooked Julia, whose life-story is full of the glare of authentic tragedy. He was quite right. Julia's life makes up a chapter beyond compare in the annals of womanhood. Within its savage sensuality, there flower, now and then, pure roses of attractiveness and romance. I shall deal with it soberly.

Tiberius's second marriage, to Augustus's daughter Julia, is another essential point in our understanding of him. I have already set on record Suetonius's opinion that the desire, or the caprice, which she felt for Tiberius was one of the reasons for this unhappy union. But who could be sure then, and still less who could reason today, about what went on in the heart of this woman whose immorality knew no bounds? Whom did she love, among all the fleeting men who passed beside her as lovers or as husbands? Not she herself could have said.

What is certain is that Tiberius did not love her, because he was in love with Vipsania; because his puritanical and reserved nature could not have been compatible with the frivolity and the shamelessness of this merry widow; and, finally, because there were many reasons, upon which I shall touch in a moment, for assuming that Tiberius's temperament, shy and somewhat frigid, was not one of those which make a man forget his habits and his conventions in the presence of an imperative desire, a mad desire such as this profligate princess was able to inspire in other Romans.

[1] Buchan, 15.

If Tiberius married her, it was solely in obedience to the will of Augustus, this time the instrument of Livia's ambition and the caprice of Julia herself.

It was under such ill auspices that their marriage began. Nevertheless, it seems that at the outset they lived in harmony and that Tiberius 'responded to Julia's love,'[1] which must have been no mean feat. Julia, who unfortunately for history was very prolific, promptly became pregnant (10 B.C.), but the male child to whom she gave birth did not survive. Suetonius, that conscientious and obliging commentator, tells us that from this moment their fleeting love vanished and they slept apart.

Moreover, Tiberius, busy waging war, was not often in Rome, and Julia was not, like her daughter Agrippina II later, a woman capable of living in the field in order to help her husband. When she was Agrippa's wife she had accompanied him on the journey which he made to the east; but this was a triumphal expedition, not a campaign. In Jerusalem she was welcomed with Asiatic pomp as though she were a goddess. Philo of Alexandria mentions the deep impression which the great city's temple, magnificently adorned for their reception, made upon the mind of Augustus's general.[2] At the beginning of her marriage to Tiberius, Julia similarly went with him to Aquileia to prepare for a military expedition; and it was there that she gave birth to the child who died. But henceforth their two lives, like their beds, remained apart for ever; and Julia gaily took advantage of the many triumphs and ovations which her husband was enjoying on the remote frontiers to abandon herself in Rome to the most shameless licence.

If the shade of Messalina had not been so close to her, Julia would have passed into history as the unexampled representative of sexual delirium. But we may judge her with more pity than harshness, since the pathological palliation of her excesses is well known. She was the daughter of placid Scribonia and Augustus, and it is through him that we must seek the germ of her wildness in the epilepsy of the Julian family. This is confirmed by the unhappy mental state of the children she had with Agrippa:

[1] Suetonius, *106, Tib.*, 7. [2] Philo, *30, 37*, 294 ff.

Caius, who was probably a schizophrenic; Agrippa Postumus, mentally backward, with indications of madness; Agrippina, with sudden fits of a decidedly abnormal nature; and Julia, given to the same erotic delirium as her mother. Doubtless the plebeian equilibrium of Agrippa's family did not suffice to neutralize the turbulent blood of the Julian family.

But environment, in this case as in so many others, played a much larger part than heredity itself. It is rare for men or women to be inexorably inclined towards evil through congenital and inherited predisposition. The heredity with which we are born is merely an invitation to follow a given path. It is easier for us, thanks to this impulse, to follow this path rather than the opposite one; but it is always the influence, casual or deliberate, of environment which, in the last resort, determines our moral path.

Julia lived in one of those difficult phases of a decadent society in which there is a sudden and dangerous transition from the rigour of the traditional to the audacity of the modern. Writers of the period such as Ovid give us some idea of what the libertinage which had invaded Rome was like, and this is corroborated by the repeated attempts to restrain it by means of severe laws and sanctions during the reigns of Augustus and Tiberius. In this conflict puritan Livia represented tradition, and Julia represented innovating modernity.[1] Livia brought up her stepdaughter Julia, and Julia's daughters, Julia II and Agrippina I, 'with such strictness that she trained them to work wool, never say a single secret word, never hide the smallest action, and have no relations whatever with the outside world.'[2]

In such cases, excessive strictness, contrasted with the free and easy air of the streets, may provoke a rebellion which leads, through reaction, to wantonness. In Julia's attitude there was, in fact, something of youthful satiety with the distaff and the irking silence of the imperial home.

But above all, by way of excuse for her, we must bear in mind what a solvent effect must have been exerted upon women not endowed with the strongest health by such sudden and continual

---
[1] This point is very well studied by Ferrero, 27.
[2] Suetonius, 106, Aug., 64.

marriages and divorces, without love ever being taken into account, even as a matter of courtesy. The most shameful white slave traffic of our time is less immoral than what then amounted to plain prostitution in the name of reason of state.

Julia's Husbands and Lovers

Julia was fourteen years old, and therefore incapable of knowing what she was doing, when she was married for the first time to Marcellus II (25 B.C.). Two years later Marcellus died, and, after two years of widowhood, in 21 B.C. she was married again, to Agrippa, a sturdy soldier, 'nearer boorishness than refinement,'[1] who was twenty-two years older. The divergence between Agrippa's harsh and unpolished character and his wife's fashionable fickleness and dissipation made impossible any harmony between them, other than that bestowed by ordinary external convention in the frivolous environment of palaces and due fulfilment of the duty of parenthood. This unequal union lasted nine years, and they turned it to good account for their fatherland, since they had five children, of whom the last was born a few months after Agrippa's death, in the year 12 B.C. In this same year, Julia was married again, to Tiberius, after his sudden divorce, upon which I have already commented, from Vipsania, daughter of the first marriage of Agrippa, Julia's dead husband.

So Tiberius, full of well-founded doubts, married the widow of his own father-in-law. There is no reason why any of these legal unions should strike us as more moral than the clandestine unions which Julia meanwhile had with her numerous lovers.

We can now better understand how her dangerous heredity, combined with a family and social environment in which surface strictness covered a fundamental absence of moral sense, produced that reckless life of hers, which has been handed down to us with a legendary halo of scandal.[2] Legend has spared her no aberration of sexual conduct. She was even accused by her own grandson, Caligula, of incest with Augustus, of which Agrippina I was the presumed offspring.[3]

[1] Pliny, 79, XXV, 9.
[2] See Suetonius, 106, Aug., 65; Velleius, 114, II, 100; Dion, 22, LV, 10.
[3] Suetonius, 106, Calig., 23.

Let us turn, to be just, to a more reputable testimony, that of Seneca.[1] 'The divine Augustus,' he says, 'exiled his daughter, who had surpassed in impudicity every infamous meaning of the word, thus covering the imperial home with scandal: lovers admitted in droves; nightly orgies throughout the city; the Forum and the Tribune, whence her father had proclaimed laws against adultery, chosen by his daughter as a place of disorder; daily meetings beside the statue of Marsyas, where, worse than an adulteress, a mere prostitute, she claimed her right to every shamelessness in the arms of the first passer-by.'

The statue of Marsyas, in the Forum, was the meeting-place of the prostitutes of Rome; and, according to Pliny,[2] Julia went so far as to put a crown on it, one night when she was drunk. Augustus later learnt about this, and, despite the deep hurt to his family pride, set it on record in the decree in which he banished his daughter.

Velleius, a trustworthy man and a contemporary, gives us a list of some of her known lovers: Iulus Antonius, Appius Claudius, Scipio, and others with names no less illustrious. Among them let us note, with sneaking sympathy, a choice specimen of hypocrisy, one Quintius Crispinus, 'who concealed the most shameless misconduct behind a mask of severity.' They are always amusing, these grave men, disguised in solemnity, who amuse themselves like students, especially when their dissoluteness is disclosed, so scandalizing the faint-hearted and terrifying other hypocrites who have similarly doffed the bearded masks of gravity.

To these known names we must add Julia's anonymous, but innumerable lovers of a quarter of a hour, picked up by chance in her erotic revels through the lanes of the suburbs.

Rome was passing at this time through a phase of the ascendancy of women in private life, and therefore in public life; and in all periods in which this occurs there appears the type of woman of shameless sensuality, insatiable and flighty, who is but one symbol the more of usurpation of masculine rôles: in this case, the rôle of Don Juan. In Augustus's and the following reigns we may note several cases typical of this variation of the feminine instinct,

[1] Seneca, *100*, VI, 32.   [2] Pliny, *79*, XXI, 6.

which crops up from time to time in the history of nations, and always with the same significance.

Several of Julia's love-affairs became famous, among them her affair with Iulus Antonius, son of Mark Antony and Fulvia, and husband of Augustus's niece Marcella I. This Marcella I had previously been Agrippa's wife, so that Iulus Antonius, not content with legally robbing the great soldier of his first wife, afterwards robbed him also of his second wife, through the more tasty means of adultery. Iulus Antonius was a great gallant and a poet, a friend of Horace, who dedicated one of his odes to him, and he was much favoured by Augustus, who, in addition to marrying him to his niece, made him consul. The emperor's indignation knew no bounds when he learnt that Iulus Antonius had repaid these favours by seducing his daughter—or letting himself be seduced by her. The seducer committed suicide to escape exile or execution.

But, amid the endless stream of arrows which rebounded off Julia's invulnerable white skin, there was one which, through the slight chink that Don Juans of either sex possess, struck her to the heart. Her most constant lover, perhaps her one true love, was Sempronius Gracchus, one of the Don Juans of the period, 'a man of exalted birth, agile mind and eloquence, which he employed for evil.' He seduced Julia while she was still Agrippa's wife, and his love-affair with her continued during her marriage to Tiberius.[1] Later we shall see how, like other frivolous men, he was capable of dying with dignity and courage, when the betrayed husband, now in power, took his resentful revenge upon him.

All the historians are in agreement that, up to the last moment, Augustus was ignorant of his daughter's licentious mode of living: a strange thing, since it was the gossip and the scandal of all Rome. Husbands, through a kindly design of the gods, are often the last to hear about such things; but fathers are not, especially when they are rulers. In this case, apparently, it was the other way round.

Tiberius, on the contrary, did know what everyone else knew:

[1] Tacitus, *107*, I, 53.

the reiterated ridicule which covered Agrippa's glorious grey hairs; and he was aware that he inherited it. He said nothing. His face betrayed nothing: he was a master at making up his expression at will. But this tremendous humiliation to his family pride was fine fuel for his resentment.

Tiberius's Sexual Timidity

The worst of it was that Julia, not content with pursuing at Tiberius's side the same adulterous life as when she was Agrippa's wife, went from bad to worse. Her numerous lovers and finally her unrestrained prostitution, described to us by Seneca, corresponded with the period of her marriage to Tiberius.

But her progress along the road of scandal cannot be explained unless we assume her husband's condonation. Whatever Julia's temperament may have been, it is obvious that such open and repeated wantonness on the part of a wife can never occur unless the husband is a cynic—which Tiberius was not—or unless he deserves the title of husband only in a nominal sense. The most virile of men, such as Agrippa was, is exposed to the danger that his wife may prefer someone else, even though he be less virile. But a case not merely of adultery, but of scandalous promiscuity, if it be tolerated by the husband, amounts to public recognition of his own conjugal incompetence.

Everything we know about Tiberius confirms this suspicion: to my mind, no mere suspicion, but a certainty. It is unquestionable that this mysterious man was a chaste man, and, since he was not so through virtue, he was so through necessity, or in other words through timidity: a diagnosis which fits in very well with his melancholic and reserved psychology. This is one of the points in the psychological life of Tiberius—very similar, in this respect, to that of other tyrants known to history—which it is essential to clear up.

He was married for the first time at the age of about twenty-three; and the seven or eight years which elapsed before Vipsania became pregnant may be regarded as an index of that matrimonial apprenticeship, sometimes very long, which many sexually timid men require before living together calms their initial fear.

It is true, on the other hand, that Julia, his second and bolder spouse, promptly became pregnant; and I should not like to cast doubts on Tiberius's responsibility for this event, though every doubt is admissible when we are dealing with such a heroine of polyandry. But the significant thing is that, after his breach with Julia, this man of thirty-two renounced all amorous activity.

This fact is doubly significant in the case of a man like Tiberius who was a candidate for the emperorship and later became emperor; for he had only one son, and that, in those days when death gloated over distinguished victims, only remotely guaranteed the succession. So it is singular that he made no attempt at even one of those endless divorces and remarriages that filled the lives of other emperors up to their old age.

That Tiberius's failure to remarry was not offset by clandestine love-affairs seems equally certain, since we do not find the least reference to them in that ebullition of gossip and facile calumny which gives such a particular character to his reign. Only Suetonius[1] mentions a certain Mallonia, 'whom Tiberius, now elderly, tried to seduce, but who persistently refused his shameful petitions'; but this reference forms part of the accusations of libertinage and degradation against Tiberius during his latter years in Capri, which I am unable to accept.

Tiberius's Left-handedness

We may take it, then, that Tiberius was a sexually timid man, as are many other resentful men, who may be so precisely because of their timidity. Tiberius's timidity, soothed by the sheltering influence of Vipsania's affinity to him, suffered a relapse when her place in his bed was taken by impetuous Julia, the prototype of the brilliant, exacting and notorious woman who not merely terrifies the timid, but may even make men timid who normally are not.

This very common anomaly of the sexual instinct particularly affects men of tall stature like Tiberius. It also affects left-handed men; and we know that Tiberius was left-handed. Suetonius

---

[1] Suetonius, *106*, *Tib.*, 45.

tells us that 'his left hand was stronger and more nimble than the other.'[1]

This fact that Tiberius was left-handed is very important. Hirschfeld, and I myself, have pointed out its frequency in men with anomalies of the sexual instinct, such as homosexuality and timidity, which have some of their roots in common, and for this reason are often mistaken for one another. Tiberius was not homosexual, and, strange to say, this infamy, one of the first charges to be hurled against any unpopular public man, was never imputed to him. Indeed, if I am not mistaken, Tiberius was the only one of the Cæsars, including Julius Cæsar and Augustus, to whom such a sin was not imputed, save for the calumnies surrounding his later years in Capri, which are of no account. Leonardo da Vinci is another immortal left-handed man who was also accused of sinning in this way, whereas in fact he was only a timid man.[2]

Julia's Scorn

But there is also a passage in Tacitus, obscure and much disputed, which in my judgement is cleared up by this assumption. It is that[3] in which the great historian relates that Julia, who, as we have seen, at the outset set her cap at Tiberius, years afterwards alleged that their marriage 'was unequal.' According to Tacitus, Julia's 'scorn,' which derived from this fact, was the main cause of her husband's retirement to Rhodes. What was this 'scorn' of hers, what was the reason that made Julia shun her husband, and made him retire to an island, filled with humiliation?

Baker[4] rightly rejects the hypothesis that Julia's scorn was based, as some authors have suggested, upon difference in birth, since the blood of the Julians was neither much more nor much less aristocratic than that of the Claudians. The Julians had rapidly made themselves famous through Julius Cæsar's feats of

---
[1] Suetonius, *106*, *Tib.*, 68.
[2] On this point see my book 63. Recently I encountered a very typical case of a sexually timid man, who regarded himself, with no reason, as homosexual; and he was a left-handed man, who wrote inversely, looking-glass fashion, like Leonardo da Vinci. Henting (39) also notes the frequency of left-handedness in schizophrenics such as Ludwig II of Bavaria, whose sexual instinct was confused.
[3] Tacitus, *107*, I, 53.   [4] Baker, *8*, p. 65.

arms and Augustus's triumphs. Their aristocracy was, therefore, an upstart one; and, accordingly, when Mark Antony attacked Augustus, he threw it in his face that his great-grandfather had been a freedman, his grandfather a usurer, and another of his ancestors an African, a baker and a perfume-seller.[1] Even after the Julian stock ranked as 'divine,' the true aristocrats regarded it with that tacit disdain which a new nobility always inspires in an old one. We find a passage in Seneca which doubtless refers to this when he says 'one must distrust those who, in speaking of their ancestors, when they lack a man, put a god in his place.'[2]

A new-born divinity is lower, from the viewpoint of patrician pride, than an old aristocracy. So the Julians could not regard with contempt the Claudians of ancient tradition; and least of all could Julia, widow of Agrippa, such a plebeian that Caligula was ashamed of his descent from him 'because of the lowness of his origin.'[3]

It is unquestionable that Julia's contemptuous attitude was based upon her intimate relations with Tiberius. About this time Julia wrote a famous letter to her father, in which she was abusive of her husband.[4] Baker assumes that in it she related abominations and abnormalities such as those which were later imputed to Tiberius in Capri; and he adds that it is possible that it was from the text of this letter, and not from the *Memoirs* of Agrippina II, Nero's mother, as is generally believed, that Suetonius informed himself about Tiberius's sexual and sadistic delirium, which has covered his memory with dishonour.

But all this is pure supposition. All we know about the letter is that in it Julia was abusive of her husband and that she justified to her father the contempt which she felt towards him, and at the same time, to a certain extent, her own more than irregular mode of life. It was said on all sides that the missive was drafted by Sempronius Gracchus, Julia's true love, who must have been well acquainted with all her secrets after so many years of adulterous relations with her. Instead of imagining that the letter contained charges of sexual abnormalities and excesses, of which no

---

[1] Suetonius, *106, Aug.*, 2 and 4. [2] Seneca, *99*, III, 28.
[3] Suetonius, *106, Calig.*, 23. [4] Tacitus, *107*, I, 53.

one had hitherto thought of accusing Tiberius, it is much more logical to suppose simply that Julia denounced her husband's conjugal incapacity.

Sexual monstrosities are rare; timid and impotent men are numerous; and a historian of a man's life should choose, between the two hypotheses, not the one which is more entertaining for the reader, but the one which has the greater human probability of being the right one.

There is another item of evidence, interesting although indirect, which supports my way of thinking. It is that Tiberius, when he became emperor, laid down the dogma that sexagenarians were incapable of procreation:[1] a great biological mistake, which was probably based upon his own experience as a man who prematurely became sexually weak.

Another hypothesis which strikes me as worth consideration, though it has not hitherto been considered, is that Julia was repelled by the ulcers and scabs which, as early as this, were beginning to spread over Tiberius's body and face. He himself felt ashamed of them. Later we shall see that these lesions, which were possibly leprous or syphilitic, were horrible in appearance and had a foul smell.

Tiberius's Flight through Timidity

At this moment of conjugal tragedy occurred the episode, already mentioned, of Tiberius's retirement to Rhodes, which has much bearing upon my thesis. I shall show later that there were, at the same time, political reasons which contributed towards this strange flight. But we shall see also that the genesis of Tiberius's flight was mainly bound up with reasons of a biological kind: his resentment, a passion which often finds vent, through a tendency towards flight, in a demand for solitude; and, in addition, the motives of a sexual kind with which I am dealing. So much is hinted at by Tacitus, the greatest expert in the human soul among the historians of the period.

There is no doubt that Tiberius was wounded by the environment of scandal in which his wife placed him; and, over and above

[1] Suetonius, *106, Claud.,* 23.

this, what impelled him to flee was the fear inspired in him by a bedfellow beyond his strength. It is very significant that, when he had been four years in retirement on the island, and when Augustus, now assured of his daughter's moral degradation, thundered against her his edict of exile and divorce, Tiberius, as soon as he heard about this, wrote several letters to his father-in-law asking him to diminish the severity of his sentence upon Julia. This attitude on the part of the betrayed husband has been attributed to his kindliness; but it was merely an expression of relief from his burden, which was removed with the exile of his wife.

The proof of this is that he never forgave Julia. When he became emperor, he did not set her at liberty, but on the contrary accentuated the despair which led to her death. Meanwhile the soul of this timid man breathed more freely in the knowledge that he was free from his exacting spouse;[1] and soon afterwards, thus comforted, he sought Augustus's assent to his return to Rome.

From this moment onwards, no one ever referred to any love-affair on the part of Tiberius, legal or illegal, normal or abnormal, until his retirement to Capri, in A.D. 26, when he had reached the age of sixty-seven. It was then that the story began of his unrestrained sexuality, which deserves to be considered at some length.

The Legend of Capri

Most of Tiberius's defenders, from Voltaire onwards, attribute this alleged madness of Tiberius in his old age to the calumnies of impudent Suetonius.[2] They forget that another historian, Dion, of whom they themselves make much use as their authority for their apologias, explicitly says about Tiberius that 'the incontinent love which he showed for men as well as women of the highest birth earned him general contempt.' Dion adds that his friend Sextus Marius was accused of incest by Tiberius in revenge for keeping his daughter out of the emperor's way, fearing lest he should dishonour her. 'These scandals gained him the reproach of infamy.'[3]

[1] Suetonius, *106, Tib.*, 11.   [2] On this point see my book 66.
[3] Dion, 22, LVIII, 22.

Modern historians, therefore, are not telling the truth when they say that Dion does not refer to Tiberius's sexual scandals, since, as we have just seen, he does speak of them, and in the plainest terms. Nevertheless, Suetonius[1] is the principal author of the legend, when he paints, with coarse crudity, a series of erotic and sadistic pictures which have as their setting obscenely decorated rooms in the palaces of Capri and the marvellous grottoes of the island, and, as their subject, the libidinous and bloodthirsty old man and a chorus of girls, youths and boys.[2] Everyone is familiar with these stories, which for century after century have haunted the dreams of young students of humanity.

I am among those who believe in the absolute improbability of these wild excesses. But I do not agree with the historians for the reason given by them as though with one accord, namely the impossibility that a man who had lived a life of physical austerity and almost complete chastity should launch out into the licence and the erotic fatigue which Suetonius describes, at an age when most men are thinking rather about sitting peacefully in the sun and commending their souls to God; just as the Emperor Charles V did in Yuste, and as Tiberius probably did in Capri. The argument to which I refer appears for the first time in Voltaire and later in his henchman Linguet.[3]

Without mentioning Voltaire, La Harpe refutes him through Linguet, an innocent liberal who served many purposes, among them that of a scapegoat, and, in the end, did not escape the guillotine. La Harpe, with his experience as a priest, must have known the mysteries of love much better than vain Voltaire, and he points out, very rightly,[4] that a lusty young man needs no such devilries to enjoy his hours of love; the purest love is always that of the most virile, and that it is precisely the weak, and therefore the

---

[1] Suetonius, *106, Tib.*, 42 *et seq.*

[2] It is interesting to note that one of the scenes described by Suetonius, ridiculous in their sheer unlikelihood, refers to Tiberius as bathing in the blue, lukewarm water of a grotto, surrounded by lascivious boys swimming like little fish alongside an old shark. Amiel, who may have been confused in his chronology and in his social categories, but was certainly not in his sexual instinct, delighted in playing with little boys and saying much the same thing to them: 'I am a big fish, and you are little fish swimming beside me.' See the prologue to my book *63*.

[3] Voltaire, *117. Sur la tolèrance*, XXV, 46 and 47. Linguet, *56*.

[4] La Harpe, *53*.

elderly, who, when they lose their heads, have to resort to the wildest follies in order to continue the obstacle-race of love.

We doctors have painful experience to what an extent even men who were models of continence into old age may fall into these disorders. The most scandalous case of sexual perversion which I have encountered was that of a man well known for his exemplary life until he was past seventy. It was after this age that his sexual instinct went astray.

So the madness ascribed to Tiberius might have overtaken him in an abnormal phase of senility, and it would have been quite compatible with the continence of his youth and his middle age. But it is improbable that this was the case. It is improbable because Tiberius was a sexually timid man, and perhaps from an early age an impotent man. The timid man never ceases to be so, and he never exchanges his habitual bashfulness for such orgies as Suetonius describes, especially at an age when the causes of the inhibition of his sexual instinct are increased by physical decline. Besides, the melancholia and the implacable resentment which embittered his soul when he retired from Rome are incompatible with such dramatic bacchanalia.

My scepticism about them is therefore founded not on any sentiment of unconditional admiration for the emperor, which I do not feel, or on the childish arguments of Voltaire and other defenders of him, but on the psychosexual and social grounds to which I have just referred.

What, then, was the origin of the story of Tiberius's profligacy? It leaps to the eyes that the alleged episodes in Capri are a legend, taken neither from Agrippina II's *Memoirs* nor from Julia I's letter to Augustus, but created by public imagination. This was a really 'punitive legend,' with which society punished a man whom it hated on other grounds, and it punished him, as the arbitrary mind of the masses, of which Suetonius was the mouthpiece, is in the habit of doing, by the exaggeration of his actual vices and the fabulous invention of fresh ones into the bargain. Later we shall note the relationship which exists in the public mind between sexual excess, this time false, and cruelty, in this case undeniable.

Not without reserve, posterity has absolved Tiberius of any such infamy. It would not be just, however, that this absolution should carry with it that of other misdeeds which he undoubtedly committed, and for which this legend was precisely a punishment.

Julia's Exile

The epilogue to Julia's life was cruel. Whatever were her sins, and I have not concealed them, we are repelled by her father's cold persistence in his severity towards her; and we are led to think that perhaps those authors are right who suppose that, together with her licentious living, there were other grounds, perhaps political, which serve to explain his sternness. Pliny says that 'Julia had parricidal plans.'[1] This does not appear to be true; but only on some such grounds is the emperor's relentless wrath to be understood. Suetonius says that Augustus at first intended to put Julia to death;[2] but finally he contented himself with exiling the adulteress to the island of Pandataria (2 B.C.), whither her mother, humane and magnanimous Scribonia, bravely followed her.

Exile at this period did not always mean much physical hardship. For those who suffered it there were sometimes chosen not sterile rocks, but the enchanting islands of the Mediterranean to which wealthy people from more than one continent resort today for pleasure and amusement, such as the Balearics. It was on one of them that Votienus Montanus, the writer, spent his exile under Tiberius; and we may assume that he dreamed and worked beneath its blue sky, just as Chopin did centuries later, without excessive bitterness. The comforts which personages of sufficiently high rank enjoyed in exile were, on occasion, so great that Seneca was able to say that 'the viaticum of some exiles of today is worth more than the patrimony of the powerful of yesteryear.'[3]

But this was not what exile meant in Julia's case. She was forbidden any comforts, including wine, and any relations with men, even her slaves: perhaps the greatest deprivation for her. Five years later she left the island for Regium, where she died

---

[1] Pliny, 79, VII, 46.   [2] Suetonius, 106, Aug., 65.
[3] Seneca, 99, 12.

soon after the assassination of her last son, Agrippa Postumus, in A.D. 14. For some time already she had suffered much pain in her stomach, perhaps a legacy from her long nights of orgy, and found no relief in the plant extracts which her doctors prescribed for her.[1]

In the endless hours of her exile, she must have remembered her earlier life as exiles always remember it, as though it were another life, the wonderful life of another Julia, to whom the whole world bowed down. With that clairvoyance with which one understands fate in the hour of irremediable misfortune, she must have realized that in this world everything is absurd and everything is logical at one and the same time: apotheosis and persecution alike, contrasting cards of the destiny that rules our lives beneath the influence, inaccessible to human reason, of the will of God.

Perhaps the one thing of all which she could not understand was the unquenchable wrath of her father, who not only never forgave her, but even, carrying his animosity beyond the grave, forbade her and her daughter, the other Julia, no less full of sins of the weak flesh, to be buried in the imperial mausoleum.[2]

Punishment of the Lover

So harsh was Julia's father, Augustus, who was to leave behind him in history a trail of semi-divine glory. Tiberius, her husband, humiliated, resentful, incapable of any generous gesture, coldly clinched his cruelty. After Augustus's death, he increased the severity of Julia's exile. He prevented her from leaving her house, and deprived her of the small pension which her father had allowed her.[3]

As for her lover, Gracchus, who had spent the last fourteen years confined on a rocky island off the north coast of Africa, Tiberius ordered him to be put to death. At the sight of the soldiers arriving, Gracchus hastened to the beach, where he learnt his impending fate and faced death bravely. After writing to his wife, he calmly bent his neck before the executioner,[4] steadfast in the

---

[1] Pliny, *79*, XIX, 29.   [2] Suetonius, *106*, *Aug.*, 101.
[3] Suetonius, *106*, *Tib.*, 50.   [4] Tacitus, *107*, I, 53.

knowledge that his blood would for ever stain Tiberius, who, incapable though he was of senile excesses in Capri, was only too capable of calculated, cold-blooded revenge upon those who offended him.

The Populace and Julia

There is a moving feature in connection with this sad story, namely the affection which the populace showed for Julia during her days of misfortune, partly just because her name was Julia and the illustrious blood of the Julians, beloved by the man in the street, ran so freely in her veins; and partly by way of reaction against the cruelty of the punishment inflicted on her, which was largely attributed to Livia, her stepmother and mother-in-law. This was one of the reasons for the lack of affection which Rome displayed towards the empress. Besides, the popular mind is always disposed to pardon sins of love, and it was especially so when they were committed by a woman as beautiful as Julia against a husband so unlikable as Tiberius.

People flocked to petition the irate emperor that he should allow his daughter to return to Rome. Augustus replied that he would see fire and water mix first. Then the people of Rome, not knowing what else to do for the unhappy princess, flung flaming torches into the Tiber, in the hope that the miracle of a union of the two elements would come to pass. Naturally it did not. All that was achieved, by dint of petition, was Julia's transfer from her solitary island to Regium.[1]

We may be sure that Julia was comforted, not so much by the betterment of her position, as by this breath of the affection of the populace which was wafted from Rome to her in her exile.

Portrait of Julia

Historians of the period say that Julia was very beautiful, and that she possessed all the other graces in addition to perfection of feature. Her mode of living was sumptuous. Her luxury and extravagance knew no bounds. One of her fads was dwarfs, who even at this time served as an inhumane amusement for the

[1] Dion, 22, LV, 13.

mighty. Her daughter, Julia II, so like her mother, copied her in this and in worse things, and went everywhere with a little monstrosity in whom she delighted, to the great annoyance of Augustus, who hated deformity.[1]

Such likenesses of her as have been handed down to us convey either a coarse and somewhat virile face, as in the case of the Chiaramonti bust,[2] or else a hawk-like, sensual profile, as in the case of coins stamped with her effigy. It is said that white streaks made their appearance prematurely in her black hair, much to the mortification of such a flirtatious person.[3]

As for her traits of talent which the historians describe in their books, they convey simply a childish smartness, which would have left no trace if it had not borne the imperial stamp. In short, Julia was, in my opinion, a commonplace woman with her morality torn to pieces by heredity and bad example. But she fills me with pity, this woman so weak in her human failings, so harried by the strength of men ironclad in their hypocrisy.

In the last phase of her life she was intensely unhappy, as intensely as only those can be who have earlier been lucky beyond their deserts. She never knew the great consolation of pardon, human or divine. She died in infamy in her exile without hearing the superhuman voice which was soon to speak: the voice of Him who was able to understand the Magdalene.

[1] Pliny, 79, VII, 16. Suetonius, 106, Aug., 83.
[2] The psychological traits which Baring-Gould (10) deduces from contemplation of this bust seem to be suggested by prejudice, since, like everyone else, he knew beforehand what Julia was like. This is a mistake very easy to make in this class of investigation into the iconography of dead and gone persons with a strongly marked personality.
[3] Women whose hair goes prematurely white are, in fact, usually highly sexed and very prolific. Many medical authorities regard white streaks as a sign of excessive activity of the thyroid, and this often coincides with obvious hypereroticism.

PART II
The Clash of Clans

I

JULIANS VERSUS CLAUDIANS

Warring Passions

TIBERIUS'S relations with his mother, and with Augustus, his stepfather and father-in-law, have been interpreted by historians according to their fancy. His apologists depict him as an almost angelic being, and among his virtues they include an unbounded filial love. Others stick to the classical version that the son and his parents did not get on well together.

But the truth is that we are not concerned with a mere family dispute, and it is puerile to consider the problem in such terms. Deep and confused feelings due to a complex of childhood made up the woof of this relationship; and with it were intertwined unbridled hatreds and ambitions concerned both with politics and with clans.

In Tiberius's eyes, Livia was always the morally adulterous mother: the mother who had deserted her home and brought sadness upon her husband's venerable head. Augustus was the stepfather, doubly hateful because he had offended and humiliated the noble old man in addition to robbing him of his wife. Tiberius never forgot this. His puritanical and disciplined spirit makes him seem to us respectful towards the emperor and submissive to the authority of this stepfather and his mother. But, beneath his formal deference, his passion slowly fermented.

The story of this passion, which is in fact the psychological basis of the reigns of Augustus and Tiberius, is in itself the story of the struggle of the Claudians against the Julians: a struggle full of dramatic episodes, in which the characters succeed one another, sometimes rising almost to the point of seizing power, sometimes falling headlong into exile or death.

This long battle lasted from Augustus's marriage to Livia until

Tiberius's death. The two sides were captained in the fight respectively by each of the married pair, Livia and Augustus. Rarely has history presented us with so striking an example of the interplay of passions.

Tiberius's mother Livia, united by marriage to Augustus, preserved all her life a family spite against the clan of Augustus, who had persecuted the Claudians until shortly before he married her. Like the females of certain insects, she conquered Augustus and made him her spouse in order to get the better of him. Perhaps, given her temperamental frigidity, she respected Augustus as a man; for such respect is compatible with family hatred. But it is obvious that her whole life was made up of one gigantic effort of her woman's will to hitch the destiny of her own family, the Claudians, to the fabulous chariot of the imperial power.

In this enterprise she was the ally of her son Tiberius, although an abyss of instinctive passion separated them. Thus family ambition and ambition for power united Livia to her son and separated her from Augustus; and, in its turn, the sexual link which united her to her husband separated her from Tiberius.

The great struggle between Claudians and Julians developed mutely, but implacably, beneath the shelter of the puritanical palace. When Augustus died, the Claudians triumphed with the raising of Tiberius to power. But the fight went on between Tiberius, always the instrument of his mother's ambition, and the surviving branch of the Julians, that of Germanicus and his wife Agrippina, which in the end, when Livia and Tiberius were both dead, got the upper hand with the succession to the throne of the last, and the worst, of the male Julians, Caligula.

The story of this struggle is the subject of this and the following chapters.

Tiberius's Triumphs

On the death of his father, Tiberius was taken into the home of his stepfather, in the year 33 B.C., when he was nine years old. From this date until 26 B.C. he remained there with his mother, who took care to give him a first-class education, proper to the lofty destiny which the astrologers had predicted for him.

His relations with Augustus, often away from home on journeys of inspection or waging war, were not close until the year 26 B.C. In that year, when Augustus set off for Gaul and Spain, he took with him his stepson, now just sixteen years old. From then until A.D. 14, when Augustus died, Tiberius's political collaboration with him was continuous, save for the period of Tiberius's eclipse during his retirement to Rhodes. The histories of the two emperors were so closely linked that it is impossible to write them separately.

Young Tiberius seemed to have been chosen by the gods to be crowned with good fortune. He was endowed with all the talents and with unusual, though perhaps rather feminine, good looks. In the course of these thirty-nine years much glory, many triumphs, came his way. I shall record them briefly.

In the year 24 B.C. he was made eligible to receive honours, five years before the legal age. In the following year he became quæstor. In the year 20 B.C. he was sent to the eastern provinces, stopping on the way enchanted with Rhodes, where his misanthropic love for islands began. In 19 B.C. he became prætor. In 16 B.C. he accompanied Augustus on another journey to Gaul and Spain, that remote and diverse land which must have much interested his contemplative mind: a land sunlit and strange, where there existed both the fierce heroism of the barbarians of Cantabria, that perpetual thorn in the flesh of Rome, and the subtle, forward-looking mind of the south, which was to produce Seneca, the most profound thinker of his time, and Trajan, restorer of the empire and greatest of its rulers.

In the year 15 B.C. he began his military successes in the Central Alps, side by side with his brother Drusus I. He repeated them during the years 12 B.C. to 9 B.C. on the Danube; in Germany from 9 B.C. to 6 B.C., and, on his return from Rhodes, from A.D. 4 to A.D. 9, when he returned victorious to Rome. He continued to wage war at intervals from A.D. 10 to A.D. 14, that is to say, until the death of Augustus,

In addition to ovations and warlike triumphs, he was twice consul (13 and 7 B.C.), once tribune (6 B.C.), and attained various other rewards and honours which his merits, the intrigues of his ambitious mother, and the adulation of the Senate laid at his feet. He shrank from accepting all of them and his manner in doing so (with which I shall deal further) suggests not so much modesty as timidity and proud scepticism.

A mere spectator of his laurel-strewn path, which could end only in his succession to Augustus, would scarcely doubt that what underlay it was affection and generosity on the part of the emperor, and gratitude on the part of Tiberius. But the truth is that between the two men there existed only a rancorous tension which gradually turned into hatred. I have already explained its origin. We may now take it for granted that, if Tiberius managed to succeed Augustus, it was against Augustus's will; that, lacking ambition of his own, Tiberius was urged on by the ambition injected into him by his mother; and that, in order to gain the succession, he had to leap over the corpses of all his competitors.

Genealogical Memorandum

Before we embark upon the episodes of the struggle, it may be helpful to remind the reader, lest he lose his way in the tangled growth of names and relationship, how the two hostile families were constituted.[1]

The Claudian family was represented: (1) by Tiberius, son of two pure Claudians, Tiberius Claudius Nero and Livia; (2) by the son of Tiberius and Vipsania, Drusus II; (3) by the son of Drusus II and Livilla, Tiberius Gemellus. Since Livilla, in her turn, was the daughter of Antonia II, Augustus's niece, Tiberius Gemellus possessed the blood of both families, but with the Claudian predominating.

The Julian family was constituted thus: (1) Marcellus II, nephew of Augustus and son of Octavia, though he also had Claudian blood through his father, Claudius Marcellus; (2) Caius Cæsar, Lucius Cæsar and Agrippa Postumus, born of Augustus's daughter Julia I and Agrippa, and therefore direct grandsons of Augustus; (3) Germanicus, of Julian blood through his mother Antonia II, daughter of Octavia, Augustus's sister, and perhaps on his paternal side too, if, in fact, his father, Drusus I,

---

[1] For further details, see the Genealogical Tables, pp. 224–225.

was the son of Augustus and not of Claudius Nero (Germanicus was, besides, married to Agrippina I, sister of Caius, Lucius and Agrippa Postumus); (4) the sons of Germanicus and Agrippina I, Nero I, Drusus III and Caligula.

This division, somewhat arbitrary owing to the uncertainty of some paternities, had as its basis not only genealogical grounds, but also elements of attachment so strong that they sometimes outweighed those of blood itself. For example, the whole branch of Drusus I, with his son Germanicus and Germanicus's sons, though they were officially half Claudian by blood, in fact formed the most outstanding representation of the Julian faction, thanks to a strong wave of popular enthusiasm which turned all of them into a branch of legendary Julian heroes, opposed to Tiberius.

Outline of the Clash of Families

The clash between Julians and Claudians comprised five main episodes, which may be superimposed upon the above genealogical table: (1) Marcellus II, Julian, versus Tiberius, Claudian; (2) Caius and Lucius, Julians, versus Tiberius; (3) Agrippa Postumus, Julian, versus Tiberius; (4) Germanicus, Julian, versus Tiberius; (5) Germanicus's sons versus Drusus II, Tiberius's son, and afterwards versus Drusus II's son, Tiberius Gemellus.

These episodes may be grouped into two main phases. During the first, while Augustus was alive, he used his power to try to extirpate the Claudians, who were supported by Livia. I shall call this first phase 'Julians versus Claudians.' During the second, after Augustus was dead, Tiberius (and behind the scenes Livia), now in power, tried to extinguish the Julians. I shall call this second phase 'Claudians versus Julians.'

A Stepfather's Antipathy

Despite the fact that he was united to the Claudian family through his love for Livia, Augustus retained all his life a passionate affection for his own family, the Julians. Until the day of his death he was anxious that a member of it should be his successor.

The reason for his preference was, above all, the call of the blood and the family pride that play so large a part in the life of men, and therefore in history, especially ancient history. But, if ever there was a man endowed to the utmost with the capacity for subordinating all else to political considerations, that man was Augustus; and this is precisely one of the reasons why he was such a great ruler.

So, if he favoured the Julian family with such tenacity, it is legitimate to assume that he did so in obedience to some motive in addition to family affection. This motive, arbitrary but potent, was his antipathy towards Tiberius.

That Tiberius, despite his military and political talents, was disliked by his stepfather there is no denying. If Augustus, in Tiberius's eyes, was his mother's abductor and an offender against his father, Tiberius, in Augustus's eyes, was the living prosecutor of his own misdeeds.

For that matter, no one ever found Tiberius congenial. I shall deal with this point more fully later. Suetonius tells us that Tiberius's arrogance and bitterness became evident while he was still a boy, and that for this reason his tutor in rhetoric, Theodorus of Gandara, called him 'a pitcher moulded with blood.'[1] Augustus, adaptable and adept in the art of getting on with people though he was, could never reconcile himself to his stepson's resentful manner.

But, since Augustus had no sons by Livia (or, at least, no admitted son), his natural successors were necessarily his stepsons, Livia's two sons, and, in the first place, Tiberius, the elder. This chronological priority was a misfortune for Rome, for it is probable that all the embroilment which the succession to Augustus involved would have been avoided if he could have been succeeded by Drusus I, who reconciled the rights of the Claudians with the emperor's own preference. We have already seen that Augustus clearly showed this preference for Livia's second son, who may have been his own son too. A further proof of this preference is that he had married Drusus I to his niece Antonia II, who was of the illustrious Julian blood, whereas he had married Tiberius to Vipsania, daughter of Agrippa, Augustus's general and friend, but a man of purely plebeian rank.

[1] Suetonius, *106*, *Tib.*, 57.

Perhaps Augustus might have associated the two brothers in the succession, and left to chance—which in those days often meant a sinister alliance with the will of the mighty—the possibility that the younger brother would reach the goal first. But Drusus I was killed in an accident, and unlikable Tiberius remained alone. Then a new candidate for the succession presented himself, in the person of Augustus's nephew Marcellus II, son of his sister Octavia. So began the first episode in the struggle between Julians and Claudians.

Marcellus versus Tiberius. Agrippa's Anger

Augustus's preference for Marcellus II very soon became public property. Marcellus II was not of pure Julian blood, since his father, Marcellus I, belonged to the Claudian clan.[1] Nevertheless, for the reasons which I have already stated, socially and in sentiment he represented the Julian race. This presumptive heir, according to Seneca, was 'a youth of active mind and much talent, thrifty and strictly continent':[2] virtues which, to be sure, did not do him much good, since he died young. He was the same age as Tiberius.

In Rome, where court ceremonial attained a high degree of hierarchical significance, Augustus's leanings towards Marcellus were taken for granted when, in the year 29 B.C., in the great triumph which celebrated the emperor's victory in the battle of Actium, Marcellus rode on the right of his triumphal chariot and Tiberius on the left.[3] Velleius, who was alive at the time of this event, declares that henceforth 'everyone thought that Marcellus would be the emperor's heir.'[4]

So certain seemed this intention of Augustus, that Agrippa, angered at his preference for Marcellus, absented himself from

---

[1] Marcellus I was a descendant of Claudius Marcellus, the famous general who defeated Hannibal. It was doubtless through him that Tiberius inherited his prudent military skill.

[2] Seneca, *98*, 2. Horace dedicated an Ode to him (*45*, I, 12), in which he praised him highly; but, as always, we must not attach too much importance to the eulogies of this excellent, but courtier-like poet. It is also supposed, as I have already remarked, that Marcellus was the youth whom Virgil extolled in his debatable *Eclogue* IV.

[3] Dion, *22*, III, 1.

[4] Velleius, *114*, II, 93. We find similar statements in Suetonius, *106*, *Aug.*, 66, and Dion, *22*, XLIII, 32.

Rome. Velleius himself tells us that, if Marcellus had been formally raised to the succession, 'Agrippa would not have let him enjoy it in peace.'[1]

At this time Augustus's health was very precarious. It was for this reason that there were such heated intrigues about his presumptive heir. It is probable that the emperor, so small in stature, was tubercular. As early as the year 29 B.C. he had been gravely ill; and in the years 24 and 23 B.C. he was on the point of death. He was saved by his doctor, Musa, by means of cold hydrotherapy, a treatment, then first coming into repute, which was to reappear so often in the course of medical history. It was believed in Rome that, since Musa had cured the emperor's illness with his cold water, it must necessarily cure all other diseases. Such is the sad fate of a doctor who makes a reputation.

Musa's first resounding failure was with poor Marcellus. This caused his professional star to wane; but Musa was by this time wealthy and so honoured that a statue had been erected to him. Doubtless his easy circumstances helped the court doctor to bear the injustice of the charge, brought against him from all sides, that he had cut short Marcellus's days, and even the insinuation that Livia had used him as an instrument to hasten Marcellus's death and so restore the prospects of succession in favour of her own family. But one man was grateful to him for his professional stupidity, and that was Agrippa.

Agrippa, 'the plebeian, the new man who made himself illustrious,' was indeed inordinately ambitious. His military genius gave him a right to be so; for, without detracting from Augustus's political qualities, it may be said that a great part of his fame fairly belonged to his admiral and general. A loyal but boorish man, he felt no sympathy whatever for Marcellus, despite the fact that he had been groomsman at his marriage,[2] and Marcellus's favour with the emperor infuriated him.

He was a great figure, this Agrippa. His head, lost amid the great collection of famous statues in the Augustus room in the

---

[1] Velleius, *114*, II, 93.

[2] It was owing to the fact that Augustus was ill that the marriage of Marcellus II and Julia I was presided over by Agrippa.

Louvre, at once attracts and holds the visitor's interest. There is in this self-willed effigy more intelligence, more nobility, than in all the other Cæsarian personages put together, including the great emperor himself.

But it remains a mystery what was the limit of Agrippa's ambition, and therefore what was the inner meaning of his anger and his retirement from Rome. In most cases, the ambitious man himself does not know the measure of his ambition; so how can anyone else know it? Some authors incline to believe that he aspired to be associated with Augustus in power, and eventually to succeed him. Such an ambition would not have been preposterous. If Marcellus II was the son of Octavia, Agrippa was married to Marcella I, who was Octavia's daughter. His mature age (he was about the same age as Augustus) and his great experience made him preferable to young and delicate Marcellus.

It appears, moreover, that Augustus himself had already encouraged such hopes on the part of his general. Dion tells us that in 23 B.C., when the emperor thought he was going to die, he gave his ring, the symbol of supreme power, not to Marcellus, but to Agrippa.[1]

All this would explain Agrippa's disillusionment when he found his young brother-in-law favoured instead of himself. But we cannot be sure whether this was just what happened. Suetonius explains the general's retirement on grounds of sensitiveness rather than disappointed ambition.[2] Whether it was through justifiable disappointment or mere delicacy, it is unquestionable that Agrippa could not stand Augustus's nepotism, and that he deliberately excluded himself from public life until Marcellus died in 23 B.C.

His death was a blow to his mother which Seneca sums up in these heart-rending words: 'the pain of her stricken soul became

---

[1] Dion, 22, LIII, 30. This historian depicts Agrippa as very devoted and submissive to Augustus (22, LV, 29); and he adds that Agrippa withdrew from Rome in agreement with Augustus himself, in order to avoid a clash with Marcellus, who disliked Agrippa (22, LIII, 32). But this explanation is less likely than that of indignation on Agrippa's part, which I give in the text.

[2] Suetonius, 106, Aug., 66. The same author repeats this idea elsewhere, saying that Agrippa withdrew from Rome 'lest he should seem a competitor and censor' of Marcellus II (106, Tib., 10).

corrupt, turning itself into her delight.'[1] Never would she have portraits of her son around her, because she had only too many pictures of him in her mind. Amid all the turbid passions of the court of the Cæsars, this pure maternal pain of Octavia's shines like a brilliant star in the night. She was, indeed, one of those few and admirable women whose virtue stood like a wall between Rome and complete depravity. Nothing could make her forget her dead son. We are told that once when Augustus sent Virgil, who was a great orator, to entertain her by reciting some of his heavenly verses, and when he mentioned Marcellus in one of them, Octavia fell to the ground in a faint, overcome by emotion.[2]

Augustus also gave public expression to his sorrow as one of the greatest of his life; but, although he was very fond of Marcellus, his regret was doubtless even more that of an emperor than that of an uncle. Marcellus's death shattered his plans for succession in the Julian line. So ended the first episode in the clash of clans, and the second began.

The new Cæsars

Now that fate had frustrated Augustus's intention of succession in favour of the Julians, it seemed inevitable that he should be forced to turn to the Claudians. Seneca tells us that Octavia, in her despair, hated Livia, 'who seemed to have inherited for her son (Tiberius) all the good fortune promised to hers (Marcellus)';[3] and perhaps we may find in these words a reference to the rumours of Livia's share in the death of the presumptive heir.

But so tenacious was the emperor that he would not admit defeat. He conceived the idea of marrying Agrippa, now over forty, to his daughter Julia, whom Marcellus had just left a childless widow, only eighteen years of age.[4] Possibly it was Agrippa himself who demanded this marriage, with all the strength conferred upon him by his recent disappointment, so that his ambition

---

[1] Seneca, *98*, I, 1.   [2] See Budé, *16*, p. 53.
[3] Seneca, *98*, I.
[4] This was Agrippa's third marriage. His first wife was Pomponia, by whom he had Vipsania, Tiberius's future wife. His second was Marcella II, daughter of the first marriage of Octavia (Augustus's sister) to Claudius Marcellus I. Agrippa divorced Marcella in order to marry Julia as his third wife.

should not be frustrated for the second time. It is certain that he had the support of Mæcenas, that well-known matchmaker, who approached Augustus with this forceful argument: 'You have made Agrippa so powerful that now there is nothing for you to do except either make him your son-in-law or put him to death.'[1]

The marriage took place a little later (21 B.C.) and, to Augustus's great delight, in the following year Julia gave birth to a son, Caius, and three years later to another, who was named Lucius. Lucky Augustus, happy to find that fate submitted to him with the same docility as men, adopted both of them. The two of them received the title of Cæsar, were brought up in the imperial household as Augustus's sons, and were obviously intended to be his successors.

The Julian inheritance thus seemed assured. Augustus sought to make it still more secure by ordaining that, if he died before the two boy Cæsars were old enough to rule, their own father Agrippa should act as regent for them, thereby fulfilling his own ambition for power.

But once more the divine will wrought havoc with human calculations. Agrippa, the strong, died prematurely, in the year 12 B.C., much earlier than Augustus, the weakling, whose death had so often been feared.

The general was carried away by an attack of gout, caused by his great gluttony all his life. Perhaps a contributory cause of his death was the torture of the ridicule with which Julia, his second wife, covered his glorious grey hairs.

Apart from his fame as a soldier, Agrippa was an unhappy man. According to Pliny,[2] he deserved his name; for Agrippa means 'born with difficulty,' and, in fact, he came into the world feet first, instead of in the normal posture, head first. Among the Romans this was regarded as an ill omen, contrary to the belief among the Spaniards, to whom being born feet first is a sign of good fortune in life. That the omen was fulfilled is borne out by the gout which tormented him from his youth; by his marital misfortune; and 'above all,' says Pliny, 'by the fact that he begot Agrippina,' with whose stormy history I shall deal later.

[1] Dion, 22, LIV, 6. [2] Pliny, 79, VII, 6.

Lucius and Caius versus Tiberius

Agrippa's death presented Augustus with the problem of finding a regent to take his place as guardian of the young Cæsars. The choice fell—this time there was no help for it—upon Tiberius, whom Augustus married in the following year (11 B.C.) to his daughter Julia, Agrippa's widow, for which purpose Tiberius, as we have already seen, had to divorce his first wife Vipsania, by whom he already had one son and another child coming, which was stillborn after the divorce.

It is certain that astute and tenacious Livia inspired this arrangement, in order to thrust Tiberius towards the possibility of power,[1] and that she was helped by the erotic caprice of Julia herself. With no less certainty we may assume that Augustus accepted Tiberius as son-in-law and guardian of the young Cæsars 'much against his will.'[2]

It is no less easy to suppose what must have been the attitude of Tiberius, who, remote from these intrigues, was campaigning beyond the frontiers with great success. The only information we have about him at this time is that which tells us how deeply grieved he was at his divorce from Vipsania. We may be sure that the gift of his new wife, Julia, already notorious for her shameless licence, was scarcely the best means either of consoling him for the loss of his beloved Vipsania, or of providing him with a fresh companion suited to his taciturn and timid character. So it was doubtless full of resentment that he accepted his new matrimonial position.

As for his political position, which set him below Caius and Lucius in precedence, he had rendered military services which he was entitled to regard as meritorious; and to these could be added his rights by birth, which were higher than those of the young Cæsars. Dion,[3] among others, underlines the inevitability of Tiberius's sense of a grudge against these Cæsars who had been preferred to him. Some modern authors deny this, basing themselves on the gratuitous assumption that his character was exem-

[1] This is the opinion of most modern authors: Gardthausen, *32*, I, 3. Dessau, *20*, I, 467. Ciaceri, *17*, II.
[2] Dion, *22*, LIV, 41. [3] Dion, *22*, LV, 9.

plary. But we have only to recall that he was a man, and one certainly not exempt from passion, in order to be assured that he could only regard the position of Agrippa's sons as heirs to the throne, contrasted with his own position as a mere guardian, as nothing less than a usurpation. As Ferrero puts it graphically, 'Tiberius could not swallow this affront.'[1] Caius and Lucius, for their part, did not feel the least liking for Tiberius, and, as we shall see, were not slow to show it.

Undoubtedly this resentment fermented darkly in his soul during this time, when, as Tacitus depicts him, aloof and dignified in his distant camp, he lived as hard a life as his legionaries, keeping military discipline among them with all the puritan severity of an upright man, but a man despairing in love.

Perhaps, too, it was during these melancholy days that he sought relief from his pain in wine, thus earning the wit of his troops when they changed his name from Tiberius to 'Biberius,'[2] His fondness for wine, which seems certain, does not, as his alarmed apologists believe, contradict the fact that he was a temperate man, as it is equally certain that he was. At that time, much more than today, wine was a gift of the gods which a sensible and even a learned man might use, not so much for the sensuous pleasure of drinking it, as for its specific virtue in effacing sadness of heart. Sombre Tiberius could scarcely aspire to be more virtuous than Cato himself; and Cato openly declared his liking for wine. A little later Seneca, the stoic, laid it down that wine 'washes away our troubles, cleanses the soul to its depths, and, among its other virtues, assures the cure of sadness.'[3]

---

[1] Ferrero, 28, 184.

[2] Suetonius, 106, Tib., 42. Pliny also says that Tiberius in his youth was addicted to wine (79, XIV, 28); and further on that his son Drusus had the same fondness for wine as himself. It is to be noted that Tacitus, who attacked Tiberius so strongly, does not mention his alcoholic addiction. La Bleterie (52) supposes that this omission was due to the fact that the great historian did not wish to annoy Trajan—during whose reign he wrote—who was also a great drinker.

[3] Seneca, 97, 17. Seneca's eulogy of wine was not echoed by other authors of his period, such as Pliny, who paints a terrible, and admirable, picture of the dangers of drunkenness. Above all, as particularly harmful he stresses drinking without eating, a very bad habit which, he says, was introduced in Tiberius's time through the fault of the doctors, 'seeking reputation with any novelty' (Pliny, 79, XIV, 28). It is only fair to Seneca to add that his eulogy of wine was cautious,

Sadness was a chronic disease in the case of Tiberius, and entitled him to a regular medicine. The love-affairs of his new wife, Julia, reached the ears of his soldiery like an echo of the brothel. As he reviewed his legionaries, suspicious Tiberius must certainly have seen in their eyes furtive reflections of roguish thoughts humiliating to his dignity.

Death of the two Cæsars

Once again fate was to upset the designs of men. Caius and Lucius had inherited the physical and mental weakness peculiar to so many princely families. Neither of them was worth much. About Lucius we have scarcely any data, apart from that of his early death, which occurred in A.D. 2. He died suddenly, at Marseilles, on his way to Spain. It was rumoured that the cause of his death was poison provided by Livia[1]—that insatiable poisoner, in the imagination of the Roman populace—bent on clearing the way for Tiberius. This was just one more legend; but, like the other crimes of which she was accused, it points both to the fact of Livia's opposition to the presumptive successors of the Julian family, and also to popular dislike of her.

About Caius we do know something. We know that he was a degenerate. Even honey-mouthed Velleius, who accompanied him on his last expedition to the east, and who, on the smallest provocation, compared all generals or princes with the gods themselves, speaks of him without the least enthusiasm. With all his adroitness as a court chronicler, he tells us that 'his vices were fostered by his courtiers,' and that 'his conduct was so changeable that it might offer abundant matter either for praise

since in other parts of his work he too paints a sinister picture of the evils of drunkenness; but even in these passages he insists that a drunkard is not always indiscreet. As an example he mentions Cossus, governor of Rome in Tiberius's time, to whom Tiberius, always suspicious though he was, saw no harm in revealing secrets which he would never have told his other officials, despite the fact that Cossus was almost always drunk. Such a drunkard, indeed, was Cossus that on one occasion he fell asleep in the Senate, and had to be picked up and taken home, without his knowing anything about it. In this passage, Seneca confirms what some historians say, but others deny: namely, that Tiberius gave an important office to L. Piso solely for the reason that he had drunk for three days without stopping (Seneca, *102*, LXXXIII).

[1] Tacitus, *107*, I, 3. Dion, *22*, LX, 11.

or for blame.'¹ In the mouth of so great an adulator, this ambiguous judgement was equivalent to the severest condemnation.

But Augustus, blinded by family affection, adored Caius. 'Light of my eyes,' he calls him in his letters, written with pathetic tenderness.² In Caius's expedition to the east, which Augustus prepared for his heir with a large escort of illustrious men, in order to train him for the office of emperor, the pomp of his journey was extraordinary. Ovid³ tuned his lyre to celebrate the apotheosis of the start of this journey, which was to end so tragically. He made lyrical prophecies about the victorious return of the heir, thus showing how far he lost his sense of divination when he took adulation as his muse.

Caius, who had just married Livilla, a very interesting woman about whom I shall have something to say later, showed obvious signs of mental dullness on this expedition. Not the least of them was falling into an ambush laid for him by his enemies, in which he was wounded. According to tradition, as a result of this event his mind became clouded, and, seized by profound melancholy, he withdrew into a life of solitude. Abandoning all his honours, he sought refuge, out of humility, on board a merchant ship,⁴ despite Augustus's frantic lamentation. Finally Augustus, in A.D. 2, persuaded him to return to Rome. But Caius was so ill that he died on the way, at Limyra, on the coast of Asia opposite Rhodes, before reaching the shores of his fatherland.

Even though it is true that a traumatism may cause madness, if this explanation is to hold good we have always to reckon with an innate predisposition to derangement. In Caius's case it is obvious that this was what happened. His wound, at the most, precipitated the disorder bequeathed him by his heredity. It is easy to see that this came to him through his mother, who was an amoral hysteric, with the same epileptic background as all her family, and not through his well-balanced father—if, indeed, Julia's promiscuity permits any assumption about her children's paternity.

[1] Velleius, *114*, 102 and 101.
[2] Malcovati, *61*, 13.
[3] Ovid, *75*, 1.
[4] Dion, *22*, LV, 11.

In this case, however, study of the portraits of Caius Cæsar seems to banish any such idea. The two in the Louvre, in fact, show a likeness between the young prince and Agrippa which indicates Agrippa's paternity, especially in the strong space between the eyebrows, which appears in Caius's weak face as a fleeting reflection of that which gives so much individuality to his father's fine bust.

Augustus adopts Tiberius

With the two Cæsars dead, the path was once more free for Tiberius, who had now returned from Rhodes (A.D. 3) and was living at Mæcenas's villa, aloof from all political activity. Meanwhile Augustus, beaten by fate and weakened by age—he was now sixty-six and overwhelmed with work and suffering —surrendered one more trench to the demands of Livia, more exacting than ever as she too grew older.

We may take for granted the contemporary account that it was she and not Tiberius, ever more haughty and withdrawn, who, with indomitable tenacity, garnered for her son the possibility of future power. Popular imagination held the empress capable of going to all lengths to achieve her long-standing desire. If so, the ambitious woman won an apparently complete triumph: three months after Caius's death, Augustus adopted Tiberius.

But the struggle was not over. Augustus still had two trenches left in which to defend the blood of the Julians: Agrippa Postumus and Germanicus. Agrippa Postumus was brother of the two dead Cæsars. Around him was to rage, in its third episode, the great battle between the two rival families.

The Elimination of Agrippa Postumus

It was impossible that Augustus should transfer to Agrippa Postumus the same fervent favour that he had shown towards Lucius and Caius; for this prince, born after his father's death, was notoriously abnormal: 'brutal and of violent temper,' 'extremely depraved in mind and character,' 'grossly ignorant and stupidly proud of his physical strength.'[1] So his contemporaries describe

[1] Suetonius, *106, Aug.*, 75. Velleius, *114*, II, 112. Tacitus, *107*, I, 3.

him, with irrefutable unanimity. A contemporary English historian finds only one pretext for defending him, namely, that he was an angler, and adds that anglers are never wholly bad.[1]

It would have been too much of a scandal for Augustus to repeat, in the case of this poor angler, the process of favouritism which he had carried out in the cases of Marcellus and the two Cæsars. But, at all events, Augustus ventured to adopt him at the same time as Tiberius, though he gave Tiberius precedence over him; and, in addition, he made Tiberius, in his turn, adopt Germanicus.

Fresh military successes increased the prestige of Tiberius, who received yet another triumph and was granted tribunician power for a further ten years. Nevertheless, Livia was not satisfied. Three years later (A.D. 7), by dint of intrigue, she contrived that Agrippa Postumus, who, though stupid as ever, had done nothing deserving condemnation (as Tacitus points out), should be exiled to the island of Planasia, near Elba, where centuries later another much more distinguished castaway of political storms was to set foot for a while.

The conditions of Agrippa's exile were so severe that they amounted to a living death. Tacitus adds that this time the ambitious empress achieved her design 'not by obscure intrigue, but with full publicity.' I shall deal in the next chapter with the last tragic phase of this unhappy prince's life.

So Agrippa Postumus, too, was eliminated from political life. But there still remained a whole family, that of Germanicus, which enabled Augustus, at once vacillating and stubborn, to pursue his underhand campaign against his stepson. The fourth phase of the struggle now began.

Germanicus versus Tiberius

Although Tiberius already had a son, Drusus II, aged fourteen, Augustus, when he adopted Tiberius, compelled him, as we have already seen, to associate himself with Agrippa Postumus and to adopt his nephew Germanicus, who, in addition to his half-Julian blood, possessed the prestige conferred upon him in the

[1] Buchan, 15, p. 249.

public mind by the fact that he was, so to speak, the reverse of Tiberius. By way of accentuating this preference, in the following year, A.D. 4, Augustus married Germanicus, who was nineteen, to his granddaughter Agrippina I, sister of his never forgotten grandsons, the Cæsars Caius and Lucius, who was just eighteen. Among the gossipers of Rome the report promptly ran that the emperor was bent at all costs on securing the succession for Germanicus, of whom he was very fond.

We can imagine the effect of this open demonstration of Augustus's preference upon the mind of Tiberius, resentful of the favour which he had already shown to Marcellus, Caius and Lucius, and Agrippa Postumus. Tacitus tells us that, in the last resort, only Livia's tears prevented Augustus from publicly proclaiming Germanicus's succession, which seemed inevitable.[1]

Augustus's Death. Tiberius's embittered Triumph

So we come to A.D. 14, in which year Augustus died. Tiberius was pursuing his campaign in distant Illyria, satisfying his addiction to war and chewing the cud of his resentment.

At the time of his death, which took place at the height of summer, Augustus was in Western Italy, at Nola, near Naples: the place where Claudius Marcellus, his great ancestor, had routed Hannibal in all his pride. Summoned in all haste when the emperor, now seventy-six years of age, was taken gravely ill, Tiberius reached Nola just in time to hear him breathe his last sigh. He died on 19th August.

Of course, it was said once more that what killed him was neither old age nor illness, but the inevitable Livia, who was supposed to have poisoned, actually on the branch, some of the figs that the old emperor enjoyed picking and eating while he was walking in the garden.[2]

Tiberius was now Emperor of Rome. But in Augustus's will, read by a freedman in the Senate, there remained recorded for ever the repugnance with which he had designated as his heir this displeasing representative of the Claudians, after all the candidates of the Julian family had fallen in the fateful contest, one after

---

[1] Tacitus, *107*, IV, 57.   [2] Dion, *22*, LVI, 30.

the other. 'Since the cruelty of fortune,' said the document, 'has robbed me of my sons Caius and Lucius, let Tiberius Cæsar be my heir.'[1]

'This wording,' says Suetonius, 'confirmed the suspicion of those who thought that Augustus had chosen his successor not so much through affection as through necessity.' Public rumour coincided with this impression. It was said that the slaves who watched beside Augustus during the last night heard him say, when Tiberius left the room, 'I pity the people who are going to fall into those slow jaws.'[2] It was also rumoured that the astute old man had decided to adopt Tiberius in order that his own fame should be increased by the contrast between his own life and that of his successor, 'so haughty and so cruel in mind.'[3]

All these, no doubt, were malevolent inventions; but they were embroideries on the unquestionable fact that Augustus disliked Tiberius. There is no doubt about it: Augustus's choice was enforced by fate and by that irresistible pressure which is exerted on a public man by his home environment and especially by his wife, whose instinct lies in wait for that fleeting moment, unknown to the outside world, when his will weakens and lends itself to any concession, especially if he is an old man.

So, together with the supreme honour, Tiberius received the supreme motive for his resentment. It was doubtless for this reason, and not through modesty, or entirely through timidity, or on any other of the superficial grounds which were suggested at the time, that he hesitated so much before accepting the imperial power. Tacitus[4] tells us about the supplications of the senators and the specious replies of the new emperor, whose thoughts

---

[1] Augustus had drawn up this will during the previous year. Suetonius gives such exact details regarding it that no doubt about this episode is possible (Suetonius, *106, Aug.*, 101, and *Tib.*, 23). We may recall, moreover, Augustus's suggestions about the possible designation as his successor of men outside the imperial family, such as Lepidus, Arruntius or Asinius Gallus. His resistance before he gave in to accepting Tiberius was, in fact, desperate.

[2] Suetonius, *106, Tib.*, 21. This historian impartially refuses to accept these rumours. He gives it as his opinion that judicious Augustus 'must have carefully balanced Tiberius's virtues and vices, and found that the former outweighed the latter.' 'Those slow jaws' appears to have been a reference to the deliberation with which Tiberius said anything or did anything.

[3] Tacitus, *107*, I, 10.   [4] Tacitus, *107*, I, 11 and 12.

'were wrapped in a darkness thicker than ever.' His haggling led to a tension which broke out in personal clashes, such as that between him and Asinius Gallus, his first wife's new husband. Finally he decided to accept the emperorship.

But he accepted it with no enthusiasm. By this time it had become for him a duty, and no more. This lofty position was, so to speak, the apex of a pyramid of intrigues, base passions, tragedies and deaths, in which it was hard to distinguish those designed by fate from those to which crime lent a hand.

So, from the outset, the festering thorns of resentment increased the evident unfitness of Tiberius, disappointed with life and bordering on old age, to govern the empire; and at the bar of history his rule was to reek of antipathy and bitterness.

The struggle of the Julians against the Claudians was over. But the struggle of the Claudians, now masters of power, against the Julians was only beginning.

II

CLAUDIANS VERSUS JULIANS

Livia, Virtue Incarnate

THE second part of the struggle between the two families—Claudians versus Julians—developed under the sign of Livia. The decline and finally the death of Augustus left in the foreground the figure of this extraordinary woman, who attained the title of 'Mother of the Fatherland,' *Genitrix Orbis*, but never won the affection of her people. She was a woman implacable in her ambition, frigid and tenacious, a cat or a panther as it might suit her. Her activity serves as the main plot in the story of the last episodes in the great struggle.

When a historian tries to re-create a dead and gone person, not as a mere character in public events, but as she was when she was alive in all her vibrant humanity, it is inevitable that he should succumb to a feeling of sympathy or antipathy towards her, which is quite compatible with impartiality in the judgement which her public activity may seem to him to deserve.

All the ancient writers agree in praising Livia's domestic virtues: the continence of her married life; her modesty in attire; the diligence with which she devoted several hours every day to weaving, with her daughters, her *protégées* and her servants, the simple tunics worn by her husband and herself; and, finally, the simplicity of her meals, which was not inconsistent with her drinking a few glasses a day of the generous wine of Pucinum, to which she herself later attributed her longevity.[1] But her character, which we can piece together in its typical traits from the scanty references of contemporaries, attracts some people and does not attract others, just as is the case with living persons. I count myself among those whom her character does not attract.

[1] Pliny, *80*, XIV, 7.

Livia was, in fact, one of the clearest examples of the universal species of 'intolerable virtue,' which was not uncommon in Roman life, and of which we shall later find a similar model in Agrippina I. 'Her virtues,' says an English commentator on Tiberius, 'were manifested to the point where they became a standing invitation to vice.'[1] No one who is familiar at first hand with contemporary references can dissent from this opinion; nor can he accept as legitimate the apologias of those who experience the fascination of the 'Roman matron,' whose prototype was incarnate in Livia. Many a time this legendary matron was nothing more than one of those whited sepulchres whose condemnation was about to be pronounced by a voice ready to resound in the fastnesses of history.

The Strength of Sexual Austerity

A strange woman indeed was Livia. Her strength lay in her sexual austerity. One of her admirers[2] writes emotionally: 'Legend, which imputed to her fantastic poisonings,[3] absurd ambitions, and novelistic intrigues, nevertheless could never accuse her of infidelity or immorality.' All this is unquestionable. Ovid[4] called her 'the vestal virgin of our chaste Roman women'; and Tacitus himself, never sparing in his judgement, said that 'she was pure in her morals as the women of ancient days.'[5]

The only thing of which we catch a glimpse in the classical histories is what we should today call a flirtation between the strict matron and the consul Fufius, who, according to Tacitus, 'was endowed with all the qualities which attract women'; and 'to this he owed his good fortune, which was due to Augusta (Livia).' This was a case, in other words, of patronage based on the charm of a spruce youth, such as we might find in any country in modern times. The episode must have been of some importance, since it was noted in Tiberius's inexorable records; and when, many years later, he excused himself from attending

---

[1] Tarver, *108*, VI. [2] Ferrero, *27*, II.
[3] Livia was accused of poisoning her husband, Augustus, Marcellus II, Caius Cæsar, Lucius Cæsar, Agrippa Postumus, and Germanicus: all of them because they stood in the way of her son Tiberius.
[4] Ovid, *77*, IV, 13. [5] Tacitus, *107*, V, 1.

his mother's funeral, in his letter to the Senate he made a reference to it which was that of a typically resentful man.[1]

Virtuous Livia, in any case—this is interesting to note—was not much of a prude, as are many women who are strictly chaste, perhaps because frigidity preserves them from temptation. For example, Dion tells a story which adds to our knowledge of her psychology. One day some men were being led away to punishment for the offence of going about naked. Livia saw them passing, interceded for them, and secured their pardon, on the ground that, if nakedness were an offence in the case of the living human body, so it ought to be in the case of statues.[2] This comparison of hers between statues and living bodies helps to explain her chastity.

No one disputes her virtues. But, since legend respects them, praises them, and hands them down to us as unquestionable, we are entitled to think that her defects, which legend also transmits to us, were equally unquestionable. The austerity of her life was so devoid of any warmth that it chills admiration for her. Only virtue inspired by love has any efficacy as an example; and Livia's virtue strikes me as made out of the same marble as her statues.

She was, it is true, strictly faithful to Augustus, and that in itself was a good deal in those days when, as Seneca puts it, 'the most decent form of matrimony was adultery.'[3] But her fidelity had in it the original sin of her marriage to Augustus, which took place at the cost of the dishonour and the unhappiness of two people: her first husband, and Augustus's first wife, Scribonia, whom he divorced in order to possess her rival even before her suspect pregnancy was over. We owe a few words to Scribonia, who passed into the background of history's stage surrounded by a faint and fugitive halo.

The Tragedy of Scribonia

It is with good reason that Baring-Gould[4] describes the way in which Augustus rid himself of Scribonia as 'dishonourable and cruel.' Augustus's antecedents in matters of love had, indeed, little

---
[1] Fufius, into the bargain, permitted himself some biting remarks about Tiberius.
[2] Dion, 22, LVIII, 2. [3] Seneca, *100*, 9.
[4] Baring-Gould, *10*, p. 166.

romantic about them. During the years of his struggle for power he used matrimony as an aid to his ambitions, with a shamelessness which, even given the morals of the period, strikes us as excessive. Purely as a matter of convenience, he became engaged to the daughter of Servilius Isauricus; but, before the marriage took place, he jilted her in order to become engaged instead to Claudia, stepdaughter of Mark Antony and daughter of Fulvia. His marriage to Claudia had as its purpose an alliance with Mark Antony. But the ferocity of his prospective mother-in-law, Fulvia—it was she who drove a bodkin through Cicero's tongue after his death—became so soon and so strongly manifest that Augustus, despite all considerations of convenience, jilted her in turn before the marriage. Finally he married Scribonia. Here again, however, it was not for love, but because her brother, Lucius Scribonius Libo, was a power in the party of Pompey, and his friendship suited Augustus's plans.

Scribonia was one of those few virtuous women—with a human, and not solely a Roman, virtue—who passed through the annals of the period of the emperors without a single stain. When the political reasons which had united him to her disappeared, Augustus put her aside, with the same realism as his earlier betrothed. Into the bargain, he had meanwhile fallen in love with Livia, apparently sincerely this time, though there was also the consideration of convenience that it served his ambitions to unite himself with a woman of the aristocracy.

Scribonia was his only wife who gave him children. But neither her virtue nor her fecundity did her any good. Augustus was so base as to declare in writing that he divorced her because he could not stand her unbearable character;[1] and he insinuated that her morals were not entirely unblemished, thus dishonouring her name, when her complete chastity was notorious. Neither her age —she was already past her youth when she married—nor her lack of beauty diminishes the merits of her virtue, since at the Roman court, as at all courts, her political position, rather than all the graces put together, would have accounted for her attraction to men seeking their fortune by way of love.

[1] Suetonius, *106, Aug.*, 62.

The unhappy, humiliated wife disappeared from the scene, full of sorrow and dignity. Her name never figured in that immense wave of evil-speaking which filled the reign of Tiberius. But she reappeared when her daughter Julia was exiled by Augustus for immorality in the year 2 B.C. Then Scribonia's conduct, her enlightened charity, contrasted strongly with Augustus's inhumane conduct. In his case, his position as a father did not attenuate the barbarous severity of his punishment of Julia. In Scribonia's case, her daughter's dishonour was only one reason the more for feeling herself to be a mother; and she accompanied Julia in her exile until her death, fifteen years later.

One feels repelled by the pharisaical severity with which Augustus punished his own daughter's loose living, above all when one takes into account the fact that, where love-affairs were concerned, he was in no position to cast the first stone. I have already referred to his numerous adulteries. He was even suspected of homosexuality, the corruption of boys, and incest.[1] These charges were doubtless due to the malice of his enemies; but it was malice based upon the notorious licentiousness of his life during his youth and middle age. This was so far public property, that when he introduced laws aimed at reforming morals, there were any number of jokes and jests in the Senate, since everyone thought that such repressive measures should, in all justice, begin with the emperor himself.[2] Augustus's morality ranked far below his genius for government.

Livia's Ambition

But let us return to Livia. All the evidence agrees that it was she who, at the cost of sacrificing Scribonia and for the sake of ambition, plotted the exchange of her husband, Claudius Nero, elderly and with no future before him, for the young triumvir who in the year of their marriage, 38 B.C., was already carving his way with unequivocal resolution towards the conquest of power.

Whether or not she loved her new husband afterwards, or even had any affection for him, it is not for me to say. In any case, it is enough for us to know that she respected him. But her whole

[1] Suetonius, *106. Aug.*, 71, and *Calig.*, 23.   [2] Dion, 22, LIV, 16.

character and the very tolerance, almost the complacency, with which she closed her eyes to the emperor's strayings are strongly suggestive of the fact that she placed everything, even her love for him, if she had any, at the disposal of her ruling passion, which was ambition.

Long afterwards, when she had become a widow, she was asked by what means she had managed to keep on good terms with Augustus during all the time they lived together. She replied that one of the reasons was that she 'always overlooked his infidelities.'[1]

Here we have one of the keys to her character. If a wife responds to her husband's infidelities with persistent virtue and also with ostentatious dissimulation of his conjugal failings, it is almost always because this is the twofold price she has to pay for absolute domination of his will; and, at the same time, it is an indication of her own shortcomings in love. Moreover, the whole of Livia's emotional and sexual life conveys the impression that she suffered from a defect common to many ambitious women, namely, frigidity.[2] From the lofty height of her frigidity, the wife, inviolate, impervious to that generous surrender of the soul which true love presupposes, utilizes her attractions purely to the advantage of her ambitions.

All authorities, both ancient and modern, recognize that Livia's ambition was the mainspring of her character. It is true that circumstances favoured this passion of hers. Perhaps in no other period of history was the destiny of peoples so much in the hands of women as in that of the Roman emperors. The reason was that at that time the legitimate importance of women, namely motherhood, reached one of its culminating moments. In the eyes of the Roman, the woman was, above all else, the mother, the soul of the home; and so, at the same time, her capacity for

---

[1] Dion, 22, LXIII, 2. Livia said that the secret of her power over Augustus consisted in these facts: that she had always been inflexibly virtuous (which, before her second marriage, is not entirely certain); that she had never meddled in her husband's affairs (which was certainly not true); and that she turned a blind eye to his infidelities (this does seem certain). In short, an excellent practical programme for a bride.

[2] Henting takes the same view (39).

attracting men attained one of its phases of apogee. For this reason, also, excesses of her power of attraction presented themselves in the form of imperious domination, as in the cases of Livia or Agrippina I, or in the form of feminine Don Juanism, as in the cases of the two Julias or Messalina.

Here we have the secret of the senselessness of feminism. When the woman claims to be socially the equal of the man, it is obvious that what she gains in external influence over him she loses in intimate influence. The emancipated woman has ceased to be the man's possible slave, but at the same time she has also ceased to be his possible master. She has simply turned herself into his rival, and as such the woman nearly always comes off worst.

It follows that the phases of woman's authentic historical influence are not those when she rules directly, but on the contrary those when, though apparently in the background, she uses man as her instrument. It is then, as was the case in Rome, that a strong will to govern, and also a great capacity to govern, arise in the weaker sex; that the normal rôles are reversed in whole families; and that we witness, in generation after generation, the spectacle of robust man subject to intensely feminine woman. In no other period so much as that in which he lived could Cato have written his famous sentence: 'We men rule the world, but the women rule us.'

Livia, like so many other Roman women of her time, was a memorable example of such impetuous ambition of feminine power exercised through making use of men. Its symbol was the cock with crest erect which emerged from the warmth of her young bosom and from which the horoscope of the stars foretold a ruling destiny. This ambition strengthens in the woman with the passing years—because advancing age brings her closer to masculinity[1]—just as in the man, once he is past his prime, the instinct for dominating other people usually diminishes in proportion as the impetus of his virility lessens. It is then, when he has learnt wisdom, that the average man realizes that his greatest conquest is over his own passions, and that domination over other people interests him less and less.

[1] See my book 62.

Such was Livia's strength of will that it astounded Rome at the time of the death of her favourite son, Drusus I. Seneca tells us that her grief was profound, but that once her son's beloved body was laid in the tomb Livia suppressed her sorrow lest she should disturb Augustus with her tears or lose a single moment from her household duties.[1] Her strength of mind was doubtless aided by her robust physical health, which became legendary. Ovid wrote of her: 'Illness passes you by, and in your bosom you guard chastity'; and her grandson Caligula, less lyrically, called her 'Ulysses in skirts.'[2]

Augustus's Cleverness. Torment in the Night

Livia's zest for domination was applied wholly to the task of securing the triumph of her family, that of the Claudians, over the rival family of the Julians, that of her own husband. Few things give us such a good idea of Augustus's matchless political quality as the supreme tact with which he managed to reconcile this activity on his wife's part with conjugal harmony. To maintain this ability day after day, for fifty years, with the woman who shared his home life and his bed at night presupposes more diplomacy and more strength of mind than to keep the peace among the varied peoples who made up the Roman empire.

Many a time, no doubt, if we are to believe reports about their hours of conjugal intimacy, Augustus gave way to the physical temptation of his wife, who handled her charms just as a gladiator handled his sword. Dion tells us that one night, at the time of Cinna's conspiracy, the emperor could not sleep because of his anxiety. Then the voice of the siren whispered in his ear: 'What is the matter, Augustus?' Well enough she knew, since she herself had doubtless hatched the plot for Tiberius's benefit. Disjointed conversation followed in the dark, until Livia finally convinced Augustus that he should exercise clemency towards the conspirators.[3] In this nocturnal intimacy, many other questions like that of Cinna must have been settled to Livia's advantage.

[1] Seneca, *98*, 3. This great writer contrasts Livia's stoical conduct in the presence of grief with Octavia's unrestrained sorrow, human and moving, when she lost her son Marcellus.
[2] Ovid, *77*, II, 3. Suetonius, *106*, Calig., 23.   [3] Dion, *22*, LVI, 47.

It was public property that Augustus constantly consulted his wife at serious moments in his public life. On the empress's distaff were woven not only her husband's tunics, but also the destiny of the empire. Livia, says Dion,[1] 'concerned herself with affairs as though it were she who held the supreme power.' Sometimes she carried her interference to the length of improper ostentation, since she appeared before the people 'at moments of anxiety, and was in the habit of publicly haranguing the crowds and the soldiers.'[2]

But, by some miraculous means, Augustus managed to reconcile her undue co-operation in public life with the steadfast favouritism of husband and wife for each of the two branches of the imperial family.

Psychology of the Last Phase in the Struggle

Once Augustus was dead and Livia and Tiberius had achieved their ambition, it would seem at first sight that the struggle between Julians and Claudians must have come to an end. But it did nothing of the kind. It simply changed course. It was no longer the struggle of the Julians, in power, against the Claudians aspiring to domination. It became instead the struggle of the Claudians, now masters of the resources of power, against the Julians, temporarily vanquished.

Moreover, from this moment onwards there appeared an important psychological change in the attitude of the protagonists. Tiberius had hitherto been united to his mother by common ambition, though separated from her by his resentment. Now that Augustus was dead and the reason for their alliance had ceased to exist, since they had attained power, Tiberius's dislike of his adulterous mother, the woman who had hurt his father's dignity, became accentuated.

Every year in his life, once he was emperor, was marked by a fresh wave of resentment against his mother for her injustice to his father. We can plainly see how, now that his political account with his mother was settled, the picture of his father, lonely and beaten, while 'she' had sought fortune in the arms of her

---

[1] Dion, 22, LVI, 47.   [2] Suetonius, *106, Tib.*, 50.

vainglorious and ambitious young husband, stood out ever more clearly, ever more vividly, in Tiberius's memory. The gulf which separated mother and son deepened daily. When Livia died, Tiberius concentrated in one act the whole half-century of his resentment. While still a boy, he had spoken the eulogy of his dead father with infinite affection and respect; but now, in an icy letter, he refused to attend his mother's funeral.

It was under these auspices that the long struggle continued. Of the Julian family there remained alive Augustus's last grandson, Agrippa Postumus, chewing the cud of his stupidity in exile, and Germanicus, nephew and adopted son of Tiberius, married to Agrippina I and with several children. Every one of them was a danger to the succession to Tiberius, who had only one child, Drusus II. It was around them that the last phase of the struggle was fought.

Despite the extenuations of historians who favour Tiberius, there is no effacing the impression that Livia and Tiberius zealously devoted themselves to exterminating all these potential enemies of their family, or at least helping their spontaneous extermination. From this distance we can distinguish only confusedly how much there was in this extermination of criminal intent, and how much of that mysterious fate which so often serves as accomplice to great human wrongs.

Death and Resurrection of Agrippa Postumus

About Agrippa Postumus I have already written. But we must now finish his story, which is certainly one of the darkest in the lives of Livia and Tiberius.

Livia's intrigues, as we saw in the last chapter, succeeded in setting Augustus against his grandson. We know, among other things, that Junius Novatus and Cassius of Padua, doubtless acting as agents of the Claudians, circulated letters hostile to the emperor, supposedly written by Agrippa Postumus, which later proved to be forgeries.[1] But for the time being the plot proved a success, for Augustus, in a rage, exiled Agrippa, taking account also of his notorious folly. At the last moment, however, so it was said, the

---
[1] Suetonius, *106, Aug.*, 51.

emperor repented of his decision and had an interview with the exile on the island of Planasia[1] at which Fabius Maximus, his man of confidence, was also present. Grandfather and grandson were reconciled and mingled their tears.

Despite the secrecy with which Augustus made this sentimental journey, Livia learnt of it through Marcia, Maximus's wife. Her indiscretion cost her husband his life, since Augustus, aware of Livia's hatred for his grandson, had wanted to keep the interview secret at all costs, and could not endure the violation of this secrecy. The details with which Tacitus[2] relates this episode are so circumstantial as to leave little room for doubt that in fact Augustus intended at the last moment to restore the unhappy Agrippa to favour.

In the presence of this danger, Livia lost no time. Old Augustus, already near his end, observed 'the confabulations between Livia and Tiberius with anxiety.'[3] He knew what they were plotting. It was said, as we have seen, that the empress decided to hasten her husband's death with poison;[4] and we know, too, that this was false. But it is unquestionable that no sooner was Augustus dead than Agrippa Postumus was executed on his island.

It never became clear who ordered this odious execution. The centurion who beheaded Agrippa, not without difficulty, since he was very strong and defended himself desperately despite the fact that he was unarmed,[5] declared in Rome that he 'had obeyed the orders of the emperor.' But which emperor? Here we see the crafty hand of Tiberius, master of the art of dramatic equivocation. He pretended to be surprised, and asserted that the order was not his. Then whose was it? It was put about that Augustus had left the order for execution behind him, to be carried into effect on his death, and some people went so far as to say that his own wife forced him to write it before he died, in a final abuse of her power of fascination. But almost everyone believed that the assassination was plotted by Livia and her son.[6]

---

[1] Pliny says so explicitly, *80*, VII, 46.
[2] Tacitus, *107*, I, 5.   [3] Pliny, *79*, VII, 46.
[4] Tacitus, *107*, I, 5; and also Dion, *22*, LVI, 30.   [5] Tacitus, *107*, 51.
[6] Tacitus, *107*, I, 6. Suetonius, *106*, Tib., 22. This last author asserts that Tiberius did not divulge Augustus's death until after Agrippa's assassination.

Today no one can doubt that the two of them were responsible for this crime, over which the defenders of Tiberius and his mother pass as though they were walking on red-hot coals. The air of surprise which Tiberius adopted when he learnt that 'the orders of the emperor had been obeyed' was akin to the repulsive gesture which was made a little later by Pontius Pilate, his governor in Judæa. In this crime Tiberius took the personal revenge against the Julians which he had stored up during so many years of humiliation. The resentful man, when he attains power, is capable of anything.

In this year, the very same year of Tiberius's accession to power, Julia, mother of Agrippa Postumus and wife of the new emperor, also died in her exile in Regium. Perhaps fate hastened her end; but I feel no qualms about believing Tacitus when he accuses Tiberius, and not fate, of this coincidence.[1]

Both Julia I and Agrippa Postumus were abnormal people. With Julia I have already dealt. Agrippa's imbecility was notorious. It is disclosed even in his fleeting profile on the coins minted in his honour. Nevertheless, the fact that they were descendants of Augustus and, above all, the fact that they were enemies of Tiberius sufficed to give them immense popularity. The people and the upper classes of Rome followed the fortunes of the exiled prince with the same enthusiastic sympathy as in the case of his mother. The story that Augustus, before his death, had a reconciliation with Agrippa Postumus conveys the impression that, if it were not true, it was one of those fables by which the public tries to turn its collective desires into reality. But there was another episode which demonstrated the same thing: the episode of the unhappy exile's 'resurrection.'

It seems certain that, the moment Augustus died, Clemens, one of Agrippa's slaves, tried to kidnap him and take him to Germany; this he did in order to save him from the wrath of Tiberius, which his friends could see swooping upon him. Tacitus says that the project was 'beyond the capacity of a slave,' and that it was probably planned by men of note, 'people in the prince's household, knights and senators';[2] and the fact that it was designed to

---

[1] Tacitus, *107*, I, 53.   [2] Tacitus, *107*, II, 39 and 40.

take Agrippa to Germany, where the legions were notoriously hostile to Tiberius, bears out this assumption.

But that critical moment which decides the fortune or the failure of plots was against the conspirators. The boat which was taking Clemens, Agrippa's would-be saviour, to the island of Planasia encountered adverse winds; and, when Clemens landed, the poor prince was already beheaded. Then Clemens and his supporters fell back upon the supernatural.

They stole the dead man's ashes, and the daring slave hid himself at Cosa, in Etruria, where he let his hair and his beard grow into the same shape as those of Agrippa Postumus in his exile. There was a strong physical resemblance between the two men. Meanwhile the other conspirators spread throughout the empire the rumour that Agrippa Postumus was still alive and that he would one day return to Rome. Universal desire gained credence for the fable. 'A miracle of the gods' had restored the young man of the favourite family; and so, when the supposed prince landed at Ostia, he was welcomed by an immense, emotional multitude.

Tiberius, a man inclined to believe in anything extraordinary,[1] must have had a fright. The subject of resurrection found a strong echo in his pagan soul without faith in the gods. It was for this reason that, years later, he was so much disturbed by the news of another resurrection, that of Jesus crucified in Judæa. Through credulity rather than anger, and perhaps with secret dread, he ordered the arrest of this man presumed to have risen from the dead.

Clemens, the false Agrippa, was put into prison. He endured torture heroically, and refused to give away the other conspirators. It was said that Tiberius himself was present at his torture, and that, with his misgivings masked beneath his resentful man's humour, he asked the slave, writhing in agony on the rack, 'how he had managed to become Agrippa.' To this Clemens replied defiantly: 'Just as you managed to become emperor.' So ended the story of Augustus's last direct descendant.

[1] See a shrewd study of Tiberius's credulity in Reinach, *84*. See also my book, *66*.

Germanicus, the Popular Hero

The case of Germanicus deserves to be dealt with at greater length. As we have already seen, Augustus compelled Tiberius to adopt him as his son. We know, too, what height of popularity Germanicus achieved. Through the haze of this immense popular enthusiasm for him, it is difficult for us today to judge the real merits of the young prince.

Heredity, which is sometimes trustworthy, inclines me to believe in them, since his father, Drusus I, was a model among men and princes, and his mother, Antonia II (to whom I shall refer later), left behind her deserved repute as an exemplary woman. Suetonius thus describes the son of this perfect pair: 'It is unquestionable that Germanicus united, in a higher degree than anyone had ever reached before, all the virtues of mind and body: unequalled good looks and valour; the greatest gifts of learning and eloquence in the two languages, Greek and Latin; extraordinary kindliness; and finally a wonderful talent for winning sympathy and deserving the affection of other people.'[1] It is all but the portrait of a god.

The sole defect which anyone ventured to attribute to him was weakness of the legs, and this he cured by dint of riding. Tacitus, still more enthusiastic, compares Germanicus with Alexander.[2] Besides being a great general, he was a fine poet. At least the courtiers, who, as such, are not usually good critics, said that he was. During the reign of Claudius, by way of homage to his memory, one of the plays in Greek which he had written in his youth was staged; and there is also mention of an inspired poem inscribed on the memorial statue which Augustus ordered to be erected in honour of his horse.[3]

It was also said that Germanicus was a good democrat; and everyone believed that if he came to the throne he would try to restore the old republic. The same thing was believed about his father, whom he closely resembled, even in his obsessing dreams, to which I have already referred as a trait common to the Julian family.[4]

---

[1] Suetonius, *106, Calig.*, 3. See also Dion's eulogy, *22*, LVII, 18.
[2] Tacitus, *107*, II, 73.   [3] Suetonius, *106, Claud.*, 11. Pliny, *79*, VIII, 64.
[4] See p. 33 of this book, and *Tacitus, 107*, II, 14.

It is obvious that, in this eulogy of Germanicus, on the basis of unquestionable grounds for admiration, his contemporaries, without realizing it, were presenting a rather ingenious reverse of the figure of the hated Tiberius. This is often the case in the popular genesis of heroes, to whom the subconsciousness of the oppressed masses ascribes qualities opposite to those of a hated tyrant. Sometimes this myth is so strong that it ends by creating a reality and producing qualities in the hero which he did not possess. For better or worse, many public men have been brought into being by the rough chisel of public opinion.

We need not consider here whether the popular enthusiasm for Germanicus had more myth than reality about it; but the idea of the prince's liberalism is open to question. There is no reason for supposing that either he or his father held other views than those of Augustus and Tiberius: in other words, the views of dictators.[1] Probably, like Augustus and Tiberius, they would have been dictators if they had come into power. But the people, that eternal child, believed the contrary, classed them as democrats and worshipped them as such.

So far as we know, Germanicus was an excellent general; but even in this respect he differed from Tiberius. Tiberius was cautious, slow and wily, whereas Germanicus's chief asset, which he used lavishly, was great personal dash, like that of his father and Julius Cæsar. In battle he engaged in hand-to-hand fight with the enemy,[2] of which Tiberius would never have been capable.

Relations between Tiberius and Germanicus. The old Debt

I must here stress the personal relations between Tiberius and Germanicus, to which I have already referred in the last chapter; for this is a point which is badly interpreted by most historians. Almost all of them, in fact, describe these relations as exemplary in their cordiality. It is certain that they were nothing of the kind.

To be sure, Germanicus, despite his impulsive character, always behaved most nobly towards his uncle and emperor. This is demonstrated by the fact that, when the legions in Germany rose

---

[1] On this point see Duruy, *24*, IV, p. 275.
[2] Suetonius, *106*, *Calig.*, 3.

in rebellion and Germanicus was sent to suppress them, he stubbornly refused to put himself at the head of their movement, as the soldiers desired, in order to overthrow Tiberius, who had just become emperor. It would have been easy for the young general to dethrone Tiberius, or at least put him in an awkward position. Far from doing so, 'in proportion as his authority increased, he exerted himself to strengthen Tiberius's position.'[1] His nobility on this occasion became legendary. One of the 'Enterprises' in *The Prince*, by Saavedra Fajardo, has as its main theme the hatred with which Tiberius repaid Germanicus's loyalty: 'the more faithful he showed himself in his service, the less Tiberius liked him.'[2] Such was the myth. There are still to be seen on the walls of some old houses prints of an eighteenth-century engraving which represent Germanicus, in a highly theatrical attitude, threatening to transfix himself with his own sword rather than betray his emperor.

It is, on the other hand, very doubtful whether Tiberius paid him back in his own coin. We know for certain that he did not approve of Germanicus's military leadership; and in this he may have been justified. But the people, who were closer to the truth than the commentators of twenty centuries later, clearly perceived how much impassioned censure there was in Tiberius's dismissal of the young general from the command of the legions. Mommsen[3] justifies this decision of Tiberius on the ground that Germanicus, on his own responsibility and carried away by his impulsiveness—perhaps also by that of his wife—was openly running counter to the emperor's prudent policy in the Rhineland. But the fact remains that discord between the two men existed, and that the sumptuous triumph which marked Germanicus's arrival in Rome, immortalized in the cameo in the Bibliothèque Nationale in Paris, did not suffice to disguise it. Tiberius's hereditary pride and his well-founded conceit of himself as a soldier now found their revenge. If he had been accused of excessive prudence, his subconscious mind now tacitly accused Germanicus of excessive imprudence; and so, while he surrounded him

---

[1] Tacitus, *107*, I, 34.   [2] Saavedra Fajardo, *89*, XLVII.
[3] Mommsen, *72*, IX.

with honours, in accordance with his usual tactics, he cut short Germanicus's military career in the middle.

When this became known, the people instinctively redoubled their devotion towards the dismissed general. Their disgust with the emperor and their enthusiasm for Germanicus were still further increased when, a little later, Germanicus was sent to the east.

Germanicus's Journey to the East. The Legend of Poisoning

Tiberius's apologists angrily dismiss the sinister interpretation which the ancients put upon this journey. Theoretically they are right; for an eastern journey, on one ground or another, had been made by almost all the princes of Rome. It was an occasion for pomp, and almost an award of *proxime accessit* in the government of the empire. In those distant provinces distinguished visitors sent from the capital were welcomed almost like gods. But apart from pomp and homage, there were grave political problems to be solved, and Germanicus's responsibility for settling them placed him in the category of a Cæsar.

But the fact that all this, obvious though it was, should have been interpreted in an adverse sense by the people demonstrates that, beneath all the outward show surrounding Germanicus's journey, they perceived Tiberius's rancour against him. At all times rulers, when it suited them, have known how to clothe their punishments in purple and gold or in embassies. Tiberius's reputation for hypocrisy, which was no invention of Tacitus, but a fact unquestioned by the public opinion of his time, helped to arouse suspicion; and unfortunately what followed served to give this suspicion a tragic appearance of reality.

Mere murmuring among the people was, in fact, transformed into a tumultuous wave of passion when, a few months later, Germanicus, who was then in Syria, after violent disputes with Piso the governor, fell ill and died (A.D. 19) in circumstances which suggested that he had been poisoned by Piso himself at his emperor's instigation.

Let me hasten to declare that all the data available to us agree in condemning the charge of poisoning as absurd. Tacitus himself, an exceptionally good witness, recognizes it as such.[1] The trial of Piso demonstrated his innocence. From the standpoint of our present-day knowledge, this is completely confirmed by the fact that the sole ground for the charge of poisoning was the symptoms of Germanicus's illness and death: an argument which, in the light of medical science of today, is simply ridiculous.

Amid all the startling stories, we can clearly see that the illness which carried away Germanicus did not correspond to any form of poisoning, but rather to a case of consumptive fever: perhaps a form of pernicious malaria which he may have picked up in the course of his travels about the Mediterranean; or perhaps tuberculosis. As for the 'livid blotches which covered his corpse,' the 'foam which issued from his mouth,' and the fact that 'his heart remained intact after the cremation of his body,'[2] all these are signs completely devoid of value as proof of the poisoning in which his contemporaries believed. The prosecutor Vitellus made much ado, by way of proving the crime, about this resistance of the heart to the flames. It was no good for Piso's defenders to adduce the fact that a heart equally withstands fire when it is previously affected; and this, they said, was the case with Germanicus.[3]

Everyone believed, too, that Germanicus's death had been foretold by a bad omen, since the bull-god Apis, to whom the prince offered food with his own hand during his visit to Egypt, had turned his horned head away.[4] In the depths of their minds, the people wanted to be sure that their hero had been murdered; and, when the people want to make history, they can always find an incombustible heart and a bull with no appetite.

It must be admitted that in this case chance, combined with the stupidity of men, did indeed arrange matters in such a way that in the excited minds of the Romans the suspicion of assassination was bound to be transformed into certainty. In the first place, there was the old story of the struggle of Livia and Tiberius

---

[1] The whole story of Germanicus's journey to the east, his disputes with Piso, the grief of the people, and Piso's trial and death, is admirably told by Tacitus, *107*, II and III.
[2] Suetonius, *106*, Calig., 1.   [3] Pliny, *79*, X, 71.
[4] Pliny, *79*, VIII, 71.

against the Julians, and the highly suspicious disappearance, one after the other, of all the representatives of the heroic and democratic family, from Marcellus II to Agrippa Postumus. In the next place, there was the sudden transfer of Germanicus from his command of the legions to the east, a remote region full of promises of glory but also of mystery and treachery.

Thirdly, there was the nomination of the governor of Syria, in the person of Piso, an honest man, but violent and unlikable, and a great friend of Tiberius, to the job of keeping an eye on Germanicus. This he discharged strictly, as is shown by the statement of Tacitus[1] that he 'had heard old men say that papers were often to be seen in Piso's hands whose secret he refused to divulge, but which, according to his friends, contained letters of instruction from Tiberius directed against Germanicus.' Into the bargain, Piso was married to Plancina, who was regarded as being one of Livia's most intimate friends[2] and emerged from Piso's trial without a stain on her character, thanks to decided and indeed obvious imperial protection.

Fourthly, there was the sudden death of Germanicus in the flower of his manhood—he was thirty-three—accompanied by symptoms which ignorance and malice induced the people to interpret as those of poisoning. Fifthly and lastly, there were the facts that neither Tiberius nor Livia attended the funeral held in sorrowing Rome when Germanicus's ashes arrived there;[3] that the funeral, by order of the emperor, was on a very modest scale;[4] and that when public complaints about the lack of splendour in connection with the funeral came to Tiberius's ears, he stripped the dead man's person of any importance by saying in reply: 'Princes die, but the empire remains.'[5]

[1] Tacitus, *107*, III, 16.
[2] With reference to Livia's friendship with Plancina, see Tacitus, *107*, II, 43 and 82, and III, 15 and 17.
[3] Tacitus, *107*, III, 3. It is true that Antonia, the dead man's mother, about whose grief there could be no doubt, was not present either. I shall discuss the significance of her absence later.
[4] This does not seem certain. Tacitus himself says that the funeral was worthy of Germanicus's glory; but he may have been referring to the popular emotion rather than to the official pomp and ceremony (Tacitus, *107*, II, 83).
[5] Tacitus, *107*, III, 5.

All these factors produced in the Roman people a reaction of regular collective neurosis, in which were intermingled sorrow over the death of their hero and a feeling of hatred of the emperor.[1] Overwhelmed by the wave of popular feeling, which he was never capable of resisting, Tiberius gave way like a coward and, with obvious injustice, allowed Piso to be condemned to death.[2] Piso committed suicide before the sentence could be carried out. In fact, in the eyes of the public Tiberius was condemning himself; for those who accused Piso believed that he had acted only as the emperor's instrument. The sentence on Piso involved both of them.

Henceforth a fresh and potent source remained open to feed the hidden flow of Tiberius's resentment.

Germanicus was dead. But Agrippina I was still alive, with all her dread vitality and, into the bargain, a brood of children. From this moment the affection of the masses surrounded them. Amid all the public mourning, 'nothing wounded Tiberius more deeply than the enthusiasm of the people for Agrippina. They called her an honour to the fatherland, the true heiress of Augustus, the sole model of the ancient virtues.'[3] This deep wound of Tiberius was never to heal. But all this belongs to the story of Agrippina I, with which I shall deal later.

Rupture between Livia and Tiberius

It remains for us now to note the slow snapping of the links of ambition which had hitherto held in check the instinctive and

---

[1] I cannot resist the temptation to transcribe Tacitus's narrative of the following scene, in which the historian achieves the maximum of emotion together with the maximum austerity of style: 'There was argument about what would be the proper reception as the galleys slowly came into port, rigged in such a way that, instead of the usual gaiety of the oarsmen, everything proclaimed mourning and sadness. At the moment when Agrippina landed from her galley with her two sons and made her appearance with the funerary urn in her hands and her eyes bent on the ground, a universal groan issued from the multitude, in which one could not distinguish the pain of the relatives from that of strangers, or the grave sorrow of the men from the desolation of the women. Those who formed part of Agrippina's suite, overwhelmed by their long affliction, made all the more evident the keener, because more recent, sorrow of the multitude' (Tacitus, *107*, III, 1).

[2] I should add, however, that Piso was also accused and convicted of having incited war in the east; and this charge, apart from that of poisoning Germanicus, might have involved the death penalty.

[3] Tacitus, *107*, III, 4.

irreparable discord between Tiberius and his mother. Once they had attained power, the motive for their alliance disappeared. But Livia's impulse for domination increased with age, and she could not reconcile herself to losing her participation in power now that she was a widow. Tiberius had not wanted power; but, now that he possessed it, he had no desire to share it with his mother. At the outset, he had to put up with her tutelage. But in the end the cockerel with the red crest, now transformed into a bird of prey, made up his mind to turn against his governess.

Suetonius describes the grounds of their final rupture and there is such an air of truth about his narrative that we are bound to accept it. After a dispute between mother and son, Livia, in her anger, read to Tiberius some letters from Augustus that she had hitherto kept to herself, in which Augustus 'complained about his stepson's embittered and intractable disposition.' Tiberius, says the historian, 'was so indignant that his mother should have kept these mortifying documents for so long that henceforth, until her death, he saw her again only once.'[1]

Tiberius's wrath is understandable. Few things convey so clear an idea of incapacity for generous feeling as such a production of documents denoting a past state of mind which may soon have disappeared. A letter is always sacred, because it is, or may be, the expression of a few fleeting moments of our innermost thoughts which are entrusted to the confidence of the recipient. Our responsibility for what is written in the letter—and this makes it all the more sacred—evaporates the very next moment, just as every beat of the heart effaces the preceding beats. When something is done publicly, a contract is created which can be annulled only on other grounds similarly made public. But the intimacy of a letter is an inviolable refuge, giving sanctuary to all the variety of reasons which impel our minds to change, and it may never be exhibited as though it were an anchor holding fast our responsibility for something past and gone.

After his retirement to Capri Tiberius never saw his mother again. One visit which he paid her in A.D. 22, when she was gravely ill, was the last. When she fell ill again, this time fatally, in

[1] Suetonius, *106, Tib.*, 51.

A.D. 29, Tiberius, now continually on the move between Capri and the neighbourhood of Rome, refused to see her and excused himself in writing on the ground that he was too busy. Nor did he attend her funeral. I have already commented on the profound significance of his absence.

'An imperious mother,' Tacitus called her. In her eyes, her son was solely an instrument of domination. In his eyes, his mother was an ally in his hatreds and nothing more.

When Tiberius, at the age of nine, publicly pronounced his father's funeral eulogy she must have died in his heart, that mother of his, so lovely, so frigid, so pharisaically virtuous, who began his boyhood by dishonouring an old man and bringing into scandalous doubt the paternity of the son she was soon to bear.

Livia, beyond all question, was one of the main reasons why Tiberius had a heart so arid.

III

AGRIPPINA THE MANNISH

Agrippina's Exploits and Qualities

ANOTHER woman largely responsible for Tiberius's immense resentment and its final vengeful explosion was Agrippina, Germanicus's wife. She was a woman of an intensely interesting type, ever acting upon her human environment, and a prolific mother, since, despite the shortness of her married life, she had nine children, of whom six survived: Nero I, Drusus III, Caligula, Agrippina II, Drusilla and Julia Livilla.

Agrippina may be regarded as another perfect example of the dominating woman of the imperial period. She was less subtle and more impulsive than Livia. The Chiaramonti bust, upon which Baring-Gould comments, if it is not her authentic portrait, deserves to be so, for the masculine, aggressive expression on her face, conveyed, above all, by her strong lower jaw. In the two ruling families in this phase of the history of Rome, almost all the strong jaws, that sign of energy, belong to the women.[1]

But even more than by this disputed bust, such a judgement of her is confirmed by the description of her character by contemporary writers. Tacitus, a partisan of hers, speaks in various passages about 'her haughty air and rebellious soul,' her 'pride in her fecundity and her insatiable passion for domination,' and the fact that 'her virile passions divested her of the vices of her feminine sex.'[2] This last observation does honour to the historian's psychological insight.

Agrippina's activity at the side of her husband during the war in Germany in A.D. 15 gives us a perfect picture of her character.

[1] Baring-Gould, *10*, p. 305, and Bernouilli, *12*. Even in the bust in the Capitoline Museum, which presents her as very beautiful, we again observe the strong lower jaw.

[2] Tacitus, *107*, V, 3, IV, 12, and VI, 25. Tacitus puts some of these phrases into the mouth of Tiberius; but the historian himself readily adopts them.

Tacitus presents her to us as sometimes intervening in warlike affairs so directly that on one occasion, for example, she personally prevented the soldiers from destroying a bridge over the Rhine when they were in terror of a prospective attack by the enemy. 'During these days of panic this valiant woman fulfilled the functions of a general.' Taking up her post at the bridge-head, she addressed the legions, as they passed, with words of praise, gratitude, or encouragement. Her influence over the army 'was greater than that of its leaders.'[1] She was, indeed, a truly mannish woman.

This episode suffices to give us some idea of the driving-power of Agrippina, who, through some twist of heredity, had received in her woman's mind and body all the qualities of that great captain, her father Agrippa, which normally should have been transmitted to his incapable sons. Velleius[2] tells us that Agrippa was 'avid for mastery over other people'; that he 'could not stand temporizing and passed immediately to decision and action'; and finally that 'no human power could ever overcome him.' This portrait of the general applies to his daughter without the change of a single trait.

A similar anomaly in qualities was handed on to the next generation, since all Agrippina's sons, Nero I, Drusus III, and Caligula, were craven in spirit, whereas Agrippina II, later the mother of the Emperor Nero, had just the same virile energy as her mother.[3] The mixture of a fresh, plebeian blood, like Agrippa's, with that of a family debilitated by power sometimes refreshes and renews the old and enfeebled blood; but at other times it plays strange tricks such as that I have just mentioned.

---

[1] Tacitus, *107*, I, 69 *et seq.*   [2] Velleius, *114*, II, 79.

[3] It was, indeed, with masculine tenacity that Agrippina II accomplished the task of winning Claudius; getting him to adopt her son, Nero; and eliminating Britannicus in order to rule herself, using Nero as her instrument—just as Livia had used Tiberius. Nero, when he came to power, 'left it to his mother to direct all his affairs, public and private' (Suetonius, *106*, *Nero*, 9). Tacitus, for his part, tells us that Agrippina II, during the lifetime of Claudius, presided over a tribunal sitting beside the emperor, and received the same homage from enemies as he did: 'a novel thing,' comments Tacitus, 'and opposed to the spirit of the past, that a woman should be seen at the head of the Roman standards' (Tacitus, *107*, XII, 37). It seems certain that Agrippina II had a hand in the poisoning of Claudius. The likeness between the two Agrippinas is, indeed, striking.

Germanicus's conjugal Patience and final Farewell

The popularity which Agrippina achieved by her behaviour and exploits was immense; and it would have put her husband in a ridiculous position if he, too, had not inherited an enormous popularity from that of his father, Drusus I. The people worshipped each of the married couple equally. They were regarded in Rome as an example of perfection and conjugal concord.

But almost always when a married couple get on so well, it is because one of them commands and the other obeys. There never has been found, and there never will be found, any other formula for human beings living together in peace, from the initial social nucleus, which is the bridal bed, to the nation, which is the sum of many homes, and the world, which embraces all the nations. What matters is that the inevitable yoke should be imposed by the one who commands without arrogance, and accepted by the one who obeys without humiliation.

In Germanicus's home it is unquestionable that the helm was in the strong hands of Agrippina. The husband, expert in the art of war, with skilful strategy put up with the excesses of his wife's power in exchange for her love, which was great and faithful, and her deliberately extreme fecundity; for even at that time there were women who were ashamed of motherhood because it would later betray their age, 'and at all costs concealed pregnancy, as though it were a hateful burden.'[1] But it is certain that many a time Germanicus, in order to keep the peace at home, had to play his hand with greater dexterity than he needed in order to win his battles against the barbarians.

When he lay at death's door, however, at that time when all truths can be spoken, even those that everyday convenience has hidden most deeply in the arcana of the soul, he turned towards Agrippina, who was weeping beside him, 'and conjured her by his memory and for the sake of her children to rid herself of her pride, and learn to humble her haughtiness of mind in the presence of the blows of fortune, so that she should not exasperate the holders of the supreme power with rivalry when she returned to

---

[1] Seneca, 99, 16. Voluntary abortion was also very common at the time.

Rome.'[1] It is clear that sensible Germanicus took advantage of the solemnity of the moment to tell his wife what he had kept to himself for many years for the sake of conjugal peace.

I have already remarked that it is difficult for us to see Germanicus in his true dimensions, thanks to his deified splendour as an unfortunate and romantic hero with which his birth surrounded him. But I think that those who do not credit him with much brains are wrong. His words which I have just quoted show his clear vision of the war without quarter which his wife was about to wage against Tiberius, and his prophetic certainty of its inevitable results. Nothing demonstrates his acuteness of mind so much as his capacity to see far into the future. These last words of his are also a further proof of his generous loyalty to Tiberius, which he never concealed.[2]

With Agrippina, however, faithfulness to her dying husband's injunctions weighed less than her own driving-force, enormously accelerated by her certainty that Germanicus had died poisoned by order of Tiberius. I have already dealt with this story and shown that no such crime was ever committed. But Germanicus died convinced that he had been poisoned, and his widow always believed it; perhaps because the only things in this world in which we believe with absolute faith are those which we fear or those which we most vehemently desire, and the last thing that matters is whether they are true or not.

Tiberius versus Agrippina

From this moment onwards, in fact, Agrippina became Tiberius's constant and ever more rankling source of anxiety. The old enmity between Tiberius and Germanicus, upon which I have already commented, had paved the way for this antagonism. Even at the time when Tiberius had been dissatisfied with the way in which Germanicus was waging war in Germany, Tiberius's criticism of Germanicus had been largely based upon Agrippina's intense activity, in which the suspicious emperor foresaw much danger for the future; and henceforth his counsellor Sejanus, who

[1] Tacitus, *107*, II, 72.
[2] Some historians, such as Duruy (*24*, IV), doubt the truth of these words of Germanicus on his death-bed; but such doubt is arbitrary.

was Agrippina's mortal enemy, 'made it his business to envenom this suspicion.'[1]

Tiberius, like all self-respecting resentful men, never considered his debts sufficiently paid. Not even Germanicus's death made him forget Agrippina's pushfulness and self-assertion. On the contrary, his resentfulness of them was rekindled by the dramatic public welcome which the widow received when she returned to Italy with her husband's ashes.

It is, indeed, highly typical of Tiberius's character, with its slow incubation of his reactions, that six years later (A.D. 21) Cæcina Severus stood up in the Senate and demanded that any general or magistrate proceeding to the provinces should be forbidden to take his wife with him. In his speech this senator painted a striking picture of the pernicious influence which a wife exercises upon a man in authority; and it contained obvious references to Agrippina, as when he said that sometimes a dominating wife 'goes about among the soldiers and gives orders to the centurions,' and that 'if she is allowed, she becomes cruel, ambitious and overbearing.'[2]

Cæcina was one of the commanders of Germanicus's troops at the time of the rising of the legions in Germany. He was there to serve as a guide to the impetuous young general and a brake upon him; and accordingly he was, at the same time, an eye-witness of Agrippina's eccentric exploits. When he spoke in the Senate, years after Germanicus was dead, it is more than probable that he was criticizing his widow, without mentioning her by name, on Tiberius's orders; and perhaps he was also taking his revenge for old humiliations which had been inflicted on him in camp by the imperious princess.

He was answered by Valerius Messalinus, who eloquently defended wives in general—and Agrippina in particular—and indirectly launched a poisoned arrow at Tiberius when he pointed out that Livia too had accompanied Augustus on his political and warlike journeys. There was no denying, in fact, that, if any

---

[1] Tacitus, *107*, I, 69.
[2] Tacitus, *107*, III, 33. Cæcina was a great general, and was granted a triumph in A.D. 15 for his campaigns in Germany at Germanicus's side.

woman in Rome resembled Agrippina, that woman was the Empress Livia. There the matter ended. Tiberius did not want to press it too far, but he must have made note of the lesson in the archives of his resentment.

His son, Drusus II, also intervened in the debate with a eulogy of wives which was somewhat misplaced, as must have been underlined by the malicious smiles of the senators; for at this very time it was being said that his wife, Livilla, was doing her best to justify detractors of feminine virtue. Drusus's speech may be interpreted as a piece of artfulness on Tiberius's part to cover up the effect of that of Cæcina, through whose mouth the emperor himself was speaking.

Little by little, the strife between Tiberius and Agrippina assumed an ever graver character. The energetic widow and her sons, especially her first and favourite son, Nero I, had become the symbol of Julian glory, through the strength of popular sentiment rather than by right of blood. They represented the unforgettable prestige of Drusus I and Germanicus, and, at the same time, the public hatred of Tiberius. Around them gathered a regular party in opposition to the emperor.

If, for some time, mutual hatreds were held in check, this was probably due to the efforts made by Tiberius, in whose ambivalent mind the good sense of a ruler always persisted, to try to avoid a struggle which might have fatal consequences for Rome. Besides, whether he liked it or not, he had to reckon with the prospect that he would be succeeded by one of Agrippina's sons, since his own, only son, Drusus II, had died in A.D. 23, leaving only one son, Tiberius Gemellus, whose youth and silliness made it impossible for him to assume by himself the responsibility of the imperial heritage. Accordingly Tiberius associated his grandson with Germanicus's two elder sons, Nero and Drusus, and presented them to the Senate, adjuring the senators in the name of the gods and the fatherland to safeguard and train them.[1]

---

[1] Tacitus, *107*, IV, 8. A few months earlier, when Drusus III assumed the toga of manhood, Tiberius had made a speech in which he extolled the affection that his son Drusus II had felt towards Germanicus's nephews, and treated the two families as one. Tacitus himself admits that Drusus II 'liked, or at least did not dislike,' his second cousins (Tacitus, *107*. IV, 7).

In his favour towards the hostile family at the outset, Tiberius was doubtless much influenced also by his constant fear of flying in the face of public opinion, which was so favourable to Agrippina's party. Finally, it is possible that during these years Agrippina was protected by Livia. Tacitus[1] tells us that the two women were never friends. 'Livia,' he writes, 'showed all the attitude of a stepmother towards Agrippina, and Agrippina was as little able to restrain herself.' But intellectually they were very much alike. As often happens in life, they knew and could respect each other, even though they did not like each other.

We know, too, that as the years went by and the old alliance between Tiberius and Livia became dissolved, Livia's leanings gradually tended towards her son's enemies. This psychological reaction of hers is important as helping to confirm the empress's belated benevolence towards Agrippina. I am inclined to admit that this benevolence existed, for it is a very significant fact that the letter which Tiberius later wrote accusing Agrippina and her son, and amounting to a sentence upon them, did not reach the Senate until immediately after Livia's death. Moreover, it was said in Rome that this letter was written much earlier, and that Livia, while she was alive, managed to hold it back.[2]

Agrippina's attempt to re-marry

But the truce was broken in the end, and Tiberius's wrath against Agrippina burst out into the open. This was during the emperor's later years, his years of sombre humour; and valiant Agrippina felt that she was beaten. The tyrant had the aid, too, of his minister Sejanus, who, in alliance with Livilla, Tiberius's daughter-in-law, now a widow, officially headed the league against Agrippina, that last redoubt of the Julian family. I shall deal with the incidents of the final phases of the great struggle later, when we come to the story of Sejanus. For the moment let us finish with Agrippina.

Tiring of the pitiless struggle, Agrippina allied herself with Asinius Gallus, Vipsania's widower, and wanted to marry him (A.D. 26), after seven years of exemplary widowhood. There is no

---

[1] Tacitus, *107*, I, 33.   [2] Tacitus, *107*, V, 3.

doubt about this, since Tacitus[1] tells us that he read about it in Agrippina II's *Memoirs*. Germanicus's widow, who had seemed inconsolable, one day sent for Tiberius, on the ground that she was ill—or she may have pretended to be—and asked him point blank for permission to marry. 'A woman still young' (she was now thirty-nine) 'and virtuous,' she told him, 'cannot find consolation except in marriage.' But astute Tiberius realized the political intent of the projected marriage, and refused the widow the consolation she sought. It was to be expected, for that matter, that he should do so, since Agrippina's intended husband was his inveterate rival, the same implacable Gallus who years before had robbed him of his first wife.

End of Agrippina and her Sons

Sejanus, master of Tiberius's will and at the same time instrument of his vengeance, tightened the ring around Agrippina and at last vanquished her. She was sent to Pandataria, the same island that her mother, years earlier, had bedewed with her exile's tears. Her son Nero I was confined on the island of Ponza.[2] The two of them died soon afterwards: Nero in A.D. 31 and Agrippina in A.D. 33. In this year, too, Nero's brother, Drusus III, died in prison in Rome, after a slow agony of three years, starved to the point at which, during his last days, he devoured the wool of his mattress.[3]

Floating like a shipwrecked mariner on this sea of blood there remained only Caligula, later to become emperor. Probably, as we shall see further on, it was thanks to the help of his grandmother Antonia that he was not eliminated too.

Of these three sons of Germanicus and Agrippina, whose fate was at stake at this time, Nero I was his mother's favourite on account of his prudent and modest disposition.[4] So he became her comrade in the struggle against Sejanus and Tiberius. What we can gather about him from the documents gives us the impression of a weak man, of vacillating will, but not without talent and

---

[1] Tacitus, *107*, IV, 53.
[2] Pandataria, now known as Santa Maria, is offshore from Naples. Ponza is close to it, further south.
[3] Tacitus, *107*, VI, 23. Suetonius, *106*, *Tib.*, 54. Dion, 22, LVIII, 3.
[4] Tacitus, *107*, IV, 59 and 60.

eloquence. When Tiberius denounced him before the Senate, he accused him of 'infamous loves and lack of shame,'[1] by which perhaps he meant homosexuality; but we must listen with reserve to the voice of the resentful emperor, who was fundamentally jealous of the young prince's popularity. This, as we have already seen, was immense.

When Nero made a speech in the Senate on behalf of the cities of Asia, 'all hearts felt a sweet emotion,' because everyone thought that the orator recalled his father Germanicus, whom he resembled through his air of nobility and dignity.[2] As always happens, his popularity increased with persecution. On the day when Nero and Agrippina were denounced before the Senate, a turbulent crowd—plebeians, in fact, not patricians as some authorities erroneously allege—carried portraits of them through the streets to the accompaniment of wild cheers in their defence.[3] Though they did not realize it, those who acclaimed them were hastening their death.

Drusus III, Agrippina's second son, was of very tempestuous character. Agrippina's preference for Nero drove him, through jealousy, to ally himself with Sejanus against his mother and brother. But in the end Tiberius and Sejanus eliminated him too, imprisoning him in the dungeons of the imperial palace, at the instigation, so it was said, of his own wife, Æmilia Lepida, who was later to be accused of adultery with a slave and put to death.[4]

As for Caligula, his life as emperor is sufficiently well known to excuse me from describing this shameful soul, of whom Seneca said that 'nature seemed to have created him in order to demonstrate what the most repulsive vices in the highest in the land could achieve.'

---

[1] Tacitus, *107*, V, 3. [2] Tacitus, *107*, IV, 15.
[3] Tacitus, *107*, V, 4.
[4] Drusus III's long imprisonment has been interpreted, rather arbitrarily, on the supposition that Tiberius kept him alive as a possible means of attracting the affection of the populace. It is suggested that, when Tiberius was preparing his blow against Sejanus, in case it should fail he had the idea of letting Drusus III out of prison, placing him at the head of the cohorts, and, taking advantage of the popularity of Germanicus's family, using him as a rallying-point against the favourite.

Agrippina's Guilt

There is no excusing Tiberius for his cruel persecution of Agrippina and Nero. They were, it is true, enemies of the emperor; but there is no proof that their guilt was sufficiently great to justify the severity of their punishment. There is no evidence whatever which induces me to believe with certainty that they planned a conspiracy and regicide, as is alleged by those authors who seek to palliate Tiberius's barbarity. This suspicion has no indisputable foundation. Tacitus says categorically 'that there was no question of revolt or conspiracy,' and that Agrippina was accused only because of her rebellious character and Nero only because of his allegedly shameful love-affairs. Elsewhere Tacitus writes that it was a question 'rather of Nero's imprudent words than his guilty intentions.'[1] There was nothing more than this—except, and above all, the popularity of the two victims, which Tiberius could not stand.

Some authorities have suggested that Sejanus, and not the emperor, was responsible for their persecution; but they do not explain to us why, on Sejanus's death, Tiberius did not pardon Agrippina and her sons, as the people of Rome hoped. On the contrary, he increased the severity of their punishment. Tiberius, and not his favourite, was the executioner. When Agrippina and Drusus III died, it was two years since Sejanus had been beheaded. I shall comment later on the true part which Tiberius's minister played in this tragedy.

The Death of Agrippina

Agrippina died without surrender, strong with all the strength of a mannish woman, which exceeds that of a man. She died, in short, as she had lived. When she was led away to exile, she resisted with such violence that she lost an eye in her struggle with the centurion who was guarding her. By way of excusing the centurion, an English historian says that he was probably manhandled first by the indomitable princess, as though a man had a right to resort to fisticuffs with a woman. When she finally lost all

---

[1] Tacitus, *107*, V, 3.

hope, Agrippina starved herself to death; and even this was hard for her, since, by order of Tiberius, she was forcibly fed. But at length her obstinacy won the day, and so her life ended lamentably.

Faithful to his habit of carrying his grudges beyond the grave, Tiberius insinuated that Agrippina's suicide was due to her grief at the news that her lover Asinius Gallus had just died. Thus he flung a final shovelful of dishonour both upon Vipsania's husband and upon his family's enemy. Moreover, he ordained that Agrippina's birthday should be reckoned among days of ill omen, and persuaded the degraded Senate to make an offering of gold to Jupiter to commemorate his clemency in not having her strangled.[1]

But his refinement of cruelty almost reached the sublime when, as soon as Agrippina was dead, he ordered Plancina, Piso's widow, to be put to death—then, and not before, since he knew that Agrippina hated Plancina even more than himself, and he would not give Agrippina the pleasure of knowing that she was dead.[2]

[1] Suetonius, *106, Tib.*, 53. [2] Dion, 22, LVIII, 22.

IV

TIBERIUS'S SONS

Drusus II, the Sportsman

TIBERIUS'S implacable destiny laid him open to one disappointment after another not only in the love of his parents and his wives, but also in that of his sons. I have already dealt with his adopted son, Germanicus, and his wife Agrippina. We must now turn to Tiberius's true son, Drusus II, and his wife Livilla. Their story and that of Sejanus, to which I shall devote the next chapter, are essential to wind up the history of the great tragedy of the two families.

Drusus was born about the year 11 B.C. We know little about him; and the neutral tint with which he passes across the immense background of Rome suggests in itself that his personality was so commonplace that not even his rank as Cæsar conferred any splendour upon him. The description of him given by some modern writers is ingenious. Perhaps among the shrewdest is that of Baring-Gould,[1] who depicts him for us as an attractive kind of Oxford undergraduate of the athletic type: in other words, neither very intelligent nor very cultured, but sufficiently conscientious; a heavy drinker, disorderly in his amusements, and as capable of giving someone a box on the ears in the course of a quarrel as of jovially putting his arm round him a few minutes afterwards. We know for certain that his character was very violent, and that he was given to dissipation. He inherited from his father an addiction to wine, and often got drunk.[2] Dion tells us that on one occasion, when he went with his soldiers to put out a fire, he pretended to lose his temper with the unfortunate

---

[1] Baring-Gould, *10*, p. 296.
[2] Tacitus, *107*, I, 76. Suetonius, *106*, *Tib.*, 52. Pliny, *79*, XIV, 28.

neighbours because they were desperately appealing for water.¹ So he seems to have been a bit of a humourist: another inheritance from his father.

Tiberius was amused by his son's jokes and adventures. Nevertheless, he often scolded him, sometimes for trivial things, such as his distaste for the excellent vegetable dishes on the emperor's table,² sometimes on more serious grounds, such as his cruelty, which led him to find excessive enjoyment in the bloody spectacles in the gladiatorial arena.³ Here I may remark that, among his other good qualities, Tiberius had one almost unique among the Roman emperors. Gladiatorial shows disgusted him, and on several occasions he tried to reduce their number.⁴ This, needless to say, simply increased—though this time to his credit—his unpopularity. Drusus's bloodthirstiness reached the point of alarming people, so much so that the sharpest swords were called *drusi* after him.⁵

When Drusus fell fatally ill, his father, familiar with his strength, was not in the least alarmed. He thought that his illness was merely another of the many already caused by his intemperance.⁶ As early as A.D. 16 Tiberius had sent him to Illyricum, partly to learn the art of war, but, above all, to remove him from the temptation 'of his excessive passion for the pleasures of the court,'⁷ which was incorrigible.

Despite this, Drusus, so it was said, was a good general. For that matter, so were all the princes of that time, because they were coached by the best soldiers of the empire; and also because they had court chroniclers, whose duty it was to sing their praises.

In difficult circumstances, such as that of Piso's trial, Drusus showed a tact scarcely to be expected of his youth.⁸ This, no doubt, was an inheritance from his father's excellent diplomacy.

---

¹ Dion, 22, LVIII, 14. Father Flórez relates that 'a doctor in the time of Drusus, Tiberius's son, could defeat anyone at drinking because he always took half a dozen almonds beforehand.' Quoted by Sánchez Cantón (89). This may have been the origin of the present-day custom of eating almonds before drinking between meals.

² Pliny, 79, XIX, 42. ³ Tacitus, *107*, I, 76.
⁴ Suetonius, *106*, *Tib.*, 34 and 47. ⁵ Dion, 22, LVII, 13.
⁶ Suetonius, *106*, *Tib.*, 62. ⁷ Tacitus, *107*, II, 44.
⁸ Tacitus, *107*, III, 8.

Drusus was very fond of his father. Tacitus goes so far as to say that he was an irreproachable son.[1]

Marriage of Drusus and Livilla

We do not know the exact date of Drusus II's marriage, but it must certainly have been before A.D. 14, in which year Augustus died, since it was planned by Augustus himself, with the object of uniting the rival Claudians and Julians into one family. Drusus's bride, Livilla, now the widow of Caius Cæsar, was her new husband's cousin, since she was the daughter of Drusus I, Tiberius's brother, and Antonia II, and so a sister of Germanicus. There were three children of the marriage: Julia III, who married the unfortunate Nero I, whose sad story I have already told; and twin sons, known to history by the names of Tiberius Gemellus and Germanicus Gemellus. The latter died soon after his birth, and Tiberius Gemellus seventeen years later, put to death by Caligula.

The marriage of Drusus II and Livilla was happy, but only superficially so. In an earlier chapter, I have told how, when it was debated in the Senate whether generals and provincial governors should take their wives with them or not, and Drusus spoke in praise of wives and his own in particular, she may already have betrayed her husband, since their twin sons, who had been born two years earlier, were said in Rome to be illegitimate.[2] The reputed lover of the princess and father of the twins was Sejanus, Tiberius's all-powerful minister; and if the story were true—which is doubtful—that the adulterous pair poisoned the husband, then at the very time when he publicly sang his wife's praises they must have been plotting the crime.

This is one of the most tragic of the stories that sprang to life beneath the shadow of Tiberius, and one which the reader of today finds it hard to believe. The chroniclers of the period tell us, for example, about Tiberius's satanic bacchanalia in Capri; and with unanimous certainty all of us nowadays discredit them and regard them as the offspring of legend, whatever may have been its basis. The same criterion, founded on common sense rather than on documents, must make us inclined to disbelieve in the

[1] Tacitus, *107*, IV, 11.   [2] Dion, *22*, LVIII, 23.

murder of Drusus by Livilla and her lover, and even to accept with reserve the story of their adultery.

The reason for this doubt is obvious. Drusus II was the emperor's son and his assured heir. Why, then, should his wife go out of her way to unite herself with Sejanus, who was intriguing to secure the emperorship for himself by violence? It was said, in fact, that Sejanus won Livilla over with a promise to marry her when he became emperor. But it leaps to the eye that, in order to reach the dignity of empress, Livilla had only to wait beside Drusus for the natural death of old Tiberius, without mixing herself up in murder.

If she had been in love with Sejanus, we could understand such madness; for any woman, even a criminal woman, may fall in love. But it is improbable that she fell in love with Sejanus, because he was almost as old as Tiberius;[1] because he was a mere knight; and because, though Sejanus had the reputation of a virile man and a great conqueror of virtue, Drusus II for his part was no fool of a prince, of the kind who positively invites a wife, bought by his rank, to seek revenge in adultery; but on the contrary, as we have seen, a manly, dashing fellow, such as we should today call a good sportsman.

Given these conditions, it is difficult to believe that Livilla, through sheer love of him, should make up her mind to unite herself with her elderly suitor, even to the point of committing murder. I am, therefore, inclined to think that the one thing certain is that Sejanus, for political reasons with which I shall deal later, intended to marry Livilla should she become a widow; and that, out of this certain fact of his intention to marry her, popular fancy concocted the legend of her adultery with him, just as it later concocted the legend that the two of them murdered Drusus.

Livilla's belated Beauty

Livilla was very beautiful; and beauty always lays its possessor open to the envy and the calumny of other people, especially other women. Her beauty was a belated one: the beauty typical of

---

[1] Tarver (*108*) makes this calculation, which seems to me to be approximately correct.

the *femme fatale*. As a child she was notoriously plain; but in her youth her face gradually changed, until it flowered into what Tacitus calls 'her rare beauty.'[1] Rare, indeed, is the beauty of those women who have striven in their adolescence against lack of it and have managed to create charm in its place. Then, if their features change, as usually happens at puberty, though sometimes later, and beauty emerges from their plainness, it seems to have arisen from their original charm, and it is, in consequence, infinitely more attractive than the beauty of the woman who possessed it from the outset. We may be sure that Livilla's beauty and her charm aroused the envy of other women: perhaps that of Agrippina herself, who was less physically attractive and humiliated Livilla by making an ostentatious parade of her virtue and purity.[2] It is not difficult to suppose that, in this society in which malicious rumour, calumny and informing played so large a part, the story of Livilla's adultery with Sejanus was a pure invention by plain women, women with beauty but without charm or suitors, and women excessively virtuous.

In all ages examples are to be found of the passion with which women of an inferior class from the æsthetic point of view take their revenge upon women of outstanding beauty; and their revenge almost always takes the form of inventing lovers for them.

Mamercus Scaurus. Eudemus the Doctor

This may have been the case with Livilla. In any event, Sejanus was not the only lover with whom she was credited; and, though no one would put his hand in the fire on behalf of her virtue today, it is permissible to doubt whether she ever had one. It was also said that she had adulterous relations with Mamercus Scaurus, an odious fellow whose story in itself makes it unlikely that the emperor's attractive daughter-in-law should have fallen into his clutches.

We know his story because in A.D. 34, after Livilla was dead, this person, 'renowned for his eloquence and for his infamous habits,'[3] was brought to trial. His accusers charged him

---

[1] Tacitus, *107*. IV, 3. [2] Tacitus, *107*, II, 43. [3] Tacitus, *107*, VI, 29.

with practising magic, with adultery with Livilla, and also with having produced a play entitled *Atrea*, in the style of Euripides, whose characters made political references which Tiberius believed —probably rightly—to be directed against himself.[1] Mamercus Scaurus belonged to a very noble Roman family, one of the families which Cicero took as his model in his time of youthful ambition;[2] but the honour of his nobility was sullied by the repulsive effluvium of his vices. Seneca[3] dishonoured him for ever in an imprecation which I shall bashfully transcribe veiled in its original Latin: '*Quid? Tu, cum Mamercum consulem faceres, ignorabas ancillarum suarum menstruum ore illum hiante exceptare?*'

Instead of assuming that Livilla committed adultery with this crapulous noble, it is much easier to suppose that the infamous informers of that unhappy period brought the dead princess into dishonour by way of heaping fuel on the fire of the charges against Mamercus, a wealthy man whose fall would mean choice pickings for them.

Another adultery which was attributed to Livilla was with her doctor, Eudemus. This accusation is embraced within the great fable of the poisoning of her husband, with which I shall proceed to deal, and is equally worthy of being treated with all reserve.

The Legend of Drusus's Poisoning

About the poisoning of Drusus II one may in fact assert, without fear of error, that the story is a sheer falsehood; and it is incomprehensible that some modern historians, who achieve prodigies of dialectics in order to excuse Tiberius for many of his undeniable crimes, should accept this story of Livilla's crime without the least attempt at criticism, purely for the purpose of emphasizing the emperor's martyrdom, and so helping his rehabilitation and his repute.

The so-called proofs of this alleged crime are ridiculous. When Drusus II died, the idea that he had been murdered did not enter anyone's head, not even, as we have just seen, that of his father, that mirror of suspicion. His death must, therefore, have seemed due to quite natural causes.

[1] Dion, *22*, LVIII, 24.   [2] Plutarch, *81*, Cicero, I.   [3] Seneca, *100*, IV, 31.

Tacitus says that the poison was 'of slow and gradual action, and counterfeited the process of a natural illness.'[1] Today we know how difficult is any such counterfeiting. In the whole of ancient history, rare is the important person whose death has not been suspected of being due to poisoning; and even in modern times we have to reach the nineteenth century, when poisons and their methods of working and killing were scientifically studied, in order to convince ourselves that the majority of deaths attributed to poison, slow or swift, were nothing more than fancies on the part of the public and the historians.[2] It is shocking to think how many innocent people must have been put to death since history began on charges of poisoning, when, in fact, the deaths were natural.

The period of the Roman emperors competes with that of the Italian Renaissance in these regular epidemics of suspected crimes. In the case of Drusus II, the sole ground of suspicion that his death was due to poison was the youth of the dead man, who was just thirty-three. But the vitality of races like his, degenerated by the unnatural life of power and by constant intermarriage between the same families, was so low that the majority of the individuals concerned did not need poison or any other form of violence in order to die before reaching middle age.

When we look at the busts and statues of the Roman princes and princesses of this period, they usually convey an impression of weakness which the apologetic sculptor scarcely succeeds in masking. In the families of Augustus and Tiberius almost all of them possess the convex forehead of rachitics—including those who reached old age, as did the two emperors. The heads of the boy princes, above all, look like those of imbeciles. Whenever a strong head stands out among these statues, it is that of a man with lowlier connections, like Julius Cæsar or Agrippa. Drusus, despite his apparent athlete's robustness, was just one more who came to an untimely end through his precarious heredity and his excessive mode of life. When he died, no one thought of any explanation other than this natural one.

But then, eight years after his death, in A.D. 31, shortly

[1] Tacitus, *107*, IV, 6.   [2] See Lewin's interesting book, *55*.

after the execution of Sejanus, his wife, Apicata, whom he had divorced some time earlier with the object of marrying Livilla, overwhelmed by the putting to death of her husband and children, decided to commit suicide. But before she did so she sent Tiberius a letter in which she revealed to him a terrible secret. It was that Drusus had not died a natural death, as everyone had believed, but had been poisoned by Sejanus with the complicity of Livilla,[1] and with the help of Eudemus, Livilla's doctor and (according to some authorities) another of her lovers,[2] and of a slave named Ligdus, who was entrusted with administering the fatal draught. This Ligdus, a very handsome eunuch, was, according to Tacitus, united to Sejanus by infamous bonds.

It goes without saying that everyone firmly believed in this lewd and macabre story. Ligdus and Eudemus were put to the torture and, of course, confessed what the torturer wanted, namely, their complicity. Livilla, distraught by the accusation, died soon afterwards of starvation, enforced upon her by her mother, stern Antonia.[3]

What are we to think of this story of adultery and crime? It is obviously too tall a story even for the days of Tiberius. Tacitus himself writes that 'rumour delights in surrounding the death of princes with tragic circumstances.'[4] So it did on this occasion. No one with average sense can believe today in the poisoning of Drusus, still less in Livilla's complicity. Apicata's belated denunciation, if it ever existed, has all the aspect of the final revenge of a woman driven mad by rancour and despair, who wanted to give her own death the character of a catastrophe involving the punishment of her rivals. The confession of the alleged accomplices has no value, like all the testimony that the justice of mankind stupidly extracted for so many centuries by torture.

As for Livilla's death, it does not prove anything either. She

[1] See Suetonius, *106*, *Tib.*, 62; Tacitus, *107*, IV, 3 and 8; and Dion, *22*, LVII, 22.
[2] So Pliny affirms (*79*, XXIX, 5). Despite the precepts of Hippocrates, it was not unusual for the doctors of that time to have love-affairs with their patients. There was, for example, the famous one of Messalina with her doctor, Vettius Valens. But in the case of Livilla and her doctor I repeat that any such intrigue was unlikely.
[3] Dion, *22*, LVIII, 11.
[4] Tacitus, *107*, IV, 11.

may have killed herself, like so many other men and women of that time, in which suicide was a common way of ending one's life, simply because she could not stand the shame of the accusation. Her mother may have forced her to die, for the same reason of dignity, though one shrinks from believing that Antonia was capable of carrying her Roman spirit to this cruel length. But, in any case, it is more than probable that Livilla died innocent.

Evidence of the influence which a frenzied environment exerted upon the origin of the fiction of poisoning is to be found in the intervention of the eunuch, united to Sejanus by ties or abnormality, and in that of the doctor, who in his turn was also Livilla's lover: a diabolical combination, better than anything ever invented by the imagination of any novelist. There are, moreover, various other versions of the crime, which increase our suspicion of the whole story. One of them goes so far as to say that it was Tiberius himself, at the inducement of the astute conspirators, who, without realizing it, gave his son the fatal poison to drink![1]

We may reconstruct the truth of the matter as follows: Drusus died young of a natural disease, as many athletes do, just because of their athleticism and the atmosphere of vainglory that surrounds them, especially when the vitality of their organisms is low. His widow, who had one surviving son, Tiberius Gemellus, fearing for his fate as a rival to the sons of Agrippina, decided, lest she should be worsted, to ally herself with the man who had most influence in the politics of Rome and over the mind of the emperor, namely Sejanus. She contemplated marrying him, just as other princesses of her blood had married Agrippa, a mere knight too, who had carved his way to fortune beside Augustus. Tiberius, for the time being, refused his permission for the marriage. But Livilla's intention—politically and morally justified—sufficed to create in the first place the story of her adultery with Sejanus, and afterwards, when the popular imagination was inflamed, the story of their poisoning of Drusus.

An important fact which demonstrates that the whole matter reduces itself to a frustrated political intrigue is that, at about

[1] Tacitus, *107*, IV, 10.

the same time, Agrippina, Livilla's rival, despite her legendary chastity and her thirty-nine years of age, sought, as we have seen, to remarry too. Tiberius realized that what she really wanted was to provide an influential leader for her party, just as Livilla did; and, as in Livilla's case, he refused his permission. The legalistic mind of the emperor is clearly to be seen in these two parallel decisions.

The 'Vendetta'

All this we can plainly see today; but it could not be seen by the Romans of the period, with their minds so open to any tragic interpretation of the life of princes. Tiberius was among those who gave absolute credit to the terrible news of Drusus's poisoning and Livilla's adultery. This certainty, which filled the cup of his resentment to the brim, wasted him away.

It has been said that he did not love his son; and as evidence of his lack of love for him the fact has been adduced that, the moment Drusus's funeral was over, he reverted with his usual energy to work of government.[1] But this is yet another calumny. In his old age the emperor was cold in his expression of his feelings, sparing of words, and lacking in that fatherly and affectionate cheerfulness with which his stepfather Augustus treated his family. But there is no ground which justifies us in believing Tiberius to have been incapable of paternal love. He attended his son's funeral because it was his duty, and he never neglected this kind of duty. Then, overwhelmed by grief, he sought consolation in work. Here he showed himself to be a true Roman. The fact is creditable and not to be interpreted as justifying his reputation for cruelty.

But his resentment, freshly fired by this misfortune—the last and the worst of all—exploded in a ferocious vengeance. In the following chapters I shall tell the story of his final tragic years. When we come to this point, those who seek to excuse him can do nothing more than lay down their arms for lack of arguments. Ciaceri[2] himself no longer contradicts Tacitus, and admits that

[1] Suetonius, *106, Tib.*, 52.
[2] Ciaceri, *17*, p. 303.

'for two years Rome was bathed in blood.' But he hastens to add: 'To the ancients, the "vendetta" was almost sacred.'

It was so to the ancients, just as it is to the moderns, when they are incapable of generosity. It is so to the resentful man who lives obsessed by revenge, not to the generous man, who is fortunately to be found in all ages. At that time, as at all times, there were human beings open to clemency and not exposed to rancour and to the 'vendetta.' But it is certain that Tiberius was not one of them.

V

THE DRAMA OF SEJANUS

Sejanus's Life and Ambition

I HAVE frequently referred to Sejanus, and now I must thread his story together, lest I leave it scattered in fragments. I must also do so because, in the calvary of Tiberius's disappointments, Sejanus, according to the historians, represented his disappointment in friendship. At the same time, its study will enable us to wind up the chronicle of the struggle between Claudians and Julians.

Sejanus has passed into history as a monstrosity of evil. Tiberius's partisans stress his minister's perfidy in order to excuse the emperor and transfer to Sejanus the responsibility for Tiberius's final cruelties. His enemies stress it too, in order that the emperor's infamy may be judged through his infamous minister. So, harassed from both sides, Sejanus's memory passes across the background of ancient Rome covered with perfidy and dishonour.

We have a favourable description of Sejanus in Velleius,[1] who

---

[1] Velleius, *114*, II, 127 and 128. This apologia for Sejanus was, of course, written before his fall. Velleius published his book in A.D. 30, in other words, at the time of the favourite's full power, a year before his fall and death. Velleius's pen was certainly inspired by the same unbridled adulation that corrupted so many Romans at that time. It is more than probable that he paid dearly for his praises, since all the minister's friends—and few were so notoriously friendly with him as the historian—suffered from Tiberius's barbarous persecution. Nevertheless, Tacitus, who makes such a close count of the victims, does not mention Velleius. Perhaps he managed to escape from Rome. All that is certain is that, from this date onwards, we hear nothing more about him. Baring-Gould (*10*, p. 311) justly remarks that the eloquence which Velleius displays to justify Sejanus's elevation from a simple knight to the highest posts in the empire, quoting in his support many examples of other men of equally modest origin who filled the republic with glory, seems to indicate that Velleius was really making a defence of the favourite against the aristocrats who attacked him for his lowly birth.

knew him personally. 'He is a man,' he writes, 'of quiet serenity, with a cheerfulness which recalls that of our ancestors. He is active without seeming to be so. He never demands anything for himself, and accordingly obtains everything. He always regards himself as unworthy of the esteem in which others hold him. His face is as peaceful as his life. His mind is ever vigilant.'

In contrast with this judgement, Tacitus tells us:[1] 'His spirit was daring. He was clever at dissimulation and confusing other people. At once aspiring and proud, beneath an appearance of modesty he hid an unrestrained thirst for greatness. To get where he wanted, he employed sometimes generosity and pomp, sometimes vigilance and activity.' It is difficult to find the real truth behind these two contradictory portraits, one painted with the brush of adulation, the other with that of scorn.

Sejanus—otherwise known as Ælius Sejanus, since he was adopted by the Ælian family—was the son of Sejus Strabo, a simple knight of Tuscan origin who, in Augustus's reign, became by sheer merit commander of the prætorian cohorts and under Tiberius governor of Egypt: both of them positions of high confidence. He made a good marriage with a woman of the Junian family. His son, Sejanus, making up his mind from the outset to reach a good position in life, while he was still young married Apicata, daughter of wealthy Apicius, though he does not appear to have been in love with her. Tacitus refers to this when he tells us that Sejanus prostituted himself for Apicius's money.[2]

In the year 1 B.C. we find him forming part of the suite of Caius Cæsar on his ceremonial journey to the east: a fact which suggests that Augustus, who had prepared this expedition with such care, had already handed down to the son the confidence which he had extended to the father. But clever Sejanus was already betting on the rising star, the future emperor, who, he calculated, would be Tiberius, despite the fact that at this time he was in disgrace and retirement in Rhodes. This betting on a future which not everyone believes to be assured, rather than on a

---

[1] Tacitus, *107*, IV, 1.
[2] Tacitus, *107*, IV, 1. Dion says that Sejanus had been Apicius's 'darling . . .' (Dion, *22*, LVI, 19).

present certainty, is typical of men of great ambition. I have discussed this matter in a recent book.[1]

As his chief tutor, Caius had with him Marcus Lollius, an enemy of Tiberius, who fed the fire of enmity between the two princes: Caius, whose star seemed to be in the ascendant, and Tiberius, whose star seemed to be in the descendant. Sejanus offset Marcus Lollius's bad influence in favour of Tiberius. He proved the stronger, and Lollius shortly fell into disgrace. This, we may suppose, was the starting-point of the friendship between Tiberius and Sejanus, which was to make history.

In A.D. 14, in which year Augustus died and Tiberius succeeded him, we find Sejanus in the position of deputy for his father and then his successor at the head of the prætorian cohorts. These cohorts, which had been dispersed in various parts of Rome and outside the city, were now concentrated in one camp. In this way, Tiberius hastened to assure his personal defence, leaning upon the united and disciplined cohorts under the command of a man wholly on his side. It was an act typical of his psychology, full of suspicion and precaution.

Another proof of the new emperor's confidence in Sejanus is that when, in this same year, the legions mutinied in Pannonia and Drusus II, Tiberius's own son, was sent to suppress their revolt, Sejanus, 'even then all-powerful with the emperor,'[2] went with him as his adviser. At the same time Sejanus was intriguing against Germanicus, who was simultaneously seeking to restore discipline in legions which had mutinied in Germany. We know that it was Sejanus who adroitly fed the fire of Tiberius's resentment against the soldiers' fervent adherence to Germanicus and against Agrippina I's mannish interventions.

From this time onwards Sejanus's success was remarkable. It is obvious that the prætorian leader had in his mind, as his supreme model, the not very distant example of Agrippa, a simple knight like himself, who ended by becoming Augustus's colleague, his daughter's husband, and the presumptive heir to the imperial power. Like Agrippa, Sejanus contrived that his image should figure beside that of Tiberius in places of honour in the city,

[1] See Marañón, 65.   [2] Tacitus, *107*, I, 24.

on the standards of the legions,[1] and even on coins, as on some of those found at Bilbilis; that he should be designated consul, as a colleague of the emperor himself, for A.D. 31 (the very year in which he was to be put to death); and, finally, that Tiberius should promise him admission into the imperial family through his marriage 'to one of the princesses' of his house.[2]

[1] Tacitus, *107*, III, 72. According to Suetonius, some of the legions in Syria refused to accept this glorification of Sejanus; and, when Sejanus fell, Tiberius rewarded them, though it was he himself, of course, who had ordered this glorification (Suetonius, *106*, *Tib.*, 48).

[2] It is an obscure point in Tiberius's life, this projected marriage of Sejanus to a princess of the imperial family. It is preferable to comment on it in this note rather than in the text. We know for certain that Sejanus wanted to marry Livilla, Drusus II's widow, and that Tiberius, tactfully rather than violently, refused, or, to put it better, deferred his permission (A.D. 25). Some years later, about A.D. 30, there was renewed talk that among the honours which Tiberius would bestow on Sejanus was that of 'making him his son-in-law' (Tacitus, *107*, V, 6). Who was this new prospective bride who would make Sejanus the emperor's son-in-law? Modern authors say, almost unanimously, that she was Julia III, daughter of Drusus II and Livilla, and wife of Nero I, from whom she was divorced when he was exiled in A.D. 29. This, however, is not certain, or anything like it. The idea that Julia III was the bride chosen by Tiberius to admit this minister into the imperial family appears for the first time in the commentators on Tacitus, Rickius and Reimarus. The first, in fact, confines himself to saying that the bride was not Livilla, but one of the emperor's grand-daughters, though he does not specify which of them. There were three: Julia III, and Drusilla and Julia Livilla, both daughters of Germanicus who, as Germanicus was Tiberius's adopted son, might be regarded as the emperor's granddaughters. Reimarus, more categorically, declares that the chosen bride was precisely Julia III, basing himself on a passage in the *Chronicle* of Zonaras which reads: 'Tiberius, after raising Sejanus to the summit of honours and making him his son-in-law, through his marriage to Julia, daughter of Drusus, ended by putting him to death.' But Zonaras, a historian of the twelfth century, is a doubtful authority. Juste-Lipse (*58*) declares that Zonaras's text is wrong, and that where it says 'Julia' it should read 'Livia' or 'Livilla,' since some of the ancients (Tacitus among them) call Livilla Livia. The facility with which modern authors return to the hypothesis of Julia is due to their mistake, which they copy from one another, in believing that Tiberius refused his consent to Sejanus's marriage to Livilla, and that therefore the bride must have been someone else in the imperial family. But I have cleared up this error in the text. There was no such refusal. Tacitus says that Tiberius, faced with Sejanus's request to marry Livilla, *did not reject it, but postponed any definite reply*. I quote Tacitus's exact words: 'For the rest, *I do not oppose* either your projects or those of Livia (Livilla). As for other intimate projects which I have made with regard to you and the fresh links by which I desire to unite you more closely to my person, *for the moment I abstain from telling you about them*' (Tacitus, *107*, IV, 40). There can, therefore, be no doubt that there was no refusal on Tiberius's part, but a mere, though astute, postponement. This may have been in order to allow time for the rivalry between Agrippina and Livilla to die down. It may have been in order to raise Sejanus, then a simple knight, to a rank worthy of that of his bride. Finally, it may have been in order to gain time and, as was Tiberius's habit,

An exact repetition of Agrippa's success therefore seemed assured for the aspiring minister. His mistake consisted in forgetting that he was not Agrippa, and that Tiberius was not Augustus. Augustus possessed the virtue of generosity, which is the contrary of the passion of resentment that tortured Tiberius. Agrippa was a great statesman and a great general, so great that Horace said that his deeds deserved to be praised by another Homer.[1] To Agrippa the essential thing was effective action, and triumph mattered to him only as an addition to his enjoyment of action. Sejanus, on the other hand, was a man of superficial qualities. He was hypnotized by triumph, and, intent upon his goal, did not watch where he was setting foot in order to reach it.

Like almost all men who know women well, he knew men badly. He was ignorant, for example, of the violent reaction of which a timid soul is capable. This ignorance was his downfall. He believed that he dominated Tiberius to the point of holding

---

surround the favourite with honours while preparing for his fall, which he may have contemplated long before. But, even if we admit that Tiberius bluntly rejected Sejanus's proposal, as some of his historians assert, there was no reason why, after refusing him Livilla, he should proceed to grant him Julia, Livilla's own daughter. In short, all the indications are that the suggestion that Julia was to be Sejanus's bride is a gratuitous hypothesis, and that the promised bride was never anyone but Livilla. Dion (22, LVIII, 7) says that Sejanus, on the termination of his consulate (A.D. 30), asked Tiberius for his permission to go to the Campagna, where his 'future mother' was ill. Ciaceri (17, 294) supposes that this illness was a pretext invented by Antonia, who hated Sejanus, in order that the marriage should not take place. In any case, it did not take place. In my opinion, the most probable thing is that Tiberius never seriously intended to let Sejanus marry any of his family, because he realized the political dangers of such a marriage, and that, with his promises and withdrawals, he was merely holding at arm's length the petitions and pressure of his minister and favourite. It is to this that Suetonius (106, Tib., 65) refers when he tells us that Tiberius encouraged Sejanus 'with the hope of a marriage.' In other words, it was merely *a hope*.

Apart from this project of marriage, which has been the subject of so much controversy, there was another project, that of a marriage between Sejanus's daughter, Junilla, and Drusus IV, son of Claudius and Urgulanilla. This pair, betrothed from childhood, died tragically long before they could marry. Drusus was choked at Pompeii by a pear with which he was amusing himself by throwing into the air and catching in his open mouth: an odd game, to be sure (Suetonius, 106, Claud., 27). Unhappy Junilla was strangled, after being violated by the executioner, when her father fell into disgrace with the emperor. It was doubtless to these two projects that Terentius was referring in the speech which I shall quote in the next chapter, when he said that Sejanus 'was united to the house of the Claudians and the Julians by a double alliance.'

[1] Horace, 45, I, 6.

him in the hollow of his hand; and perhaps, losing his head altogether, he contemplated carrying his ambition to the length of crime, a limit which upright Agrippa would never have approached.

Sejanus's Intrigues

So we find him involved in obscure and manifold intrigues towards the end of Tiberius's reign, especially after the death of Tiberius's son, Drusus II, had raised the problem of the succession in an acute form.

As we have already seen, the emperor had adopted his grandson Tiberius Gemellus, associating with him Germanicus's two elder sons, Nero I and Drusus III. At the outset, he maintained this judicious association. But it was not long before his good sense as a ruler began to be superseded by his resentment. Only a year later (A.D. 24), in fact, he sent a harsh reprimand to the consuls and pontiffs because they, doubtless with the idea of flattering him, recommended these two princes to the gods.[1] Tiberius's change of front was due, as we have also seen, to the fact that Nero, alongside his mother, was beginning to become popular and gather a party around him in his turn, like his father and his grandfather. Agrippina's impulsiveness encouraged his popularity, and at the same time refuelled the emperor's aggressive reaction. But it was certainly Sejanus who exaggerated to Tiberius the danger from the party of the last of the Julians, and incited him to proceed against it and especially against its heads.

That Sejanus played this rôle is beyond all doubt. Tacitus tells us that it was 'he who stirred up the emperor's wrath,' and he who made Tiberius see 'the empire eaten up by a civil war, and the name of Agrippina's party pronounced by men proud of belonging to it.'[2] It was at this time that Livilla, who wanted to assure the supremacy of her son, Tiberius Gemellus, over the other heirs, Nero and Drusus, sought the support of Sejanus and contemplated marrying him: a project which fell like rain on the thirsty soil of the minister's ambition. In order to offset this alliance, as we have already seen also, Agrippina in her turn

---

[1] Tacitus, *107*, IV, 17.   [2] Tacitus, *107*, IV, 17.

proposed to marry Asinius Gallus. We have seen, too, how Tiberius rejected, or rather prudently and craftily postponed, both these matrimonial plans, because he realized that their execution would be equivalent, not to giving husbands to two more or less inconsolable widows, but to giving efficient and formal heads to the two warring families.

Despite this evasiveness on Tiberius's part with regard to his marriage, Sejanus's influence over the old emperor remained almost absolute. Sejanus contented himself with the hope of a marriage later, and, like a clever man, far from showing his annoyance, redoubled his obsequiousness and his services to Tiberius, resentful and sickened of his environment, until he persuaded him to retire, leaving his responsibilities as emperor at the mercy of his supplanter. Sejanus made good use of this situation, and finally the balance of the imperial will inclined against Agrippina and her sons.

Trials of Silius and Sabinus

The offensive was not begun openly against them, but against two men representative of their party: Silius Nerva, a great soldier, who seven years earlier had been granted the honour of a triumph for his victories in Germany, and an intimate of Germanicus, married to Sosia Galla, who enjoyed Agrippina's close friendship; and Titus Sabinus, a distinguished knight who possessed the very rare and noble virtue of standing in misfortune beside those who had been his friends in better days.[1] Silius committed suicide to avoid execution (A.D. 24).

Sabinus's trial, contemplated at the same time as that of Silius, did not take place until four years later (A.D. 28). Condemned to death, he died valiantly, proclaiming his innocence and calling down curses upon his executioners, who had to muffle his justifiable words by gagging him with his own tunic: a futile measure, since they reach our ears to this day.

Sabinus's death made such an impression on the people that a legend soon gathered about it. It was said that the victim's dog refused to leave his body. While it was exposed on the Gemonian

[1] See the excellent account of his trail in Tacitus, *107*, IV, 18, 68 and 70.

Steps the faithful dog brought food in his mouth every day and laid it close to the dead man's mouth; and, when the corpse was thrown into the Tiber, the animal plunged into the water and kept it afloat, before the admiring gaze of the people who crowded the banks.[1] Here the dog clearly symbolizes virtue and fidelity, contrasted with the infamy of the emperor.

Both trials were models of iniquity and hypocrisy. The denunciation of Sabinus was particularly disgusting. I recall it because it seems to have been an everyday story. Four former prætors, aspirants to the consulate, in order to ingratiate themselves with Sejanus, conceived the idea of betraying Sabinus. These scoundrels' names—they deserve to be set on record—were Latinius Latiaris, Porcius Cato, Petilius Rufus and Marcus Opsius. Latiaris pretended to be a friend and confidant of unhappy Sabinus, and by his own deceitful criticisms of Sejanus and Tiberius aroused the natural aversion which Germanicus's friend felt towards the emperor and his minister. After a few conversations, Sabinus entrusted the traitor Latiaris with all his thoughts. On the day fixed for his betrayal, Latiaris invited the victim to his house and reopened the subject, to such good purpose that Sabinus set forth, in harsher terms than ever, his grief over Germanicus's death and his indignation against Tiberius and his favourite. Sabinus was not aware that three other accomplices hidden in an attic were listening to him through carefully prepared openings, and that within a few hours detailed testimony of his conversation would be in the emperor's hands. The effect which this piece of infamy created in the city was immense. 'Never,' says Tacitus, 'did such consternation and fear reign in Rome as then.' Henceforth no one doubted the fate that awaited Agrippina and her sons and followers.

I said in the last chapter that Agrippina and her family were probably protected against this threat by Livia. I must now add that another woman also watched over them, or at least over the youngest of Germanicus's sons, Caligula. This woman was

---

[1] See Dion, 22, LVIII, 1. Pliny tells the same story in detail, but applies it not to Sabinus, but to a slave of his who was executed at the same time, and whose dog showed these signs of fidelity. This historian adds that Sabinus was involved in dangerous affairs with Nero (Pliny, 79, VIII, 61).

Antonia, the impeccable widow of Drusus I, with whom I shall deal at length later.

Persecution of Caligula and Antonia's Intervention

Antonia either could not or would not avert the condemnation of Agrippina, who was the victim most threatened through her long history of imprudence and unrestrained appetite for revenge and power. With her fell Nero, her favourite son, who was involved in her own popularity, and, a few years later, Drusus III.

Henceforth Antonia concentrated her skill on defending the youngest son, Caligula, the sole survivor.

Most historians have stressed Sejanus's persecution of Agrippina and her two elder sons, but have made scarcely any reference to his persecution of Caligula. This, however, is unquestionable, and of great importance to our story.

We know, in fact, that, as soon as his mother was exiled (A.D. 29), Caligula was sheltered by his great-grandmother Livia, and that when she died, shortly afterwards, he was taken into the home of his grandmother Antonia. Caligula was then seventeen years old. He lived in Rome with Antonia until two years later, A.D. 31, when Tiberius summoned the two of them to Capri, undoubtedly not long before Sejanus's fall.[1] All this, which clearly indicates the determination of the two women, Livia and Antonia, to save Caligula, Suetonius tells us for certain.[2]

It is unquestionable that their precautions were due to the fact that Sejanus was contemplating the elimination of Caligula too: he was the last of the Julians and should perish like the rest. In the series of trials which followed the favourite's execution there figured that of Sextius Paconianus, a former prætor, who was accused of being Sejanus's instrument *in preparing for Caligula's destruction*.[3] In the charges against other accused, there also figured

---
[1] We know, in fact, that at the beginning of this same year, A.D. 31, Antonia was still in Rome, and that from there she sent to Tiberius, now in retirement in Capri, a letter denouncing Sejanus. As Tiberius thought that Sejanus's arrest might give rise to disorders—so much so that he kept ships ready for flight, in case the business should turn out badly—it was logical that he should summon Antonia and Caligula to his side in order to place them in safety.
[2] Suetonius, *106*, *Calig.*, 10.
[3] Tacitus, *107*, VI, 3.

attacks which they had directed against Caligula. Such was the case in the trials of Messalinus Cota and Sextus Vistilus.[1] These two men, friends of Sejanus, were accused of having calumniated Caligula by charging him with corrupt morals, probably homosexuality and incest. So it is certain that the death of Caligula, as well as that of his brothers, was being plotted in the highest circles.

Everything, therefore, seemed to assure Sejanus's triumph and the annihilation of the Julians, when suddenly a woman emerged, in the person of Antonia, who, by a dramatic stroke of daring courage, managed to change the emperor's mind, overthrow the all-powerful minister, and, through Caligula, secure the succession of the family which seemed to be vanquished. It is a mystery that the designs of providence should have permitted this; for the last of the Julians was the shame of his family and the horror of posterity. Here is how all this happened.

Downfall and Death of Sejanus

In A.D. 31 Tiberius, who was then in Capri, so closely watched by Sejanus that all his correspondence was carefully intercepted, received a letter from Antonia, who had succeeded in getting it to him from Rome by means of a clever and faithful freedman named Pallas. In this letter Antonia accused Sejanus of planning a conspiracy against the emperor.[2]

It is probable that Tiberius, as was his custom, had for some time back been meditating Sejanus's downfall. People were beginning to suspect this, and already some of the favourite's former flatterers were starting to turn him the cold shoulder:[3] an infallible sign that a powerful man is commencing to totter. If this is the case, Antonia's letter merely precipitated a decision which Tiberius had already conceived. The fact remains that, the moment he had read it, Tiberius made up his mind to rid himself of his minister. He did so with all the ferocity of a weak man when he rebels against his dominator, turning the submission of a lifetime into an instant's concentration of hatred.

---

[1] Tacitus, *107*, VI, 5 and 9.　　[2] Josephus, *47*, LVIII. 8.
[3] Dion, *22*, LVIII, 4 *et seq.*

But overthrowing Sejanus was no easy job, since he had on his side not only the prætorian cohorts which were under his command, but also a wide network of partisans in the city—freedmen, knights and senators—who supported him at all costs. Nevertheless, Tiberius, who still preserved all his astuteness, managed to overthrow him, thanks to a plan which he contrived cautiously and had carried into effect by Macro, the commander of the cohorts of the guard in Capri, who from this time onwards assumed Sejanus's function of weighting the emperor's wavering will. Tiberius's panegyrists interpret his manœuvre against Sejanus as a proof of his cleverness. It was no mere cleverness, but a masterpiece of double-dealing and hypocrisy.

Macro was sent to Rome bearing, so Sejanus was told, a letter addressed by Tiberius to the Senate, in which he granted the minister magnificent honours, among them the highest of all, the tribunician power. Sejanus let himself be carried away by his vanity, and light-heartedly fell into the trap which was laid for him. An ambitious man without judgement always meets his end so simply in the way he has sinned most. While Sejanus, bursting with pride, was making his way to the Senate to attend his own glorification, Macro hastened to the camp of the prætorian cohorts and showed them another letter from Tiberius, in which Sejanus was deprived of his command and Macro himself was nominated in his place.

This was the turning-point, the critical moment of the whole plot, since everything depended on whether the soldiers would prove loyal to the emperor against their own commanding officer, or loyal to their commander against the emperor. Matters turned out well for the emperor. The cohorts swore fidelity to their new commander, doubtless with the aid of the rich monetary reward which Tiberius promised them: that palm-oil which miraculously softens the stiffness of human decisions.

While he was thus being deprived of his military strength, Sejanus was listening in the Senate to the reading of the emperor's anxiously awaited letter. It was a very long letter, in which Tiberius cautiously began by praising his minister. But, little by little, praise turned into censure, and finally into accusation. The letter ended with a peremptory order for Sejanus's arrest. After a moment of stupefaction, the senators agreed to this, especially when they heard that the prætorian guard was already on Tiberius's side. It is probable that some of them—perhaps those who made the most parade of their surprise—had an inkling of what was coming. No one stood up to defend the fallen minister. That very same day, 18th October, A.D. 31, Sejanus was tried and condemned to death.

His body was dragged through the streets of Rome for three days and torn to pieces: pieces so small that, Seneca tells us, the executioner could not find one big enough to expose on the Gemonian Steps.[1] Sejanus's eldest son, Strabo, was executed soon afterwards, and so later were his three younger children, Capito, Ælianus, and Junilla: the last, a girl under age, in circumstances of revolting cruelty which I shall describe later.

The effect which the minister's unexpected fall created in Rome must have been terrific. A writer of the period calls Sejanus 'a man more famous for his fall than for his fortune,' and both were great enough. Such is the fate of all favourites of dictators. Juvenal says that Sejanus, in his zest for honours and wealth, 'built out of many stones a gigantic tower, which, from its very height, was bound to make a sudden and disastrous fall.'[2] The spectacle of the fall of the man who had been all-powerful was enhanced by the fear that, after him, all his followers would fall too. This was just what happened. The great city was bathed in blood and tears.

The Guilt of Tiberius and Sejanus

Now let us study Sejanus's conduct. That of Tiberius was repellent. Suetonius says that the emperor behaved 'rather with the artifices of deceit than with the authority of a ruler'; and he qualifies Tiberius's letter to the Senate as 'a shameful and miserable missive.'[3] This is, indeed, a mild way of putting it.

What was the extent of Sejanus's guilt? The version which we may call official tells us that the minister, proud to the point of drunkenness with power, plotted to kill Tiberius and succeed

---

[1] Seneca, *97*, II. [2] Juvenal, *49*, X. [3] Suetonius, *106*, Tib., 65.

him as emperor. But not all historians accept this explanation.¹ Some of them, in fact, express their surprise that a fact of this magnitude should be quoted only vaguely by Suetonius and Tacitus, barely mentioned by Dion, and described in detail only by a provincial historian like Josephus.² Besides, they add, if Sejanus aspired to the emperorship, it would have been easier for him to await the death of the old emperor than to involve himself in the dangers of conspiracy and crime.

When we study the facts carefully, however, no doubt remains that Sejanus was weaving some plot, whose object might be difficult to define exactly, but from which, in any case, he stood to gain. Even though some ancient historians do not speak of such a plot, we are bound to give the utmost credit to what they do say. In any science—and history ought to be a science—definite data are what counts. Tacitus himself, though the text in which he may have described the plot is largely lost, when he refers to it in later passages gives us the impression that he accepted it as a fact.³

As for the logic of this, it is obvious. In the ordinary course of events, that is to say, after the natural death of the emperor, Sejanus could not aspire to succeed him, once Tiberius had blocked the sole possible legal path, which was Sejanus's marriage to Livilla. The honours which Tiberius heaped upon Sejanus assumed, at the most, the possibility that he might attain the position of guardian to the legitimate heirs, until they had the necessary

¹ Among modern works, the most balanced one for information about this controversy is Marsh's book, *69*, VIII and Appendix VIII.

² Josephus says that Tiberius had a great respect for Antonia, because she was his sister-in-law, because of her unspotted chastity, and because she warned him about Sejanus's conspiracy, 'when it was on the point of coming to a head against him, with the complicity of a large number of senators, officers of the army, and even freedmen of the imperial household' (Josephus, *47*, XVIII, 8).

³ For example, Tacitus tells us that Terentius, one of those accused at the time of Sejanus's execution, to whom I shall refer in the next chapter, in his defence said that he was, in fact, a friend of Sejanus, but that this did not imply that he had been involved in '*the plot against the empire and the attempt on the life of the emperor*' (Tacitus, *107*, VI, 8). In another passage, referring to the fact that women were also brought to trial on this occasion, the same historian writes: 'Though they could not be accused of seeking to usurp the empire, they were accused, etc.' (Tacitus, *107*, VI, 10). It appears, therefore, that there was a plot against the empire and its ruler, in which Sejanus was involved.

experience for ruling. In no case could it be Tiberius's intention that Sejanus should be his heir. If, therefore, Sejanus really aspired to the imperial heritage, the sole path open to him was violence, in which he would rely on his cohorts and take advantage of the emperor's age and extreme unpopularity. That such a project was no absurdity is proved by the fact that, as Duruy recalls, between A.D. 14 and 96, out of ten emperors seven were assassinated, and almost all of them were succeeded by their assassins.

Even though Suetonius barely refers to a conspiracy, nevertheless he gives us a datum which in effect accords with the reality of such a conspiracy. He tells us that Tiberius wrote in his *Memoirs* that he had put Sejanus to death when he discovered his implacable hostility to Germanicus's sons.[1] Doubtless he is referring to the moment of Antonia's intervention. Antonia must have made Tiberius see that the zeal with which Sejanus was persecuting Tiberius's grandsons was so extreme that it betrayed his real intention, which was not to punish Agrippina and Nero for their disturbances, their insolence and their family hostility, but to exterminate the whole family, leaving Sejanus as the unquestionable successor, and, if necessary, sacrificing the emperor himself. It was then that Tiberius summoned Antonia and Caligula to Capri, and saved Caligula from his imminent danger. This would fully explain the intervention of Antonia, who, working upon Tiberius's fear and pride, succeeded in satisfying her grandmother's love and her zeal as defender of the Julian family, which seemed on the point of disappearing. Her mother Octavia and divine Augustus must have smiled upon her from the peace of the next world.

Why Caligula was saved

Another point remains to be explained. Why was it, when Tiberius learnt through Antonia about Sejanus's plans for extermination, that he hastened to save Caligula, but not his brothers. who were in the same danger as himself? The spectator who contemplates this immense tragedy from our own time, at a distance of twenty centuries, may establish dates and reconstruct

[1] Suetonius, *106, Tib.*, 61.

events, but he cannot penetrate the arcana of human souls except by groping in the dark. Given this reservation, however, we may assume that Agrippina and her two elder sons, who had notoriously disturbed the public peace, of which Tiberius was so zealous a defender, incurred his severity to the bitter end. Caligula, on the other hand, was saved because he never stood beside his mother but belonged to the emperor's party, either through calculation—which is improbable, given his stupidity—or thanks to the wise counsel of his grandmother Antonia.

That this was the case is shown by the following passage from Suetonius:[1] 'In Capri, despite the insidiousness with which some tried to make him [Caligula] speak, they never managed to hear him utter a single complaint. He seemed to have forgotten the misfortunes of his family, swallowed his own affronts with almost incredible dissimulation, and showed himself so submissive and respectful to his grandfather Tiberius and to those who surrounded him that it might be said of him with good reason, that never did so great a master have a better slave.' This sufficiently explains the different fates of Caligula and his brothers.

Even after the death of Tiberius, Caligula, who had now become emperor, justified Tiberius's action against his own mother and brothers, saying that Tiberius was forced to proceed sternly against them under the pressure of the senators, whom he called 'clients of Sejanus':[2] an inadmissible defence in any case, since Tiberius always contrived to have his own way, even despite the criticism of the Senate, which in fact ventured to disagree with the emperor only once in his whole reign. Besides, if this story were true, the death of Sejanus and the senators who supported him would have changed Tiberius's stern attitude towards Agrippina and her elder sons, whereas we have seen that this was not the case, and that his hatred of them—without any senators influencing him—ceased only with their death.

Thus Antonia's decisive intervention and Caligula's hypocritical conduct explain the fact that Caligula was not only saved, but was even associated, as heir to the empire, with the emperor's direct grandson, Tiberius Gemellus, and with precedence over

[1] Suetonius, *106, Calig.*, 10.   [2] Suetonius, *106, Calig.*, 30.

him. Tiberius, in fact, in his will made two years before he died,[1] named the two young men as his heirs, arranging that they should succeed each other in accordance with the difference in their ages, or, in other words, giving Caligula preference because he was the elder. But their difference in age was not great: Caligula was twenty-five and Tiberius Gemellus eighteen. This difference would have constituted no legal obstacle to Tiberius's giving precedence, if he had wished, to the younger, who was, moreover, his most direct successor. We may assume, therefore, that he had a reason of greater substance, and that this reason was to be found in Antonia's influence. Who knows, too, whether Caligula's precedence may have been affected by the rumours current in Rome that Tiberius Gemellus was not Tiberius's legitimate grandson, but the offspring of a love-affair between Livilla and Sejanus of accursed memory?[2]

Sejanus's Character

Sejanus was the prototype of the ambitious man, amoral rather than wicked, who is to be found at all corrupt courts. He was daring, generous, physically strong,[3] and good-looking. He was a great ladies' man: 'the lover of the wives of all outstanding citizens,' Dion tells us; and he got all of them into his clutches—just as students do with their sweethearts, and soldiers with servants, and as Don Juan Tenorio also did with his victims—by promising to marry them.[4]

[1] Suetonius, *106, Tib.*, 76.   [2] Dion, 22, LVIII, 23.
[3] The crowning episode which the historians relate in connection with Sejanus's physical strength is well known. It is said to have occurred in A.D. 26. Tiberius was staying in the Campagna, and, with his suite, went into a natural cave at Spelunca for a meal. The mouth of the cave suddenly collapsed, crushing several slaves. The rest, seized with panic, took to their heels, together with the guests. Only Sejanus stayed behind. Going down on one knee, with his arms uplifted and his eyes fixed on Tiberius, he held up the collapsing rocks, and so saved the emperor's life. When some soldiers rushed to the rescue they found him still in this theatrical attitude. His feat gave Tiberius confidence in him, and out of gratitude the emperor made him his minister (Tacitus, *107*, IV, 59). The unanimity with which modern authors accept this story without the least criticism is incomprehensible. No man could have been capable of holding up, by his unaided strength and for so long a time, rocks of such a size as figure in the story. It is possible that Sejanus did what he could to save Tiberius, and that legend invented the romantic picture which Tacitus handed down to us.
[4] Dion, 22, LVIII, 3.

There is no evidence in his history that he committed any misdeeds other than those likely to be committed by any reckless man in a corrupt social environment. In the end he fell headlong into the abyss of ambition; but we need not blame him overmuch. If he persecuted Germanicus's sons, it is obvious that he did so, at least at the outset, in subservience to the designs of his lord and master. If he did indeed conspire against Tiberius, before we reproach him we must consider the motives of his plot. There have been many conspiracies in history which were morally justified; for legality does not always coincide with virtue or with common sense. Probably not a few upright men of today would have been conspirators at Sejanus's side. At least in these proceedings on which history has already passed judgement, our pity inclines rather towards the conspirator who paid for his guilt with his life than towards the resentful and cruel emperor who died of old age in his bed.

The Monstrous Law

While Tiberius awaited news from Rome in Capri, surrounded by his prætorians and with a ship with sails set and the rowers on their benches, ready to flee if his plan miscarried, Sejanus was torn to pieces by the eternal, abominable barbarity of the mob.

He paid for his sins in this life. But there was a last episode in the story of his punishment which absolves him for everything, and would have absolved him even if he had been fifty times worse: the most pitiful and the most inhuman episode in all this tremendous history. It has passed through many books in Tacitus's version, but it deserves to be related once more in the same immortal words:[1]

'Although the people's wrath was beginning to decline, because the first punishments had already calmed the public mind, it was decided to take action against Sejanus's surviving children. They were taken to prison. The son foresaw his fate. The daughter was so far from suspecting it that she asked everyone what she had done and where she was being taken; and she added that she would not do it again, like a child threatened with punishment.

[1] Tacitus, *107*, V, 9.

The authors of that time relate that, as virgins could not suffer the death of criminals, the executioner violated the girl immediately before strangling her. After their strangling, the bodies of brother and sister were exposed on the Gemonian Steps.'

Many historians, beginning with Voltaire, have cast doubt upon this horrifying crime.[1] But we might just as well refuse to accept all the other crimes which Tacitus relates as this one, simply because it does not suit us to believe it. The logic of Tiberius's mind is so much in favour of our admitting this barbarous punishment that I feel that, if it were not true, it might well have been; for Tiberius was capable of the most monstrous of crimes in order to keep within the letter of the law. His justice was that of the puritan, who is always a bad judge.

It was for this reason that Montesquieu, commenting upon this passage, wrote the words which the French Revolution made famous: 'Tiberius, in order to preserve legality, destroyed morality.'[2] But, many years before him, much the same thing had been said by a great Spanish commentator on Tacitus, Álamos de Barrientos, who made this note on the margin of this same page: 'So much have the meaning and the spirit to do with the law that they are not fulfilled when only its letter is satisfied.'[3]

This great crime brought the struggle between the Julian and the Claudian families to an end.

[1] Voltaire, *117. Dictionnaire Philosophique:* art. *Défloration,* and *Essais sur les Mœurs et l'Esprit des Nations.*
[2] Montesquieu, *73.*   [3] Álamos de Barrientos, *1.*

PART III
Other Characters

I

TERENTIUS

An Exemplary Speech

IN THE years which followed Sejanus's execution Tiberius's vengeance was implacable. It was urged on by self-interested denunciation, that abominable growth in all periods of terror in human society. Those who had been friends of the unhappy minister perished one after the other; and by their side fell others in whose cases such friendship was invented as a pretext for destroying them and depriving them of their social rank or their wealth.

History reiterates the fact. Neither the classical chroniclers nor modern commentators have contrived to diminish the horror of those nightmare years. Over and above all Tiberius's shrewdness as a ruler, over and above his talent as a soldier and his occasional flair for justice, there stands out for ever the vision of the old tyrant shut up in his island with his resentment—which is worse than with his vices—and thence fulminating his implacable sentences. 'Suffering excited his cruelty,' says Tacitus; and this impression of a sadistic orgy of inflicting pain, which ended in a blind attack on the whole of society, cannot be effaced by the dialectics of all his apologists.

Tiberius's wrath, in fact, scourged not only those accused of conspiracy with the fallen minister, but also those who had simply been his faithful friends or even his acquaintances. This was an immense injustice, for in many cases being friends with the all-powerful favourite was merely a normal step towards becoming friends with the emperor; and, when Tiberius punished those who had served Sejanus, he was really punishing his own servitors and followers. As usually happens in such circumstances, Rome presented the sad spectacle of those who cravenly denied the friendship they had so recently boasted, or shamefully turned the persecution to their own selfish advantage.

Such evils are common to all times and the disgrace of all epochs of humanity. For this reason it is right that I should devote a separate record to that worthy man who is never lacking in such great moral collapses, and was not lacking either in the one which I am describing. Just as a pair of every animal species were saved from the Deluge to perpetuate themselves afterwards, so, whenever human decency seems to be on the point of disappearing for ever, there comes to the surface the example of some single, heroic soul who by his dignity saves that of all men.

This outstanding exemplar in the catastrophe of Tiberius's terror was named Terentius. In the year after the fallen minister's execution he was accused, like so many others, of having been a friend of Sejanus. Instead of denying it, Terentius made a speech in the Senate which shines through this dark period like a ray of light.[1]

'I was a friend of Sejanus,' he said. 'I sought his friendship, and I was glad when I gained it. Everyone sought it because his friendship was the best of titles in the emperor's eyes; and because his enmity sufficed to hurl him who suffered it into disgrace. I shall mention no names. I accuse everyone and I defend everyone with my words and at my own peril. In fact, it was not Sejanus whom so many men sought after, but you, Cæsar, who had united him by a double alliance to the house of the Julians and the Claudians; for Sejanus, do not forget it, was your son-in-law and your colleague as consul. You cannot judge me, Roman Senators, by the last day of Sejanus, but by all the sixteen years which preceded it, when even being known to his freedmen or to the slaves who guarded his door was in itself a title to honour.'

And he ended: 'Let conspiracy against the empire and attempts on the life of the emperor be punished. But, Cæsar, let a friendship which ended at the same time as your own be forgiven to us, as to you.'

[1] Tacitus, *107*, VI, 8.

The Eternal Voice

In the succeeding centuries the voice of Terentius has served as an accusation against Cæsars of all kinds; and as a consolation to many a man persecuted on account of a past for which he was responsible only so long as he believed it to be worthy. Public life, whatever end it may pursue, always has a decency of its own, which entitles the citizen to take part in it without harm to his conscience and without any responsibility for the future. If one day this decency should be lost (or the circumstances make it appear to be lost), the conscience of those who served it remains intact, and so does their responsibility. No one can call them to account: least of all those who were at the head of affairs and remained there afterwards.

Terentius sets us, moreover, the example that worthy deeds are always immortal, even though they may seem humble, and even though they contrast with all the strength of power. This deed of Terentius, the sole thing we know about his life, makes him, in the memory of mankind, worth more than all the pomp of his emperor. Historians give Tiberius credit for the pardon which he granted Terentius; for pardoned he was. But it would have made no difference whether he was pardoned or not. Whether he ended his mortal life in his bed by the hand of God or in prison by the rope of the executioner, what makes mankind progress, amid so much misery, is precisely the fact that, in the everlasting eyes of history, no Terentius could ever be obliterated by any Tiberius.

II

ANTONIA, OR RECTITUDE

The Happy Pair

IN THE array of grim personages who filled the stage of Rome at this period, we have seen something of Antonia, surrounded by a halo of rectitude. She deserves to have more said about her.

Antonia, Augustus's niece and daughter of Octavia and Mark Antony, was fortunate enough to acquire her moral heredity most plentifully not from her father, the triumvir, who wasted his talent and his destiny in sensuality, but from her mother, that virtuous woman whose grief over her son's death became legendary.

She was, so the historians say, the most beautiful woman of her time. The statues of her which have been preserved do not in all cases justify this judgement, though I may here usefully repeat my reservation about the authenticity of such iconographic attributions. In the two in the Louvre she presents a fine face, but with an excessive retraction of the lower jaw which gives the mouth a certain impression of silliness. On the other hand, in the bust in the British Museum she displays a beauty radiant with harmony and grace.[1]

Augustus married her to Drusus I, Livia's son and perhaps his own. The marriage took place at the same time as that of Tiberius and Vipsania, Agrippa's daughter. These were days of rejoicing and optimism in the family of the great emperor. With the marriages of the two brothers he looked forward to multiplying

---

[1] This is the so-called bust of Clytia, which Bernouilli (*12*, II, 1) believes to be that of Antonia.

the males of his family, and, through Drusus and Antonia, uniting the two great families of the Claudians and the Julians. Yet this decision of Augustus was perhaps one of his greatest mistakes. Every marriage is a riddle, whose solution is not known until years later, and the riddle becomes doubly difficult when on its solution depends not only the happiness or the unhappiness of the married couple, but also that of a whole nation. If Antonia had been Tiberius's wife, the course of the history of Rome might have been radically changed; and the history of Rome gave birth, for many centuries, to that of the world.

The marriage of Tiberius and Vipsania, as we have seen, ended unhappily. That of Drusus and Antonia, on the other hand, achieved an exemplary felicity. 'Was there ever,' asked Ovid, 'a pair more perfect than Drusus and his wife?' The husband was the idol of the people for his valour, his friendliness, and what was assumed to be his democratic ideas. The wife was the admiration of all, for the irreproachable dignity of her life even more than for her beauty. She was fastidiousness itself in her morals, and so she was physically, since she became famous because she never spat:[1] a fact which gives her a special claim to our liking.

On his warlike and triumphant expeditions, Drusus was always accompanied by his wife, even when she was pregnant, since her second son, Claudius, was born on one of these expeditions, at Lyons. The couple had three children, and about all three of them future annals were to have much to say. Germanicus became famous through his popularity, through his suspected death by poisoning, and, above all, through the fact that he married Agrippina. The second son, Claudius, a mixture of abnormality and shrewdness, became emperor by chance, the shamefaced husband of Messalina, and adoptive father of the emperor Nero. With the third child, Livilla, we are already familiar through her luckless beauty, her supposed complicity in the death of her husband, Drusus II, and her unhappy end. It seems almost incredible that a pair so perfect should have produced such a measure of grief, shame and death.

[1] Pliny, 79, VII, 18.

Drusus's Death

Drusus I died, in the prime of life and at the height of his glory, in the year 9 B.C. His gifts as a great general and a man with a strong power of attraction seem unquestionable. Tiberius himself, so cold in his affections, loved him deeply. Pliny tells us that when he received news of Drusus's accident, in order to reach him before he died he covered the 200 miles which separated them in a day and a night.[1] Tiberius's grief when Drusus died in his arms was intense. Ovid describes him at this moment as 'undone, pale, with his hair in disorder, his eyes full of tears, and his face distorted by sorrow.'[2] It is certain that the great poet could have found no other occasion to depict the emperor in terms of such human grief for the rest of his long life.

In the fatal course of destiny which cut short prematurely the lives of all those who bore the name of Drusus, this Drusus, the first, died from an accident, the fall of his horse, in which he broke a leg. Still there was not lacking, even then, the rumour that he was poisoned by Augustus himself, jealous, so it was said, of his stepson's democratic renown.[3] The story, I need scarcely say, is improbable: among other reasons, because Drusus's liberalism was, as I have already said, an illusion invented by the people. He died from a natural complication following upon his accident.

The Exemplary Widow

From the day of Drusus's death, his widow, in all the bloom of her beauty, lived only to honour the memory of her husband—'her first and only love,' as Ovid sang[4]—and to care for her children and later her grandchildren. Her conduct seems to have been a fine continuation of that of her mother. The merit of her chastity is enhanced when we recall the environment in which she lived, full not only of temptations, against which her virtue was impregnable, but also of the pressure and the obligations of reasons of State. Augustus sought to compel her to make a fresh marriage which would suit the convenience of his house. The law *de maritandis ordinibus* was invoked against her resistance; but it

---

[1] Pliny, 79, VII, 20.
[3] Dion, 22, LV, 1. Suetonius, *106, Claud.*, 1.
[2] Ovid, 76.
[4] Ovid, 76.

could not overcome her, thus demonstrating once more that dignity of conscience is much stronger than the devices of legality. As often happens, Antonia's upright attitude in face of the law, after exasperating its guardians, ended by reducing them to admiration. In Augustus's eyes, her irreducible chastity was the most profound reason for the esteem which he always professed for her. It was shared by his wife, Livia, and Tiberius inherited it from both of them.

Antonia spent the rest of her youth and middle age in Rome or in her villa at Bauli, withdrawn from any political activity, watching her children grow up and maintaining close relations with Augustus and Livia. Sometimes she was a trifle eccentric. For example, she kept an eel in the pond in her garden of which she was very fond, and adorned it with costly earrings like a woman's. People flocked from all parts to see it.[1]

The Weak-minded Son

Augustus's high-minded letters to Livia in connection with Claudius, Antonia's second son, demonstrate the affection which the great emperor felt for her. None of Augustus's great achievements arouses our admiration so much as this correspondence fragmentarily handed down to us by Suetonius,[2] in which it is touching to see how, amid his exacting duties, he found time and inclination to keep a paternal eye on the smallest and most delicate family problems.

Of Antonia's three children, the eldest, Germanicus, strong and self-willed, soon left home to seek his fortune, assured to him in advance by the emperor's protection. But her second son, Claudius, was to fill much of his mother's old age with care and anxiety. He suffered from childhood from 'various very long illnesses,' which left as their legacy 'a weakness of mind,' though he was not without intelligence. He was, so Suetonius

---

[1] Pliny, 79, IX, 81.
[2] Suetonius, 106, Claud., 4. We know from Pliny that Augustus wrote his letters on a very fine paper, and, as he used both sides of it, this made them hard to read. Livia used a stronger paper (Pliny, 79, XIII, 24). During the reign of Tiberius there was a shortage of papyrus, and a commission of senators had to be appointed to control the paper supply, as in our own times (Pliny, 79, XIII, 27).

tells us, slow of speech and unsteady on his legs. He dribbled at the mouth, and a continual tremor kept his head swinging from side to side. Juvenal depicts him in much the same terms.[1]

All this entitles us to suspect that one of his childish illnesses was encephalitis, leaving behind it deferred symptoms of this disease, which correspond almost exactly with those described. It is less easy to interpret the protuberances or caruncles that the ill-favoured prince had beside his eyes, which swelled and reddened in moments of excitement.[2]

The sole blemish which we find in Antonia's life—though it is quite in keeping with the psychology of the period—is her lack of feeling towards this sick son of hers. When she spoke about him, the historians tell us, she called him a 'caricature of a man'; and, by way of emphasizing anyone's stupidity, she used to say: 'He is more of a fool than my son Claudius.' His grandmother Livia and his sister Livilla shared the same contempt for him.[3] With this cruelty of all of them we may contrast the charity and common sense of Augustus in the advice he gave about the invalid boy to his wife, whom he asked to read it 'to our dear Antonia.'

Antonia and Tiberius

When Augustus died, Antonia continued to keep in close relations with Livia and Tiberius. She had a further link with Tiberius in the puritan outlook on life which both of them possessed. If they had married, they would have got on well together. Tiberius, soured and sickened by the frivolity and immorality of the women with whom fate brought him into close contact, doubtless felt a boundless admiration for this woman who, while equally beautiful and well-born, neither left her husband to marry another man for caprice or convenience, like his own mother Livia, nor took advantage of her position as a pretext for loose living, like his second wife Julia. Antonia, for her part, probably had a liking too for this lonely man whom no one else liked. In any case, it is unquestionable that she managed to adapt herself adroitly to the peculiarity of his character, sometimes in order to

[1] Suetonius, *106, Claud.*, 2 and 30. Juvenal, *49*, VI.
[2] Pliny, *79*, XI, 54.   [3] Suetonius, *106, Claud.*, 3.

defend her children and counteract the rebellious attitude of her daughter-in-law Agrippina.

One proof of her affection for the two emperors—or of her cleverness, or both—is to be found in the fact, to which I have already referred, that when her favourite and famous son Germanicus died, and neither Tiberius nor Livia ventured to attend his funeral, Antonia did not attend it either, out of a sense of solidarity with them and in order to lend the authority of her undoubted mother's grief to the reasons of a political kind which explained their absence.

This behaviour of Antonia's gradually gave her an influence over Tiberius, and later she was to reap its fruit. I have already dealt with her activity during the last years of the struggle of the Claudians against the Julians. By her energy and her adroitness, which was considerable, she saved the life of Caligula and made him emperor, thus achieving the triumph of her family when its cause seemed irretrievably lost.

The Final Bitterness

But with this triumph, the crown of all the patient effort of her life of virtue, was bound up her greatest bitterness. Antonia knew better than anyone else how unworthy was Caligula, the new emperor whom she had saved from death and raised to the throne. Nevertheless, her religion of family forced her to protect him.

Caligula was a madman. He was epileptic from childhood, not with larvate attacks like so many others of the Julian family, but with typical fits—'*puer comitiali morbo vexatus*'[1]—and he suffered from obvious deliriums of cruelty and sexual aberration. Impeccable Antonia had to pass through the horror of finding her favourite grandson in the arms of his own sister Drusilla, while they were still living in Rome in her care; and afterwards, when Caligula became emperor, she had to attend the monstrous marriage of brother and sister.[2] Later, when the old princess reproached him on the ground that he owed everything to her, Caligula replied in a threatening manner that she had better not forget that all power was in his hands, and that he could use it against anyone

[1] Suetonius, *106, Calig.*, 50.   [2] Suetonius, *106, Calig.*, 24.

he liked. The mad emperor refused to receive Antonia alone, and did so only in the presence of Macro,[1] perhaps at his instigation, since Macro may have feared lest she should repeat with Caligula, to his disadvantage, the clever work of undermining which she had achieved with Tiberius against Sejanus. To console her for such terrible trials it did not suffice for her to see a scion of her family on the throne of Augustus.

She was, moreover, very old, and unable to bear all these indignities and insults. She died horror-stricken, with the awful burden of knowing that she had made a tragic mistake. Family meant nothing compared with good or evil; but she did not realize this until it was too late.

It is said that Caligula himself hastened her end by poison. Then, without troubling to leave his festive table, he calmly watched the funeral pyre burning in the distance, on which lay the body of the woman—the most beautiful and the best in Rome—to whom he owed his empire.

Such was Tiberius's sole woman friend. Was it, we may ask ourselves today, a true friendship, nurtured by family affection and hierarchical respect? Or was it a calculated friendship, placed at the service of her cult of family? No one can answer these questions. But I cannot help thinking once more how the course of history might have been changed if Tiberius's wife had been Antonia, fruitful and exemplary, capable of stemming, with her generosity and her rectitude, the flood of the emperor's resentment.

[1] Suetonius, *106, Calig.*, 23.

III

TIBERIUS'S FRIENDS

Unfaithful Friends. Agrippa the Jew

TIBERIUS'S resentment was partly due to the ingratitude of his friends. The historians speak above all of the ingratitude of Sejanus, whose story I have already told. They also tell us about Macro, who inherited from Sejanus the emperor's complete confidence, but soon set himself against him and took part in barely concealed intrigues with Tiberius's heir, Caligula.

To the list of unfaithful friends may be added Agrippa the Jew, grandson of Herod the Great, who strikes us today as the perfect predecessor of those dissipated and immoral princes whom we find on fashionable beaches and in night-clubs. He was an adventurer and a gambler, always in debt. During his stay in Rome, he became great friends with Tiberius's son, Drusus II. They were bound together by the brotherhood created by a common life of licence and drunkenness. When Drusus II died, Tiberius, always inclined to carry things to excess, ordained that none of his son's friends, including Agrippa, should present himself before him. So the Jewish prince took his departure from Rome.

But he soon came back, thanks to his friendship with Antonia, a friendship which that faithful lady had extended to Agrippa because he was the son of an intimate of hers, Berenice. This friendship went so far that when Agrippa again fell out of favour with Tiberius—this time not on grounds of sentiment, but because he owed him money—Antonia lent him the money to pay his debts to Tiberius and so continue to enjoy the emperor's favour. It finally reached the point where Tiberius entrusted Agrippa with the care of his adopted grandson, Nero I. But Agrippa soon abandoned his pupil and united himself with Caligula, doubtless through their moral affinity. The two of them sought to conspire against Tiberius, or, at least, spoke ill of him.

The touchy emperor, disillusioned at this attitude, imprisoned Agrippa. After Tiberius's death, Caligula set him free and helped him to become tetrarch of Judæa, though only for a short time. The outstanding event of Agrippa's brief reign was his persecution of the Christians. It was he who ordered the beheading of James, son of Zebedee, and he would have put Peter to death but for his miraculous escape from prison.[1]

The unfaithfulness of his friends followed Tiberius like his shadow throughout all his life. But, before sympathizing with Tiberius on this account, let us consider why he had such bad friends. When a man is betrayed by those who surround him, it is more logical not to vituperate the traitors, but to seek the reason why all of them agree in betraying him. Almost always it is the fault of the man who is betrayed. So it was in the case of Tiberius, a man without generosity and therefore a standing incitement to felony in others. Treachery is always born beneath the shade of lack of affection.

Faithful Friends. Lucilius Longus.

Nevertheless, Tiberius had some real friends. He had at least two, both of them excellent friends: Lucilius Longus and Cocceius Nerva. Two friends are, perhaps, quite a number for an emperor; for what gives friendship its highest quality is unselfishness, and it is almost impossible that the friend of a powerful man should not have a self-interested aspiration concealed within his affection. Rarer still is the ruler who does not suspect such an aspiration, even though it does not exist; and such a suspicion casts an inevitable shadow upon the purest of affections. This is one of the heaviest taxes upon the enjoyment of power.

All we know about Tiberius's character entitles us to assume that in his case such suspicions must have been ever-present and acute; and not without reason, for few public men have suffered such repeated disillusionments as cut him to the quick. Of his two friends, one, at the last moment, perhaps against his will, became his harshest critic. The other died faithful to his friendship and

---

[1] See the highly picturesque narrative of Agrippa the Jew's adventures in Rome in Josephus, *47*, VIII.

Tiberius repaid him with one of the most generous acts of his life.

The second, his friend faithful unto death, was Lucilius Longus. 'He was,' says Tacitus, 'his companion in good fortune and in bad'; and that is enough to enable us to judge the quality of his affection. When Tiberius retired to Rhodes, Lucilius Longus was a senator. Abandoning all his duties, he alone among the other senators followed Tiberius into his voluntary exile. The friendship which united them remained constant until A.D. 23, that ill-fated year in which Tiberius suffered the loss of his son Drusus and that of one of his grandsons. A few days later, Lucilius Longus died too.

This faithful friend was a man of modest birth. It was perhaps for this reason that he resisted the corruption which infected most of the courtiers. Despite this, Tiberius wanted to make a pompous demonstration of his affection for the dead man and his gratitude to him. He was given funeral honours at the expense of the treasury, and, in the Forum of Augustus, Tiberius erected a statue in honour of the memory of his exemplary friend who asked for nothing in return for his friendship.[1]

Nerva's Suicide

Nerva, too, was an 'inseparable friend of the emperor.' He was a senator, deeply learned in the laws human and divine, and, into the bargain, the possessor of a considerable fortune.[2] His grandson, also a senator and a great jurist, was Marcus Cocceius Nerva, who was elected emperor on the assassination of Domitian. According to the busts of him which have been preserved, such as that in the Louvre, the shape of his skull and his face denoted high intelligence. We may imagine that he inherited it from his grandfather, Tiberius's friend.

The Nerva with whom we are concerned was a close collaborator with the emperor in the administration of justice and in the great reforms in public works which were made during his reign. He was probably one of Tiberius's best ministers, if not the best.[3]

---
[1] Tacitus, *107*, IV, 15.   [2] Tacitus, *107*, IV, 58, and VI, 26.
[3] Baker (*8*, p. 279) rightly says that historians have not paid the Nerva family the well-earned justice which is their due.

But, apart from the tasks of government, the emperor found pleasure in Nerva's friendship and wisdom. Nerva went with him everywhere, and was one of the few who accompanied him during his stay in the Campagna and his long retirement in Capri.

But one day, there in Capri, this prudent jurist made up his mind to commit suicide (A.D. 33). This is another of the events in Tiberius's reign which are hard to explain. Tacitus says that when the emperor learnt of his friend's intention 'he hastened to his side, overwhelmed him with questions, resorted to entreaties, and made him see the responsibility which would fall upon the emperor's conscience and the injury it would do to his reputation if his intimate friend should voluntarily end his life without good reason.' But Nerva, deaf to this argument, starved himself to death.

The true cause of this singular suicide is and must remain a mystery. Tacitus tells us that Nerva's confidants said 'that seeing more closely than anyone else the ills of the empire, anger and fear forced him to seek an honourable end before his fame and his repose were violated.' Dion asserts that he killed himself 'because he could not endure his relations with Tiberius,' and because the emperor would not follow his financial advice.[1]

It is certain that Nerva did not share Tiberius's views about some questions of administration and policy. These differences, together with the terrible spectacle of what was happening in Rome and of the storm which was disturbing his emperor's mind, may have induced the great minister to commit suicide. According to Dion, the differences concerned dealt mainly with Tiberius's plan to restore the law about contracts laid down by Julius Cæsar, which the existing state of the treasury made it necessary to bring into force again. Basing himself upon this fact, a contemporary author[2] endeavours to suggest that the cause of Nerva's dramatic

---

[1] Dion, 22, LVIII, 21.

[2] Dion, 22, LVIII, 21. Ciaceri, 17, p. 307. Close reading of Dion's text does not correspond with the interpretation put forward by Ciaceri. This author also bases himself upon his reading of a passage in Tacitus (107, VI, 16), which has certainly not much significance. In fact, what this quotation shows is that the same people who refuse to believe the great Roman historian when it suits them, at other times, when it does suit them, accept a mere suggestion of his as though it were an irrefutable document.

end was not an impulse of dignity, as Tacitus says—this, according to the modern writer, 'reeks of rhetoric'—but his fear of being included in the persecution which, by virtue of this law, was about to be unleashed against usurers; for Nerva himself may have been a usurer. This suggestion shows how prejudice may disturb a historian's balance of judgement, to such a point, as in this case, that he does not hesitate to besmirch the reputation of one of the most outstanding Romans of that time, and this in his fruitless zeal to vindicate the memory of an emperor who, though an excellent ruler, was a man of poor moral quality.

No one today can fathom this distinguished suicide's motives. What cannot be denied is that Nerva died because he wanted to die, doing violence to the emperor's entreaties and orders; and his act of heroic rebellion was, so to speak, a symbol of protest and retribution at this time when so many other men died against their will and contrary to all justice, solely because Tiberius wanted them to die.

Messalinus Cotta's Jests

The story of Tiberius's friends also includes another outstanding episode. One of the noblest moments in the emperor's life was his attitude towards another of his friends, Messalinus Cotta. Cotta was a sarcastic man who on many occasions had risked his freedom by making jokes about the highest personages in Rome, especially Caligula and Tiberius himself. In short, he was one of those licensed jesters, finally slaves to their own humour, who exist in all societies and in all ages, and in the end find themselves forced to sacrifice everything for the sake of their reputation as humorists.

In A.D. 32, amid the flood of denunciations which filled Rome with terror, there was one against Messalinus Cotta, who was accused on account of one of his customary sarcasms, which was regarded as coming within the law of *lèse-majesté*. Giving himself up for lost, Cotta hastened straight to the emperor. Tiberius sent a written defence of him to the Senate, which became famous for the deep despair it expressed. It began thus: 'What shall I say to you, Roman Senators? How shall I write to you? Or, rather, what at this moment should I not write to you? If I myself am capable of knowing it, may the gods and goddesses kill me more cruelly even than I feel myself dying every day!'[1]

Doubtless Tiberius wrote this in one of those hours which come to even the hardest of men, when bitterness softens the heart and floods it with humanity. After this outburst, the emperor recalled his friendship with Cotta, and begged the judges not to regard as a crime words without any significance, which had escaped him amid the joviality of a banquet. Cotta was acquitted, and his denouncers were punished.

Some modern authors call attention, with good reason, to the incomprehensible harshness with which Tacitus and Suetonius comment upon this high-minded letter, which really does honour to Tiberius. But such was his unpopularity that even his moments of nobility were lost to sight by his contemporaries, wrapped in the fog of his double-dealing and his resentment.

[1] See Tacitus, *107*, VI, 6 *et seq.*; and Suetonius, *106*, *Tib.*, 67.

PART IV

The Protagonist

I

TIBERIUS'S PERSON, HEALTH AND DEATH

Portrait of Tiberius

IT is now time for me to speak directly about Tiberius. Hitherto I have sketched his figure from the outside, from the standpoint of the men, the women and the passions surrounding him. I must now complete this profile and compare it with the findings of a direct study of his personality.

From the physical point of view, we possess sufficient data by which to estimate the emperor. His contemporaries agree that he was a man of fine person. Velleius says that from his childhood he was notable for his height and his handsomeness;[1] and the busts which have been preserved from that time, if they are authentic, confirm this impression.

The most complete description we have of him, when he was already middle-aged, is that of Suetonius.[2] He depicts the emperor as a tall man, broad-chested, with a very white skin, distinguished features and large eyes. His hair grew very low at the nape of his neck: a trait which appears to be common to the whole Claudian family, and is indeed useful to us for identifying its members among the busts of antiquity. I do not think there is any foundation for Henting's statement[3] that his hair grew low down and in a round on his forehead, in accordance with the type which anthropologists call 'bonnet-like hair,' and which we doctors are accustomed to find in infantile and eunuchoid individuals or in degenerates. Not even in his juvenile portraits is this growth to be observed. On the contrary, from a very early age he shows signs of going bald above the temples, as is normal with men

---

[1] Velleius, *114*, II, 94. [2] Suetonius, *106*, *Tib.*, 68.
[3] Henting, *39*.

almost from adolescence. We know, moreover, that Tiberius went prematurely bald, whereas individuals with 'bonnet-like hair' do not readily go bald.

This same author asserts that several portraits of Tiberius, such as the Florence cameo, betray sexual vacillation. In fact, in this cameo, in which his profile and that of his mother appear, Livia's is more masculine than her son's. Henting also finds Tiberius's posture in his seated portrait suspect for its excessive affectation. But this is an extravagant idea, worthy only of a schoolboy psychoanalyst. In some of Tiberius's juvenile busts, the perfection of his features has something feminine about it; but, as I have already said, there is nothing in the emperor's life to support the suspicion of homosexual abnormality which this commentator suggests. Tiberius was a sexually timid man, perhaps an impotent man, I repeat; but nothing more. I have earlier commented on his left-handedness in relation to these disturbances.

His Strength. His Short-sightedness

Tiberius's strength was so great that he could perforate a green apple with his finger, or, with a flick of one, badly hurt the head of a baby or a boy.[1] It would be interesting to know why so serious a man should make such unseemly experiments on childish heads.

Moreover, lest any outlandish trait should be lacking in his mysterious personality, the historians tell us that Tiberius possessed the faculty—alone among all the men in the world, declares Pliny[2]—of being able to see in the dark, like an owl, though only for a few minutes after opening his eyes on waking. On the other hand, in the daytime his sight was bad, and this was one of the defects he put forward when he dallied about accepting the emperorship.[3] Pliny adds that Tiberius's eyes were glaucous, prominent, and with very large whites, like those of a horse. All this suggests that he was simply short-sighted, and that he peered forward because he could not see very well.

[1] Suetonius, *106, Tib.*, 68.
[2] Pliny, *79*, XI, 54. See also Suetonius, *106, Tib.*, 68.
[3] Dion, *22*, LVII, 2.

His Fetid Ulcers

Tacitus[1] gives us a very brief but masterly description of him when he was an elderly man, on the point of retiring from Rome. He was then, according to the historian, very thin, with his tall figure bowed by years, his head bald, and his face seamed with ulcers which he hid with plasters.

It is difficult to define the nature of these ulcers, which were the final phase of so-called 'tumours' which covered his face even from his youth, according to Suetonius's description. They were apparently due to some contagious disease of the skin, which, so Pliny[2] tells us, made its appearance in Italy about this time and chiefly attacked people of high rank. The disease, according to the great naturalist, was not fatal. It was very slow in its evolution, and so unpleasant that those who suffered from it would rather have died.

This explains the bashfulness which, according to Tacitus, the emperor felt about appearing in public, and the pitch to which his deformity and the sense of other people's repugnance aroused his resentment. 'In his old age,' says this author, 'his appearance filled even himself with shame.'[3] The report of these lesions became so legendary that when, more than three hundred years after Tiberius's death, Julian the Apostate spoke of him in a fantastic dialogue, he represented him as marked by his repulsive aspect on account of the great ulcers, scabs and scars from cauterization, which gave him the appearance of a leper.[4]

Medical specialists were sent for from Egypt to cure this plague; and they attacked it with cauterizations so deep that the red-hot iron went down to the very bone, leaving such profound hollows when the scar formed that the cured lesions looked even worse than the ulcers themselves. The doctors charged highly for this barbarous treatment, since we know that one of the persons

---

[1] Tacitus, *107*, IV, 57.
[2] Pliny, *79*, XXVI, 3. In addition to the details of this disease given in the text, I may add here that, still according to Pliny, the ulcers broke out first on the chin, for which reason people called the disease *mentagra*. Then they spread to the neck, the chest and the hands, forming foul scabs, ash-red in colour. The disease was brought to Italy from Asia by a knight of Perusia.
[3] Tacitus, *107*, IV, 57.   [4] Julian the Apostate, *48*.

attacked, Manlius Cornutus, had to pay the Egyptian doctor who scarred him 200,000 sesterces.[1]

It is hard to give an opinion about what this disease of Tiberius's may have been. Pliny's description of slow-forming lesions, not fatal in character, with ash-red coloured scabs and ready contagion through kissing, suggests syphilis. I have seen no commentary on this passage in the historians of syphilis. The problem opens up others with which I cannot deal here, such as the much debated question whether syphilis existed in Europe before Columbus's discovery of America. If the lesions were syphilitic, this would help to explain the emperor's mental disturbances in his old age. But we cannot ignore the possibility that the lesions were leprous, since leprosy was a disease widely diffused at that time, and, though it was known, not always diagnosed.

A poetical echo of this prosaic chapter is to be found in a mediæval legend according to which the emperor was finally cured of his pustules by Veronica herself, who came to Rome with the Holy Cloth soaked with the sweat of Christ. This achieved the miracle, beyond the doctors' power, of cleansing the sores on the body of Pilate's emperor.[2]

Tiberius's Busts

The numerous busts and statues of Tiberius which are known to us largely agree with these descriptions, except, of course, that they omit his tumours and scars, unworthy of being immortalized in marble. In these pseudo-portraits we have to discount the apologetic spirit which moved the chisels of the imperial artists. All of them made it their business that their models—whether the emperor himself or some member of his family—should recall the gods in their nobility and perfection. In the portraits of Tiberius, as in those of other persons of the outstanding families of his time, there is evident a desire, half-conscious, half-unconscious, that his features should resemble those of Augustus.

For these reasons, the Mahon bust[3] has more value than others,

---
[1] With reference to doctors' fees at that time, see some curious notes in Pliny, 79, XXIX, 5. [2] Graf, 35.
[3] Photographs of this portrait, with an excellent commentary, have been published by Babelon, 6.

since it was made at a time when the distortion of adulation did not yet apply to the future emperor. In it we see a youthful head, well proportioned though asymmetrical, with the nose slightly turned towards the left, and the left ear sticking out more than the other.[1] Nevertheless, even in this effigy there is an attempt to make it similar to the portraits of Augustus as a youth.

Heads of Tiberius dating from the time of his first service as a soldier, between the ages of twenty-five and thirty-five, are numerous.[2] In these there is to be found an accentuation of the gravity always possessed by the future emperor, who with good reason was known from his childhood as 'the elderly boy.' Above all, in these heads, bordering upon the definitive form of middle age, we note the triangular shape of the face, due to the great, and somewhat rachitic, width of the brow, and to the pointed chin, narrow and not very firm: an index of weakness of will. In none of his portraits is to be observed that prognathism of the lower jaw pointed out and commented upon by one author.[3] There is simply this sharpness of the chin, which is not true prognathism, and has the opposite significance. In his busts as an old man, which are rarer, the pointedness of the chin becomes more marked through the loss of the teeth. This detail is to be seen still more clearly in the profiles on coins.

In his portraits at a more advanced age, this accentuation of the sharpness of the chin is linked with the transformation of the youthfully horizontal line of the mouth into a drooping line, due again to the loss of the teeth, which in Tiberius's case, as in that of many men of his period, must have happened quite early.

Unlike the other emperors, in Tiberius's case his busts become rarer as he leaves his youth behind him. The effigies of him which we possess at an age past his youth are mostly coins, and accordingly the likeness is highly stylized. This fact demonstrates his

[1] This same defect is to be observed in the heads of Augustus, above all in the bust in the Louvre, clad as a pontiff, in which the mantle covering the head makes the left ear stick out noticeably, as is usual with those who suffer from this defect, which is accentuated when the head is covered with a mantle or hood.

[2] See a record and criticism, not always fair, but interesting, in Baring-Gould, 10, p. 387.

[3] Henting, 39.

concern about his physical deterioration, which is very common in misanthropic and resentful characters. Of highly significant value is the little bronze bust in the *Cabinet de Médailles* in Paris, in which, on his middle-aged face, the features to which I have referred are very clearly marked, and so, above all, is an accentuation of the bitter sneer of the mouth.

The Baldness of the Emperors

The fact that he went prematurely bald seems to have had an extremely depressing effect on Tiberius. This deserves a digression. I have recently studied the importance of the loss of hair upon psychological reactions in man and woman;[2] and I have referred to a regular 'triconeurosis' which we doctors very frequently observe: in other words, the case of men of high talent whose moral tone is disturbed, and sometimes transformed into resentment, by the fact that they lose their hair. In the case of women, the problem is less important because with them baldness is exceptional.

In these individuals, the loss of hair causes a sense of social and sexual inferiority, which may lead to a condition of true melancholia. That the same thing happened in the time of the emperors is shown by the frequent references which we find in contemporary writers to the misfortune of baldness. In incomparable verse Ovid celebrates the tragedy of a woman friend who had lost her hair. The same poet tells us that unfortunate slaves from the barbarian countries were shorn of their hair to make wigs for fashionable Roman men and women.[3] These wigs were highly valued, since in countries whose people are swarthy, such as Italy and Spain, the glamour of blonde women has always been extraordinary. At the time of the emperors this was so to the point described for us by Juvenal, and also by Martial in his epigram: 'I send you, Lesbia, these tresses from the countries of the North, so that you may see that yours are still more golden.'[4]

---

[2] Marañón, *67*.   [3] Ovid, *75*, I, 14.
[4] Juvenal, *49*, VI. Martial, *68*, V, 68.

But not women only were concerned. Grave Roman men mourned, like young dandies of today, when they found their heads being shorn by baldness. No less a person than Julius Cæsar spent hours at his dressing-table arranging his sparse hair to the best advantage, 'and was inconsolable to find himself going bald, since many a time he had found that this misfortune provoked derision among his detractors.'[1] In the portrait which Seneca has left us of Caligula—which, like so many other of his pages, might have been signed by his disciple Quevedro—he lingers over describing 'the ugliness of his desert skull, which seemed to have wept in order to preserve a few oases';[2] and, by way of conclusion, he speaks of 'his nape like a mane': in other words, the typical nape of the Claudians, which remained very hairy despite the baldness of their heads.

This was one of the reasons for degenerate Caligula's fits of peevish rage. To look at his head was a crime, and since, as is often the case,[3] his baldness coincided with abundance of hair on his body, it was dangerous to talk in his presence about goats, since he regarded this as a reference to his hairy body and legs.[4] Nero, too, went prematurely bald—'Nero the bald,' Juvenal called him[5]—and this blemish was one of the reasons for the bitterness of his character. Tiberius, despite his seriousness, also felt depressed by his baldness. One of the very large number of people brought to trial after Sejanus's conspiracy was charged with having made fun in public of the emperor's baldness.[6]

Psychology and Appearance

Several authors have published their views on Tiberius's busts, and have endeavoured to find in his features the explanation, in terms of modern psychology, of the mystery of his soul, so full of contradictions.[7] We need not pay too much attention to them, not only because of the basic fallacy of their deductions, but also

---

[1] Suetonius, *106, Cæsar*, 45. [2] Seneca, *96*, 18.
[3] See Marañón, *62*. [4] Suetonius, *106, Calig.*, 50.
[5] Juvenal, *49*, IV. [6] Dion, *22*, LVIII, 19.
[7] The most interesting iconographic study of Tiberius and his family, in my opinion, is that of Bernouilli (*12*, II, 1), for the very reason that it is made without scientific prejudices.

because of the distortion of reality in these busts, to which I have already referred. Let us recall, for example, Caligula's head, whose repulsive ugliness Suetonius and Seneca describe for us, whereas in several of the marble statues which are supposed to represent him he looks almost like an archangel.

In Tiberius's case, the useful conclusions to be drawn from study of his effigies are the following: the rachitic convexity of his forehead; his facial dissymmetry; the weakness of his pointed chin; and the characteristic expression of his lips, half-sly, half-contemptuous, which is to be observed in his youthful portraits and becomes more marked as he advances in age. Gregoriobus calls his mouth, for some reason, a 'jesuitical mouth.'[1]

The 'colum'

Tiberius's health was always robust. From his youth until his middle age he was always campaigning, and he hardened himself by long stays in camp in Spain, in the Alps and on the banks of the Danube. His biographers do not refer to any fatigues and illnesses such as kept on interrupting the youthful activity of Augustus. Only in Pliny[2] do we find a reference to his contracting a disease called '*colum*', which invaded Italy and found one of its first victims in the emperor.

No one knew what this disease was (it may have been a form of dysentery); and its name came as a great surprise to the Romans when they read it in an edict in which Tiberius announced a suspension of his activities on the ground that he was suffering from it.

His Sobriety

Tiberius was chaste. It was probably, as I have already said, an enforced chastity, due to his timidity. Apart from some excess in wine-drinking, to which I have also referred, proper to warlike life and perhaps a mitigant for his bitter memories, it is known that he was temperate all his life. Pliny himself tells us about the puritanically affected frugality of his meals, consisting almost

[1] Gregoriobus, *38, Die Insel Capri.* [2] Pliny, *79.*

entirely of vegetables,[1] with a few draughts of the bitter wine of Sorrento. When he drank it, he was in the habit of saying that it was 'a good vinegar,' and that the healthful virtues attributed to it were one of the many inventions of the doctors. Humorists like Tiberius need doctors more than the sick; for without them they would lack the main subject of their humour.

From his mother, Livia, and from Augustus he had learned the lesson of moderation. That he learnt it well is shown by the fact that in his old age he was thin and did not suffer from the gout which embittered the lives and hastened the deaths of so many well-known Romans of his time and was due, in most cases, to the disgusting and almost incredible gluttony of their feasts. Among the great sufferers from gout who were a warning to Tiberius were his father-in-law Agrippa and his nephew Claudius.[2]

Tiberius and the Doctors

As is the case with many habitually healthy men, Tiberius was much concerned about the sick. Velleius tells us that during his campaigns in Pannonia and Germany every sick or wounded man was a source of anxiety to the future emperor. He laid aside his most urgent duties in order to see after them. He put his own doctors, his cooking utensils, his baths, his stores and everything else at the disposal of every suffering soldier. When he retired to Rhodes, he visited all the the sick in the city.[3]

[1] Pliny gives us ample details about Tiberius's diet. He was especially fond of asparagus and cucumbers, which his gardener grew in boxes with wheels, so that they could be taken into the sun or the shade, according to the weather (*79*, XIX, 23, 64). He also ate radishes, sent for from Germany, which he took with wine and honey (*79*, XIX, 28, 90). I have already mentioned that he quarrelled with his son Drusus II because he refused to eat these vegetables. Tiberius was very fond of fruit, especially pears. He was a great lover of trees, and prided himself on the fact that one at his villa on the Tiber was the tallest in the world.

[2] I have already referred to Agrippa's gout. Claudius did not follow the temperate tradition of the imperial family in which he was brought up. He ate so much that, lest he should choke when he went to sleep, he had to be made to vomit by tickling his gullet with a pen: this was easy because he slept with his mouth open (Suetonius, *106*, *Claud.*, 33). He was a drunkard from his youth (Suetonius, *106*, *Claud.*, 5). He went so far as to publish an edict that people present at feasts should break wind freely in both directions, because he thought this was good for the health (Suetonius, *106*, *Claud.*, 32). It was no wonder, then, that he was gouty. As Seneca put it, 'despite his gout, it did not take Claudius long to reach Pluto's gate ' (*95*, 13).   [3] Velleius, *114*, II, 114. Suetonius, *106*, *Tib.*, 11.

On the other hand, he despised doctors. From the age of thirty onwards he gave up consulting them, and, thus showing sound sense, kept an eye on himself and attended to his own health in the light of his experience.[1] Charicles, the doctor who attended him in his last illness, so Tacitus tells us, 'did not usually control the health of the emperor':[2] in other words, he had no regular doctor.

When Tiberius was already near his end, in order to feel his pulse my far-off colleague had to pretend that he was taking his leave, and, as he kissed his hand, slid his finger on to the artery. This hasty manœuvre, which demonstrates his skill, showed him that the emperor was failing. Charicles was very different from those pedantic doctors of the eighteenth century who, copying the Chinese, spent whole hours discovering the secrets of the pulse. But, despite the doctor's swift skill, Tiberius realized the trick that Charicles was playing. Such was the emperor's tenacity that, in order to deceive him and show that he was in good health, he invited Charicles to dinner, despite the fact that he had just dined, and deliberately prolonged the fresh banquet more than usual. This double meal helped in hastening the end of the old man, who was probably suffering from hardening of the arteries and uræmia. Into the bargain, he attended a military festival and cast a few javelins himself, almost on the point of death though he was.[3]

The Emperor's Death

I shall speak later about possible mental disturbances during the emperor's last years. Physically he remained healthy until he was approaching the age of eighty—he died when he was seventy-eight—apart from skin suppurations, which did not affect his general health. The historians tell us that towards the end he

[1] Suetonius, *106*, *Tib.*, 68.   [2] Tacitus, *107*, VI, 50.
[3] Tacitus, *107*, VI, 50, and Suetonius, *106*, *Tib.*, 72. It is curious to note a similar refusal to be attended by doctors on the part of Frederick the Great of Prussia. Doubtless the enormous prestige of ancient history in his time created the legend of his death, copied from that of Tiberius, as it was communicated to the French in the *Supplement aux nouvelles extraordinaires des divers endroits* (issue of 12th September 1786). This periodical says that 'during the fourth day the king had a long fainting fit, of which advantage was taken to introduce Doctor Salle, who felt his pulse and found it fair; but the king opened his eyes and the doctor fled.' To this similarity with Tiberius's death may be added the fact that Frederick, like the Roman emperor, afterwards had an excessive meal, which hastened his end.

became increasingly feeble: a fact which cannot surprise us in view of his age and his long life of cares and sorrows.

His death was due, almost certainly, to pneumonia, which in the case of old men may be regarded as one of the most common causes of death. Suetonius, in fact, tells us that during one of his constant and imprudent journeys during the last years of his life he was taken ill at Messina. But he refused to give in until he was attacked by a severe pain in his side, together with a high fever and violent shivering fits.[1] After this, he had a worse relapse. It is a typical description of an old man's pneumonia, unexpected until the final episode.

With the news of his death, rumour, inevitable in those days in which infamy was a normal guest in palaces, would have it that his end was hastened by poison. Others said that, of his own free will, the emperor had refused to eat. Finally, others again—and they were the most numerous—alleged that Macro, his last friend, and Caligula, his successor, between them smothered him with his own pillows.[2]

These are certainly legends. The final bulletin of the discreet doctor Charicles, together with Caligula's and Macro's known impatience, sufficed to give them currency. The true story, beyond doubt, is that of Seneca, who describes the delirium which usually brings to a close an illness such as that which ended Tiberius's days. The emperor, the great Spanish historian tells us, obsessed about the succession, took off his ring as though to give it to someone. Then he put it back on the ring-finger of his left hand. He stayed still for some time, with his fist clenched. Doubtless, with the last consciousness of a dying man, he realized that this ring, which someone must inherit, would be the source of sorrowful days, which he could already see gathering around Rome. Suddenly he stood up, calling for his servants. As he made this effort, his heart stopped for ever. He dropped dead beside his bed.

Emperors, whether it suits legend or not, sometimes die just like other mortals.

---

[1] Suetonius, *106*, *Tib.*, 72. This historian, making the common mistake of the uninformed, says that he wrapped himself up well when he felt the pain in his side and then started shivering. Such shivering is always attributed to a chill which does not exist. [2] Suetonius, *106*, *Tib.*, 73, and *Calig.*, 12. Tacitus, *107*, VI, 50.

II

THE OGRE'S VIRTUES

Tiberius's Governmental Tradition

TIBERIUS'S good qualities and virtues—for he had some—have been repeatedly extolled by modern historians. They refer, quite properly, to his unquestionable gifts as a soldier and a ruler, or, to put it more exactly, a good civil servant.

Tiberius was, in fact, an excellent administrator of his empire, and there was no reason why he should not have been. On both sides, his father's and his mother's, he was a scion of the Claudians, those proud aristocrats, famous for the distinguished services they had rendered their country: services so many and so great that they had earned the family, when Tiberius was born, thirty-three consulates, five dictatorships, seven censorships, six triumphs and two ovations. Tiberius's inherited professional capacity was rounded off by his long exercise of public office beside his stepfather Augustus, who was the best of masters, because he had learned to master himself; and also beside the great ministers and generals of the time, such as Mæcenas, who was the essence of ability, and Agrippa, an outstanding warrior on land and at sea.

His Military Qualities

I have already referred to young Tiberius's very rapid political career. At the age of nineteen he was quæstor, and had to cope with one of the gravest famines from which Rome ever suffered.[1] From the age of sixteen he accompanied Augustus on his political and military expeditions; and at the age of twenty-seven he started campaigning as commander-in-chief, first the Central Alps, and afterwards in Germany and on the Danube.

[1] Velleius, *114*, II, 94.

Tiberius's characteristics as a soldier were the strictness with which he maintained discipline; the endurance and the frugality with which he shared, almost like a common soldier, the hardships of camp life; the meticulous caution with which he planned operations during long vigils in his candle-lit tent, taking omens, going to almost any length to save the lives of his men. For this he was more than once censured by those heroes—common to all times—who showed their military skill and their courage at home. Whenever he could cut short a war by diplomatic action he did so, scorning the glory of battle, traditionally so magnificent in the minds of his contemporaries.

His military qualities may be debated or exaggerated—one of his enthusiasts has compared them with those of Julius Cæsar or Napoleon—but no one can deny them. If they have been handed down to us obscured, this is due to the fact that the first plane of emotion in Tiberius's life is occupied by his directly human tragedies.

Tiberius's Culture

Tiberius was a highly educated man, though not, perhaps, so much so as to justify the statement that he was 'one of the most cultured persons in Roman society of his time.'[1]

He acquired his education in the first place during the nine years he spent with his father, whose addiction to study was well known. Then, when he was living with Augustus, he had various tutors who taught him Latin and Greek letters, with such success that he wrote verse in both languages. Theodorus of Gadara, the great grammarian, was one of his masters. Tiberius wrote his *Memoirs* and some *Records* which, many years later, were the favourite reading of the Emperor Domitian,[2] an admirer who did him no honour. He was taught eloquence by Corvinus Messala,[3] with less success, since, though he spoke impromptu naturally and fluently, his prepared public speeches were very confused and obscure, despite the constant care of Augustus, whose theme was the same as that of Don Quixote: 'plainness,

---

[1] Ciaceri, *17*, p. 278. [2] Suetonius, *106*, *Domit.*, 20.
[3] Suetonius, *106*, *Tib.*, 70 and 71.

boy, plainness,' in other words, clarity before everything, even at the cost of grammatical correctness.[1] Tacitus attributes his obscurity of language to a deliberate intention to mislead; and he adds that, if it was a question of doing something wrong, then his slow speech became, as though by magic, easily understood and very fluent.[2]

Tiberius was a great patron of art. Despite his miserliness, he went so far as to pay 60,000 sesterces for a picture by the famous Parrhasius of Ephesus.[3] He acquired more cheaply a beautiful statue by Lysippus, which Agrippa had placed in the public baths. Tiberius took a fancy to it and, without more ado, carried it off to his palace; but the people protested and he had to put it back.[4]

The works of art which filled his palace were in contrast with the plainness of his furniture, which was ostentatiously puritanical by contrast with the showy tastes of the rich men of his time. He made a point, for example, of having a dining-table of quite ordinary wood, whereas his freedman Nomius possessed a fine one, carved out of the largest piece of wood in the world.[5] At this time rich Romans had brought into fashion tables of rare wood, such as those from the forests of the Atlas mountains, which were highly valued and very costly. Asinius Gallus, Tiberius's rival, less modest than the emperor, had one for which he paid 1,100,000 sesterces; and Cicero himself, though he was not a wealthy man, also paid a million for another.[6]

His Political Mistakes

With all his experience, it was easy for Tiberius, succeeding Augustus in his fifties, to make a good administrator of the vast empire which his famous predecessor had created, and even to improve some of his laws and regulations. It is no exaggeration to say, and it is the highest tribute that can be paid to him, that Tiberius consolidated and completed the prodigious and successful administrative work of his stepfather.

Until his last years, when it became clouded by his age and his

[1] Suetonius, *106, Aug.*, 86.
[2] Tacitus, *107*, I, 11 and 33, and IV, 31.
[3] Pliny, *79*, XXXV, 36.
[4] Pliny, *79*, XXXIV, 18.
[5] Pliny, *79*, XIII, 29.
[6] Pliny, *79*, XIII, 29.

resentment, his efficiency as a good ruler and administrator was unimpaired. One cannot say as much for the clearness of his sense of politics, for in this respect he made grave mistakes in the excessive power which he entrusted to Sejanus, in his retirement to Capri, in his persecutions which terrorized Rome, and in the inept solution which he found for the family quarrels on which the succession depended.

In fact, quite apart from these definite mistakes, in themselves very much bound up with his state of mind, Tiberius was never a great politician. His idea of the empire was excessively traditionalist, and did not correspond with the needs of the time. Barbagallo[1] rightly says that he wanted to act like another Sulla, and this had become impossible. The danger of the traditionalist politician is that he falls into anachronism, which is a grave fault: as grave as that of utopianism, into which progressive politicians usually fall when they lack a sense of balance. For all these very important reasons, it is not fair to say, as his panegyrists do, that Tiberius was a great emperor. He was simply a good, and at times an excellent, administrator and soldier; nothing more.

His Concern for Discipline

Tiberius owed these capacities not only to his long apprenticeship, but also to certain qualities of his character from which they necessarily resulted. The most important of these was his concern for order and discipline, the irreplaceable basis of all good government. When he was in command of the legions, he carried the maintenance of discipline to the utmost limits of severity.[2] All his reactions tended, in fact, towards excessive puritanism, which is wholly efficacious only when it is administered with a sufficient dose of affection, or at least of liking. Tiberius set in his own life, which was as severe as that of his soldiers, a practical example of his zeal for discipline. But, if he was capable of making himself respected and even admired, he was incapable of making himself beloved by his troops, who, on the other hand, worshipped Drusus I and Germanicus, less strict, less virtuous, but more magnanimous, more human. For this reason he suffered the

[1] Barbagallo, 9.   [2] Suetonius, 166, Tib., 19.

disillusionment of seeing these legions, to whom he had devoted so much of his life, rise in rebellion against him.[1]

He had the same concern for order in civil life. His greatest enemy, Suetonius, describes with a wealth of detail all his efforts to keep down thieves in the city, bandits in the country, and all manner of disturbers of the public peace.[2] He himself was the first to conform strictly to rule in his private life. In the midst of a depraved society he was, like his mother, chaste. The biologist may be interested to know whether his chastity was a virtue or the outcome of a defect in his make-up; but, politically, it must be ranked as a merit. He was as frugal in his living as his stepfather, and with greater credit; for Augustus was frugal of necessity, since his health compelled him to be so. Tiberius's sense of duty was overruling even in connection with the deepest affections of his life. As we have seen, he did not interrupt his duties and 'sought consolation in the cares of the empire' on the death of his son, which, together with the death of his brother, was perhaps the saddest chapter in his life.

Philanthropy and Charity

He was very generous, but no spendthrift. He was generous, that is to say, in his own way. He contributed large sums of money at times of public disaster, such as the Fidenæ catastrophe, the Mons Cœlius fire, and the famines from which Rome suffered during his reign.[3] But he was, on the other hand, niggardly in small, personal, everyday charity. This gave rise to a false legend that he was a miser, a legend created by his enemies, and

---

[1] Historians who defend him quote to the contrary a passage in Velleius (*114*, II, 104), who depicts the frenzied delight with which the soldiers welcomed him when, after his retirement to Rhodes, Augustus adopted him and once more put him in command of the army in Germany (A.D. 4). This testimony possesses the value that Velleius accompanied Tiberius and actually saw what happened, instead of merely hearing about it. But against this we have this historian's incorrigible tendency to adulation. He refers to Tiberius's doings as his 'divine deeds.' Nevertheless, it is unquestionable that this was the moment of Tiberius's greatest popularity in his public life: perhaps the only moment when he was popular at all; for reasons which I shall explain later. But the fact that the legions welcomed him with enthusiasm at this time is not incompatible with the fact that some years later they should rise against him, as indeed they did.

[2] Suetonius, *106*, Tib., 37.   [3] See Tacitus, *107*, IV, 62 *et seq.*

rancorously reflected by Suetonius.[1] Close reading of this historian's text clearly shows the distinction to which I have just referred. He tells us, for example, that Tiberius gave his travelling-companions no provisions of their own, but contented himself with sharing his meals with them. On the other hand, for such public purposes as I have mentioned he emptied his purse freely.

This distinction between public and personal charity is a failing very common in great philanthropists. They help a public work with any amount of money, but they are incapable of presenting a beggar with a shy, kindly copper without asking him why he wants it. Such is the difference between philanthropy and charity. Philanthropy is above all a matter of quantity; charity, above all, a matter of sympathy.

Tiberius's Austerity

Among Tiberius's virtues should also be reckoned his austerity towards human vanities, proper though these might be to his rank. 'Tiberius's mind,' Tacitus generously recognizes, 'possessed the strength which makes a man despise honours.' He hated flattery and sometimes repelled it with violence—and in doing so lost merit—even where flatterers of high social position, such as senators themselves, were concerned. It is related that, when one of them wanted to kiss his knees, he pushed him away so forcibly that the two of them fell to the ground.[2]

If he was praised to excess in a speech, he bade the orator be silent, and he always rejected high-flown titles intended to be bestowed on his position and his person, among them that of 'Father of the Fatherland.' His most highly praised act of modesty was his refusal to allow a temple in Ulterior Spain to be dedicated to him. But this action undoubtedly had a deeper explanation, to which I shall refer in the next chapter.

I shall then deal with its psychological significance. For the

---

[1] Suetonius, *106, Tib.*, 46, 48 and 49. Pliny also refers to his niggardliness in *79*, XXXV, 10.

[2] Suetonius, *106, Tib.*, 27. Tacitus, referring to this scene, says that Tiberius's brusque action was not due to dignity in the presence of flattery, but to fear, since he thought that the senator, Quintus Haterius, was about to attack him (Tacitus, *107*, I, 13).

moment, speaking solely as a historian, I am not entitled to diminish Tiberius's merit on the ground that his motives were less noble than they appeared to be. History judges solely by results, not by motives; and everything I have said in this chapter, with its somewhat stilted air of catechizing Roman morals—though I make no claim to be the embodiment of virtue—redounds unquestionably to the credit of the much-discussed emperor.

III

TIMIDITY AND SCEPTICISM

Tiberius's Timidity

THE classical historians themselves refer to Tiberius's timidity, which, mingled with his more elemental emotions, makes its appearance at every turn of his life. Tacitus tells us, for example, that the emperor 'at one and the same time loved and feared Sejanus': a typical expression of Tiberius's ambivalence. Among modern commentators, some, such as Baring-Gould, Ferrero and, above all, Henting, stress the significance of this timidity in the emperor's life. Others, such as Marsh and Ciaceri, make less of it. But on this point argument is idle. Tiberius's timidity and its importance in his public and private life are not to be denied.

Men of tall stature, including giants, are especially predisposed to suffer from the defect of timidity, sexual and social, both closely linked. Such was the case with Tiberius, who was a tall man. Even in his military life, his well-known desire to spare the lives of his men was often interpreted as lack of decision. The failure of the Roman legions against the insurrection of the Dalmatians during Augustus's lifetime was attributed to his irresolution, and so was the unsuccessful campaign in Gaul in A.D. 21.

I have already said that these criticisms must have wounded him. His forte was diplomacy rather than military assault; perhaps because he did not feel himself to be sufficiently strong for it. Cleverness is the resource of the weak; and some men have been great diplomats simply because they were fundamentally weak.

But it was above all in Tiberius's civilian life that evidence abounds about the timidity which he hid behind his severe cast of countenance. I have already mentioned several instances of it, some apparently trivial, but all of great significance in the march of events. I may recall the absence of the emperor and his family from the funeral of Germanicus, which was undoubtedly due to fear, and the notoriously unjust condemnation of Piso, which was dictated by the emperor's timorous yielding to public clamour.

With his more than probable sexual timidity I have already dealt adequately.

His Mother and His Favourites

But what most clearly conveys his weakness of will was his constant need to lean on someone else's will. Tiberius lived always in the shadow of other people's imperious strength. In the first place, there was that of his mother and also that of Augustus, semi-divine. We have seen how he was dragged along by Livia's manœuvres and protection in the long struggle between the two imperial families. His present and his future swung backwards and forwards, like an inert object, at the mercy of two contrary forces, that of Livia, who pushed him forward, and that of Augustus, who pushed him back.

When he became master of the empire he was past fifty: an age at which the mind, at its maturity, may still yield its best fruits, but at which it is hard for it to be cast in a new mould; and this was what was needed in Tiberius's case. The long apprenticeship of his youth and middle age had been excellent for his training as an administrator, but fatal for the strengthening of his will.

He could give orders to the whole Roman empire, but he could not make himself independent of his mother. Ambitious Livia, toughened by her years, was ever his empress. We have already seen how he tried to react against her tutelage, but beneath his superficial rebellion we can sense that her yoke, forged and tightened over so many years, was stronger than he thought. To gain his independence he had to break openly with his mother. He had first to absent himself from Rome, and then to sever all relations with her. In short, like all timid men, he sought refuge in flight.

But, fleeing from one slavery, he fell into a worse one. Like all weak tyrants, he had a constant need for an omnipotent minister, a favourite. Sejanus became his favourite. Dion tells us that during the latter years of his reign it was said that 'Sejanus was the emperor of Rome, and Tiberius was merely the governor of Capri.'[1] Like all favourites, Sejanus sought to devour his master—this is a just biological law—but, as happens to many a man, he died the victim of one of those sudden violent reactions of a weak man. When his minister carried his tyranny too far, and thereby attracted the lightning-stroke of public wrath, the submissive emperor turned on him with the support of popular opinion.

To rid himself of Sejanus, Tiberius found another support also, that of Macro, a useful man though a bad one, who took the place of the fallen favourite in the command of the prætorian cohorts, and in the ruling of the empire by his influence over the emperor's will. To obtain some idea of the laxity of Tiberius's will, we need only consider this absolute submission of his to second-rate minds, vacuous and intriguing, like those of Sejanus and Macro, whereas he put to death men of political talent like Nerva. We may also compare this excessive influence of his favourites over Tiberius with the strictly defined and never excessive rank allotted to ministers of the stature of Mæcenas and Agrippa by an emperor of strong will and real political talent like Augustus. Augustus, let us not forget, also had Livia at his side for the greater part of his life, and, what was worse, during the nights of many a long year. Nevertheless, he managed to evade the same danger from this imperious woman who made a prisoner of Tiberius.

Crises of Will-power

The most characteristic crises of Tiberius's wavering will were his doubts about accepting the emperorship, and, above all, his flights, to Rhodes in his youth and to Capri in his old age. These two latter episodes belong to the nebulous region of his abnormalities and I shall deal with them later. As to his dallying about accepting power, the references of the classical authors present it as one of the typical manifestations of his hypocrisy, since while

---

Dion, 22, LVIII, 5.

he was resisting in the Senate he was handling the troops as though he were already emperor. But close reading of these references conveys the impression that his doubts were sincere, being the offspring of his indecision, and that what he was trying to conceal with his confused language and his mysterious attitude was his own weakness.[1]

The Timid Sceptic

Tiberius's scepticism also played a large part in his behaviour. I study it here because of its immediate connection with his timidity. The timid man has, in fact, two possible defensive attitudes. When he is lacking in intelligence, he defends himself from his weakness by believing in everything, and lives, like a parasite, clinging to the strength of other men or to one of the great superhuman symbols. When the timid man is intellectual and proud, his defence usually consists in believing in no one and nothing. This is the case of the resentful timid man; and so it was with Tiberius.

Not in the whole course of his life did he show a single trace of enthusiasm for anyone. It is said that he admired Augustus, but his admiration was undermined by resentment. This is sufficiently shown by the speech, to which I have already referred, in which he refused the consecration to his name of a temple in Spain. His inner mind, in fact, betrayed itself in this speech when he said that he had accepted one earlier consecration because Augustus had accepted all those that were offered to him, but that, having once observed this precedent, he would not go on following the example of his predecessor; for fame consisted in deeds, which future history would judge, and not in temples and stones erected by contemporaries.

Rarely has the violence of a man's subconscious mind risen to the surface so clearly. On an occasion such as this, to refuse an honour was no humility but sheer pride, sheer eagerness to outdo another man who had accepted all honours before him. For the

---

[1] With regard to Tiberius's doubts about accepting power, see Tacitus, *107*, I, 11, 12, and 13; Suetonius, *106*, *Tib.*, 24 and 25; Dion, *22*, LVII, 2; and the critical study by Fabia, *26*.

same reason, Tiberius refused to accept the title of 'Father of the Fatherland,' in which Augustus had taken such pride.

By way of increasing his scepticism, to his innate tendency towards it was added the lessons that life taught him. In the preceding chapters I have analysed the reasons which explained why Tiberius could not believe in the virtues of the home, or in those of marriage, and barely in those of friendship. In order to overcome so many adverse proofs he would have needed a very large measure of magnanimity, and this he never possessed.

Persecution of Religion

Finally, Tiberius did not believe in the gods. Suetonius declares that he was absolutely indifferent to those of his religion.[1] Like many intelligent men of his time, Tiberius foresaw the end of the grotesque pagan theology, perhaps better than anyone, for the very reason that historic destiny, which forms part of our souls, had assigned him the rôle of supreme, though unconscious, witness of the birth of the new faith.

Tiberius persecuted all the official religions. Today it is difficult to judge the political significance of his persecutions;[2] but it is obvious how great was the element of resentful atheism in his attitude. In A.D. 19 he expelled from Italy all those professing the religion of Isis. These, thanks to the passion for following the fashion of the upper classes in Rome, were becoming numerous. Egyptian fashions, in all their aspects, made him furious. He had some of the priests of Isis, accused of various crimes, crucified beside the Rhine. He also persecuted the Druids. Finally, he expelled the Jews.[3] About four thousand of them were transported to Sardinia on the pretext of suppressing banditry in that island, but with the secret intention that they should die victims to its unhealthy climate.

[1] Suetonius, *106, Tib.*, 69.
[2] On this point see Mommsen, *72*, XI, 75. It was in this connection that Mommsen wrote his sentence, famous because it became the great starting-point for the argument of Tiberius's apologists: 'He was the cleverest of all the sovereigns the empire ever had.'
[3] See Suetonius, *106, Tib.*, 36. Tacitus, *107*, II, 85. Josephus, *47*, XVIII, 5. Philo, *29* and *30*.

It seems certain, nevertheless, that Tiberius had a sneaking sympathy for the Jews. This is proved by the benevolent judgement passed upon this expulsion, and the excuses found for it, by historians such as Josephus and Philo, the latter a stalwart champion of his race. With this sympathy was bound up Tiberius's supposed interest in the doctrine of Christ—in some authors' eyes, his real zeal for it—or at least the wonder in his mind, so ready to believe in miracles, when he learnt that the Rabbi crucified by Pilate had vanished from his grave, wrapped in a cloud, towards Heaven.[1]

Tiberius and Omens

For Tiberius believed in omens and portents. Men, like nations, without faith are always exposed to humbug. But this was, in any case, a trait of his time. In his century, and for many centuries afterwards, there were few minds capable of rising above faith in omens, which, together with dreams, are a relic of the primitive soul that still subsists in our civilized souls. It possessed greater power then than now, not because of the distance in time that separates us from the classical age—for this is only a brief moment in the immense history of the universe—but because of the effect which the happenings of the past twenty centuries have had upon the evolution of human reason.

It was, therefore, nothing out of the common that Tiberius was terrified of lightning, against which he protected himself with a wreath of laurel; for this plant, so we are told by Pliny, the great naturalist of the period, had a well-known resistance to fire.[2] Tiberius was not alone in this terror, since the great Augustus also suffered from it, though he preferred to safeguard himself with a sealskin; and so, of course, did stupid Caligula, who, without any sense of dignity, hid under his bed when he heard the first peal of thunder.[3]

Nevertheless, it may be presumed that Tiberius believed less in omens than many of his contemporaries, including the most outstanding, such as his own historians, Tacitus, Suetonius and Dion. Suetonius tells us that the emperor was what we should

---

[1] On all these points see my book 66.
[2] Tacitus, *107*, VI, 20. Pliny, *79*, XV, 40.
[3] Suetonius, *106*, *Aug.*, 90; *106*, *Calig.*, 51.

now call a 'realist'; and so, on the eve of battle, he had no taste for consulting augurs, but preferred, during long night vigils in his tent, to devote himself to hard thinking and detailed study of such data as his captains could give him. The sole sign that inspired him with confidence during his military career was the sudden extinguishing of his lamp; but once when he trusted this omen he found himself on the point of being assassinated,[1] and with this event his disbelieving mind must have lost its last flicker of faith in the supernatural.

Consolation in the Stars

His cold, but curious soul led him to seek relief from scepticism in astrology. This addiction of his cannot, as a modern historian suggests, be put to the credit of his virtues, by being regarded as the expression of an assumed scientific spirit. Astrology in those days possessed barely a nucleus of strict scientific inquiry, though not less, to be sure, than almost all the dubious natural science of his time; but around this nucleus grew a monstrous edifice of all the prejudices, all the humbug, of the classical mind's superstition. Then, as always, superstition was most dangerous when it had a varnish of science.

From the time of his retirement to Rhodes, when he was thirty-six, Tiberius devoted himself to the so-called science of the Chaldeans. His master was the famous astrologer Thrasyllus, whom he took with him to Capri and with whom he maintained a close friendship after making him pass—for even in dealing with the supernatural Tiberius carried caution to excess—through strict proof of his good faith. Tacitus tells us that Tiberius consulted with his astrologers in Capri in the highest of the twelve villas which he built in the island, every one of them dedicated to a god.[2] Thrasyllus was, so to speak, the head of them, and they

---

[1] Suetonius, *106*, *Tib.*, 18 and 19.
[2] On Tiberius's residences in Capri, see Weichardt (*118*); M. Boutteton's reconstruction, of which *l'Illustration Française* of 2nd February 1924 gives a summary with photographs and plans; and especially Maiuri's book, *60*. This matter of the Capri palaces and their annexes—villas dedicated to the gods, mysterious grottoes, etc.—is one of the things that gave rise to the greatest fantasies among the many that surround Tiberius's figure.

were many. Juvenal, indeed, writes about the emperor in his charming island 'surrounded by a swarm of Chaldeans.'[1]

The astrologer on duty, according to the legend, climbed up to the emperor's retreat every evening by a path skirting the cliffs; and when he was on his way down, if Tiberius had suspected any fraud in his horoscope, the robust slave who accompanied the unfortunate Chaldean pushed him over into the sea. The first time it came to Thrasyllus's turn, Tiberius questioned him about his future. Thrasyllus consulted the stars, turned pale, and bravely told his master that a great danger threatened him. The emperor, thus assured of his honesty, gave him a kiss, and from that moment they were friends.

I should not like to take leave of Thrasyllus without expressing some liking for him; for in those terrible days of denunciation and persecution, he proved to be the providential man who always emerges at such times where he is least expected, and devotes his astuteness and his influence over the tyrant to doing good to others. It is said that Tiberius did not want to die before seeing all his sentences of death carried into effect. The worthy astrologer deceived him by leading him to believe that he still had a long life before him. Thus he saved the lives of many unfortunates, who were set at liberty as soon as the emperor was dead. Perhaps this is only yet another legend; but its significance is that, on this occasion as on so many others, science is most sacred when it deliberately puts its prestige at the service of deceit in order to do good.

What did Tiberius seek in the meaningless language of the stars? Perhaps, as his defenders say, he felt a need to dwell upon the mystery of life, which would serve as a support to the sterility of his soul. Perhaps again, in the immense disillusionment of his faith in the gods, he eagerly sought some other and higher truth, which, though he did not realize it, was already within his reach. It may have been for this reason that he spent so many hours with his eyes fixed on the endless pathway of the stars. But the real aim of his longing was not in the stars, but so hidden in the depths of his soul that even he never suspected it.

[1] Juvenal, 49, X.

IV

ANTIPATHY

Two Kinds of Antipathy

THE success or the failure of men depends much less upon their assessable virtues or failings than upon the subtle but decisive question whether they are likable or unlikable. Tiberius was fundamentally antipathetic; but historians, with few exceptions,[1] fail to estimate this feature in the emperor's psychology.

Much has been written about likes and dislikes and it is common ground that their essence and the reasons for them are very hard to explain. But it is obvious that there are two great groups of both feelings, or, to put it better, two poles of the same feeling, as in the case of electricity; or, if you like, a head and a tail of it.

In the first group we have an exclusively subjective feeling. A man or a woman, for profound reasons of instinctive affinity or of instinctive opposition in the presence of his or her personality, is attractive or unattractive to *us*: perhaps only to us and to no one else. In the second group we have an objective feeling. Individuals, owing to fixed conditions of their personalities, are attractive or unattractive not merely to some of us, but, practically speaking, to everyone who knows them.

If we seek the reasons for this attraction or repulsion in human beings of the second group, we find sometimes certain reasons, sometimes others; but, with absolute constancy, we discover the presence of magnanimity in the attractive person, and the lack of this virtue in the unattractive person. The measure of magnanimity in every soul is that measure of its capacity for attraction.

---

[1] Marsh concerns himself repeatedly with Tiberius's antipathy, 69, pp. 106, 131, 219, 224. Homo (43) also refers to it.

This also explains the relationship between antipathy and resentment, since the root of resentment itself lies also in lack of magnanimity. The bitterness of the resentful man gradually filters through all the strata of his soul and increases his initial antipathy. For this reason, the cycle of the resentful man's antipathy is endless.

The Displeasing Gesture

Tiberius belonged to the category of the universally antipathetic man. Tacitus tells us that 'he lacked affable manners, and his repulsive appearance inspired horror.'[1] But we find a more exact description of the antipathy which he aroused in Suetonius. 'He carried himself,' Suetonius writes, 'with his head held proudly high and his face set. He was almost always silent, never saying a word except now and again, even to those who habitually surrounded him; and even then he did so with extreme reluctance, at the same time always making a disdainful gesture with his fingers.'[2]

This last detail is highly realistic. The *'digitorum gesticulatione'* which Suetonius speaks about must have greatly annoyed people, since the chroniclers go out of their way to mention it. All of us have had experience of the stifled irritation aroused by reiterated gestures, among them those of the fingers, on the part of unattractive people. Seneca tells us about children set crying by a harsh word, a movement of the fingers, and various other disconcerting gestures.[3] A repeated mannerism like that of Tiberius may become more unendurable than a terrifying gesture like that which Seneca himself describes in the case of Claudius: 'a gesture of his limp hand, which became firm only when he began the sign for decapitation.'[4]

Tiberius's Unpopularity

Suetonius adds that Augustus often had to apologize for his stepson before the Senate and the people, 'on account of his displeasing manners, full of haughtiness,' which he attributed

[1] Tacitus, *107*, IV, 7.   [2] Suetonius, *106*, Tib., 68.
[3] Seneca, *96*, 5.   [4] Seneca, *96*, 6.

to a natural failing—in other words, to antipathy—and not to deliberate intention to offend. Tacitus must have been referring to the same thing when he tells us that, when Augustus sought the position of tribune for Tiberius for the second time, into his speech of eulogy 'he slipped one or two censures, disguised as apologies, about his mien, his appearance and his manners.'[1] Doubtless Augustus was sensitive to this antipathy which his stepson and son-in-law aroused, since he himself, on the contrary, possessed in the highest degree the gift of attraction, which was the secret of much of his success. Who knows whether Tiberius's antipathy did not also give him a secret satisfaction, as was said at the time, in finding his own virtues exalted in contrast with the opposite failings of his stepson?

This antipathy, rather than his failings and his cruelties, was the cause of Tiberius's immense unpopularity, admitted by all authors, even his present-day whitewashers. The first outburst of this unpopularity occurred when Tiberius retired to Rhodes (6 B.C.). The people were not wholly aware of the reason for his retirement or of the haughtiness which accompanied it, or even of his conduct in his voluntary exile; but it infuriated them and they turned against him. He aroused 'hatred and contempt,' Suetonius tells us, to such a point that his statues were thrown down in Nîmes and there was talk of assassinating him.[2]

Nevertheless, after this wave of hostility, on his return to Rome and his adoption by Augustus (A.D. 4) Tiberius enjoyed perhaps the sole moment of popularity in his whole life. I have already referred to the passage in which Velleius describes, although with obvious and servile exaggeration, the rejoicing of the Romans at this period; and even allowing for his self-interested adulation it is clear that this time he is telling the truth. But the public rejoicing was based on political reasons, not on specific affection for the prince. The death of the Cæsars, Caius and Lucius, had left Augustus without a successor, thus creating a grave situation for the empire. Tiberius therefore became, of necessity, a hope for the future. Probably, too, exile, that eternal creator of prestige and infallible cleanser of all kinds of stains on

[1] Tacitus, *107*, I, 10.   [2] Suetonius, *106*, Tib., 13.

public men, had tended towards forgetfulness of the antipathy of this hitherto hated man.

But such popularity, due to circumstances, had already disappeared when, in A.D. 14, Augustus died and his stepson was called upon to succeed him. Up to this time Tiberius had been much better known by the legions which camped and fought on the frontiers than by the people of Rome; and it was, in fact, among the legions that protest against his succession emerged. First the legions in Pannonia rose in revolt, then those in Germany. It is true that there was widespread discontent among all of them, due to bad treatment and poor pay, and to latent indiscipline engendered during the tedium of prolonged peace. All this had nothing to do with the personality of the new emperor, and it was chiefly these general motives which inspired the mutiny of the legions in Pannonia.[1] But in Germany the military movement, which was much stronger, was definitely against Tiberius.

There the soldiers 'refused to recognize an emperor whom they had not chosen,' Suetonius tells us;[2] and Tacitus confirms this, stressing the personal disaffection of the soldiers towards Tiberius, whom they contrasted with the congeniality of Germanicus, his nephew, who was the troops' candidate for the throne. 'Indeed, the democratic spirit and the affable manners of the young Cæsar [Germanicus] contrasted profoundly with the ways and the speech of Tiberius, always haughty and mysterious.'[3] So it came to a struggle between Germanicus's congeniality and Tiberius's antipathy. As we have already seen, only Germanicus's loyalty saved Tiberius's emperorship from lasting, perhaps, only a few weeks.

Strictness without Warmth

Once discipline was restored, Tiberius exercised absolute power for more than twenty years, without any internal disturbance

---

[1] Tacitus says that the rising in Pannonia was 'a revolt without reason, unless it were the change in the emperorship, which opened the way to disorder and to the prizes which a civil war may always bring with it' (*107*, I, 16); in other words, that whoever the new emperor had been, the soldiers, corrupted by indiscipline, would still have risen. This was not the case with the rising in Germany, which was specifically against Tiberius.

[2] Suetonius, *106*, *Tib.*, 25 and *Calig.*, 1.

[3] Tacitus, *107*, I, 31 and 33. See also Dion, *22*, LVII, 5.

except the Libo Drusus conspiracy. He ruled well, but somehow without graciousness. I have said earlier that he gave money to the needy without sympathy, as philanthropists usually do, which is the reason why they get no thanks. In the same way, he gave the people excellent administration and strict discipline, but without showing a single trace of warmth of heart; and for this reason he was never beloved. It was not, as some of his panegyrists say, that his strictness irritated people. A ruler's strictness may be annoying, but it does not stand in the way of affection on the part of his subjects. A pliant ruler may, on the other hand, be hated by his people. What matters is that the act of ruling, mildly or severely, should always be accompanied by something that makes the privilege of power pardonable; for power, even the most legitimate, is always a privilege, and it is, just for that reason, always within an ace of becoming hateful to other people. Tiberius was incapable of understanding power in this way.

Another factor which contributed towards his lack of popularity was that his policy tended to favour the privileged classes. His conception of policy was 'a downright adherence to the policy of the upper classes and the Senate. The new emperor acted, in fact, just as Sulla had acted years earlier; and there is reason to think that this must have figured among the major causes of his unpopularity.' Such is the shrewd judgement of a present-day historian, who can in no way be suspected of systematic hostility towards Tiberius.[1]

But the progress of his unpopularity until his death was linked less with political causes than with the directly human characteristics of the emperor. Today we have the impression that the façade of Tiberius's life, what was seen of him from the market-place, was his endless family quarrels, bristling with intrigue, tragedy and death. His administrative qualities remained in the background. In all these passionate quarrels, public opinion invariably sided with the Julian party against the emperor. First it sided with Germanicus against Tiberius at the time of the rising of the legions, and when the young general was relieved of his command and sent to the east. Next it sided with Agrippina and

[1] Barbagallo, 9, pp. 18 et seq.

her children against Piso, Germanicus's supposed assassin, and against Tiberius, suspected of being the instigator of the crime. Then it sided with the indomitable widow and her son Nero against Sejanus, who persecuted them in the emperor's name; and so it went on siding against Tiberius.

For this reason, the people regarded the accession of Caligula, the last scion of the beloved family, as a triumph and a liberation, though with that lack of judgement which marks all popular movements. This mistake always arises from the same thing, namely, the fact that the masses are moved by emotion, by feeling, or in other words by liking or dislike, never by reflection. This is the original, the irremediable sin of absolute, uncontrolled democracy. When it does hit the mark, it is for the same reason that a number which we have chosen in a moment of impulse proves to have won a prize in a lottery.

From Unpopularity to Hatred

The continual trials, sentences and executions which filled the latter part of Tiberius's reign multiplied the causes of his unpopularity to the point of paroxysm and turned it into hatred. Some modern writers, especially the conscientious Marsh,[1] have tried to justify many of these persecutions. But the defence of the emperor's advocates—and Marsh writes as an advocate, not as a historian—though it may modify the opinion of the erudite, can never affect the equity of the judgement of history. This is as it should be. If Tiberius was responsible for only one of the heads that fell, for only a single unjust sentence of death, that sole infamy suffices to make him a cruel emperor, responsible for all the cruelties of his reign. Otherwise one might as well seek to clear a woman's reputation for adultery by saying that her lovers were fewer than had been supposed. By way of proving Suetonius's exaggeration in describing Tiberius's reign of terror, a reputable historian adduces his sentence that 'the executioners violated virgins before strangling them.' This, he comments, does Tiberius a grave injustice, since this infamy was committed only once,

---

[1] Marsh, 69. See especially Appendices IV, V, and VII.

in the case of Sejanus's daughter. But it is obvious that this one infamy suffices to make the man who ordered it abominable.

The atmosphere of informing and calumny that afflicted Rome induced, towards the end of his reign, a blaze of hatred of Tiberius, which was relieved only by the hope of his early death. Terrorized and discontented peoples always put all their hopes in that magic but dangerous word 'change.' The masses never stop to think that they may lose by change. The days of greatest popular rejoicing that history records are those which have followed changes of rulers or régimes; but never is this joy disturbed by the memory of the endless disappointments which in human history have followed this illusion.

In A.D. 33, Tiberius, in a letter to the Senate, complained about 'the hatred which his person had aroused, because he had done his duty to the empire.'[1] The fumes of public resentment had, therefore, reached his nostrils; and this must have been one of the reasons for his retirement to Capri. But the distance which separated him from Rome, with the sea and the cliffs of his island in between, was still too small to enable him to escape the wave of hatred which pursued him. Sejanus had to establish a special guard so that no one should approach the fugitive emperor, and a strict censorship to intercept recriminating letters to him, especially anonymous letters, which disturbed him extremely. For example, Suetonius says that 'his uneasy mind was ulcerated'[2] by the libels which he sometimes found on his presiding seat in the Senate; and Tacitus tells us that on one occasion 'he was exasperated by some anonymous verses which were being circulated about him.'[3] But despite all his favourite's precautions it is certain that the well-aimed arrows of anonymous letters, which always find a chink through which to attain their mark, reached him even in his solitude in Capri.

The morbid fear which overcame him during his latter years shows us that he did not succeed in isolating himself from the hatred of his people. It is, to be sure, a calumny to say that he shut himself up in a grotto in his lonely island and indulged in

---

[1] Tacitus, *107*, VI, 15.   [2] Suetonius, *106*, Tib., 66.
[3] Tacitus, *107*, I, 72.

eccentric obscenities with girls and boys recruited by the whips of his slaves. But it is, on the other hand, beyond all question that, as his best historian tells us, Tiberius, 'overwhelmed by public hatred and weakened by years,' came to realize that power cannot be maintained by force alone, without a single breath of public opinion to support it.

Despite all force, public opinion had overthrown him even before he died. The most favourable of his apologists can find no arguments to offset the barbarous but significant outburst of delight with which Rome greeted the news of his death. Great though the general rejoicing was, the people could scarcely believe that 'the lion,' as the Jew Agrippa Herod called him, would never roar again.[1]

No longer did the people reflect—perhaps they had never reflected—whether he had ruled well or ill. They thought only about the immense, though negative, power of his antipathy. It was for this reason that they shouted themselves hoarse through the streets with a cry that comes down to us with the tragic singsong of a drunken populace; a cry that we have heard since in different words, but with the same rhythm, and that we may therefore take to be true: 'Into the Tiber with Tiberius! Into the Tiber with Tiberius!'[2]

[1] Josephus, *47*, XVIII, 8.   [2] Suetonius, *106*, *Tib.*, 85.

V
RESENTMENT AND INFORMING

Tiberius's Ambivalence

IN THE preceding chapters I have stressed Tiberius's dual personality: on the obverse, his strictness as an administrator, his zeal for order, his qualities as a general; on the reverse, the dark passions of his soul. If we try to judge him in modern terms we might say that he was an excellent technical expert with a depraved soul: a combination, to be sure, in no way exceptional. His glorification by recent authors is a typical expression of modern ethics, which, so long as a man is efficient, will forgive him all else.

This dual personality of Tiberius is interesting because it very well explains the ambivalence of his soul: his respect, as a subject and a son, for Augustus and Livia, and his hatred of them, because they had built the virtue and the glory of the imperial home on the foundation of his father's sorrow; his compassion for Julia, his lawful wife, when she was exiled, and his implacable rancour against her for the ridicule with which she had covered him; his alternations of protection and persecution towards Germanicus and Agrippina and her children; his attitudes of friendship and mortal enmity towards Sejanus, his friend and his enemy at one and the same time; and so on, always the same.

All the time, through the chinks of his excellent administrative armour, we can see the fumes of his resentment escaping, and so giving his life that ambiguous aspect which his contemporaries interpreted as hypocrisy and later historians have been unable to confine within the definition of a personality all of a piece.

The Cycle of Resentment

As we survey Tiberius's life, we can see clearly how, in proportion as his resentment fermented, the troubled, passionate reverse of his personality gradually overcame the clear obverse of his political life. For this reason the ancients regarded him as a disconcerting man who kept on changing all the time. Let me again recall the words of Pliny, who described him as an austere, but sociable prince, who as the years went by turned severe and cruel. Some of the classical historians assign a fixed date for his change from good to evil, associating it with the death of his son Drusus, or that of Germanicus, or that of Livia.[1] These misfortunes, indeed, gave sudden spurts to the cycle of his passion of resentment. But, still more than any of them, what brought about its final paroxysm was Sejanus's treachery and the alleged assassination of his son.

This outburst of his later years was also influenced by the intoxication of power. It is typical of the resentful man, and especially of the man both timid and resentful, as I have already remarked, that, when he acquires a power dependent alike on force and cunning, he makes a barbarously vindictive use of it. The test of power divides men who achieve it into two great groups: those who are sublimated by the responsibility of ruling, and those who are perverted. The reason for this difference resides solely in the capacity for magnanimity of the first, and in the resentment of the second.

To quote only examples historically close to Tiberius, among the great leaders who were ennobled by the exercise of power I may recall Julius Cæsar, an immoral demagogue at the beginning of his career, and a fine ruler in the second part of his short official life. Then there was Augustus himself, whose youth, full of profound and shameful moral failings, was transformed by the imperial responsibility into a balanced, patriarchal middle age, with unquestionable gleams of greatness. Examples of the degenerating influence of power, on the other hand, are to be found in Tiberius, Caligula, Claudius, Nero and Domitian.

It is no fancy of the ancient historians, as Ferrero[2] suggests, but a positive fact, this change which, in all cases of weak-willed and

---

[1] Tacitus, *107*, VI, 71. Dion definitely relates the change in Tiberius with Germanicus's death (*22*, LVII, 5).

[2] Ferrero, *28*, p. 192.

especially resentful men, is brought about by the intoxication of power, and indeed gives their reigns a clear appearance of two phases: a first, which is good, and a second, which is bad.

We must bear in mind what the supreme power meant at the time of the Roman emperors. Nothing can give us a better idea of it than the words which Seneca puts into Nero's mouth at the beginning of his emperorship: 'I am the arbiter of the life and death of peoples. The destiny of everyone is in my hands. What fate is to befall everyone, it rests with me to say. On one reply of mine depends the happiness of cities. Without my consent, none of them can prosper.'[1] It would be understandable that demigods should stand this almost supernatural power without its going to their heads; but not men of flesh and blood.

Finally, it is not certain that in his later years, when he was an old man, hurt by so much misfortune, and perhaps syphilitic, Tiberius's mind remained normal. I shall deal a little later with his flights, his incessant comings and goings between his retreat in Capri and Rome, which have a suspicious appearance of madness. Only Antonia's sound sense linked him with normality. But it was a link too weak by contrast with the forces that impelled him, without reason or justice, into his reign of terror: a reign of terror which sent a shudder through history and possessed all the characteristics of the spite of a resentful man, because it was not directed—like the spite of hatred or envy—against those who had offended him, but against *everyone*; for *everyone*, human and divine, was his enemy.

Informing

Typical also of the revenge of the resentful man was the use of informing which Tiberius favoured as a means of carrying it out. The resentful man in power resorts immediately to informers, his brethren in resentment. At his invitation, any number of resentful souls open the valves of their passion. Then a stream of anonymous and open informing pours forth. Sometimes this is a shameless expression of self-seeking; but, almost always, it is an

---

[1] Seneca, *101*, 1.

outlet for a resentment, perhaps impersonal, but one to which a victim has to be sacrificed.

Suetonius describes 'the fury of the informing which was let loose under Tiberius and exhausted the country in the midst of peace more than all the civil wars.' 'People,' he writes, 'watched for a word spoken in a drunken moment or the most innocent of jokes, for any pretext was good enough for denunciation. There was no question about the fate of those accused: it was always the same. The prætor Paulus was once present at a banquet. He was wearing a ring with a cameo on which Tiberius's portrait was engraved. With the hand on which he wore this ring he drew a urinal towards him. His action was observed by one of the most notorious informers of his time. But one of Paulus's slaves noticed that his master was being spied upon, and taking advantage of his drunkenness slipped the ring off his finger, just at the moment when the guests were being called upon to witness the insult which Paulus was about to pay the emperor by putting his effigy next to the urinal. At this moment the slave opened his hand and showed that Paulus was not wearing the ring.'[1]

The point of this story is that, but for the slave's astuteness, Paulus would have been imprisoned and put to death; and the informer against him would have received part of his fortune.

Only by reading, one after the other, accounts of the trials during those years of Tiberius's persecution can one realize their infamy and their horror. Many cases, such as that to which I have just referred, began comically and ended tragically. Others were tragic from the outset. Sons denounced their fathers. The vilest tricks were employed to bring about the downfall of an enemy or the unworthy gain of the informer, as in the case of Titus Sabinus to which I have referred earlier. Not only infamous creatures like the one mentioned above, but also well-known people, famous advocates and orators, made informing their business and enriched themselves by its means. 'Even senators descended to the lowest denunciations.'[2] Unquestionably, however, most of those who laid information did so for an end more pleasurable

[1] Seneca, *100*, III, 26.   [2] Tacitus, *107*, VI, 7.

than the money, the position, or the clientele of their victims. the satisfaction of paying off old causes of resentment.

Tiberius contemplated all this informing with the gesture of Pilate, which was habitual with him. But if any brave man, like Calpurnius Piso, protested against the informers, it was not long before he was put to death himself.[1]

There is nothing more effective in destroying the morale of a people than the fear of informing, which of all fears is the most unpredictable, the most subtle, the most difficult to combat and overcome. Anyone who has lived through a similar period will find no exaggeration in these words of Tacitus: 'Never so much as then [after some infamous informings] did consternation and nervousness reign in Rome. People trembled even in the midst of their closest relatives. No one dared to approach anyone else, still less speak to him. Whether he was known or unknown, everyone's ears were suspect. Even inanimate and mute objects inspired misgiving. Uneasy glances passed over walls and partitions.'[2] Walls, indeed, have ears when justice falls silent.

Such was Tiberius's reign of terror, as vile as any of the violences of weak men made proud by power. It was the reign of terror of a resentful man, maintained by informing, which proclaims the arbitrariness of power just as surely as the stench and the livid blotches of a corpse proclaim death.

[1] Tacitus, *107*, IV, 21.   [2] Tacitus, *107*, IV, 69.

VI

SOLITUDE AND ANGUISH

Tiberius's Resentment and His Humour

It remains for me to comment upon one last aspect of Tiberius's life: his feverish, irresistible and morbid tendency towards solitude. The relationship of the resentful man with his human environment is different from that of other men. Between him and those who surround him—even, if he is a personage, between him and the sticky swarm of his official associates—there is always a fissure which widens and gradually becomes a gulf. Lack of cordiality creates a kind of vacuum all about him, till at last the resentful man no longer possesses any family affection, any friends or confidants.

Such was Tiberius's position as his life went on: alone amid the multitude, with his eternal air of disdainful abstraction and his 'very sad' countenance. At times, like many resentful men, he showed traces of humour, almost always permeated with venomous bitterness. I have already explained the relationship between humour and resentment. Axel Munthe, the present possessor of one of his villas in Capri, inspired by the enthusiasm of a grateful guest and a sympathy for the terrible emperor which his predecessor in the ownership of the heavenly island never succeeded in arousing in any of his contemporaries, writes rapturously about 'Tiberius's rare sense of humour.'[1]

In the historians of the period we find, in fact, frequent samples of his humour. On one occasion, for example, his guests showed signs of surprise at seeing only half a boar on his table. The emperor pointed out to them that half a boar was just as tasty as a whole boar. On another occasion, he received envoys from

---
[1] Axel Munthe, 74, XXI.

Troy, who brought him condolences on the death of his son. As they had arrived very late, he seized the opportunity to reply: 'In return, I offer you my condolences on the death of your most glorious citizen Hector.'[1]

In such retorts, displaying a disdainful but inoffensive humour, Tiberius delighted in employing Greek proverbs or verses, of which he knew many by heart. On other occasions his humour masked a terrible cruelty. Dion tells us that, soon after his accession to the emperorship (A.D. 15), he was busy paying legacies which Augustus had left citizens in his will. One day as a funeral passed the Capitol, a bystander approached the corpse and pretended to whisper in its ear. Asked what he had said, he replied that he had asked the dead man to tell Augustus, when he reached the other world, that he had not yet received his legacy. When Tiberius heard about this, he had the man put to death so that he himself might give his message to the dead emperor.[2]

Thus Tiberius gave expression, veiled in his humour or in Greek verse, to the profound contempt which he felt for his fellow men. A ruler who comes to look upon his subjects without warmth of feeling commits the worst of sins if he does not at once lay down his mandate; for only affection confers the right to rule. Tiberius's relations with the Senate were typical of this aspect of his mind. As he was a punctilious ruler, his behaviour towards this assembly was always irreproachable; and the beginning of his reign was marked by an attempt to restore the political dignity of the Senate. But the senators, many of them venal and cowardly, others rancorous, informers or resentful men like himself, ended by inspiring him with absolute disdain. Tacitus tells us that every time he left the Senate he murmured, naturally in Greek: 'Always ready for any servility!'[3]

'Island' Psychology

So it was that Tiberius was alone in the great, bustling swarm of Rome; and in his loneliness he instinctively sought solitude, where he might encounter his own company, hard to find amid

---

[1] Suetonius, *106*, Tib., 52.   [2] Dion, *22*, LVI, 14.
[3] Tacitus, *107*, III, 65.

the multitude. This is the main explanation of his retirement, while still a young man, to the island of Rhodes, and now, as an old man, to the island of Capri.

Every misanthropic man has this same tendency towards 'the island,' which separates him from the outside world, yet at the same time gives him a limited world in which his sense of inferiority may breathe with less distress. If the misanthropic man is also a resentful man, this attraction becomes all the stronger. Indeed, a man born in an island, even if he be a normal man, suffers from the influence of an island environment, which is full of a dangerous ambivalence. In the island he may be self-sufficient—like Robinson Crusoe—better and more easily than on the immense mainland; but this self-sufficiency is irremediably limited. The stress of this twofold influence weighs upon the minds of almost all islanders. By way of relieving it they are very often alcoholics.

But the problem is clearer in the case of the man who deliberately seeks the island. I doubt whether this question has been studied with the attention which it deserves. The man from the mainland who shuts himself up in an island does so precisely because his soul needs a little, limited cosmos, just as certain birds prefer the gilded world of their cages to the outside world, full of effort and danger. Any observer may catch that unmistakable glance, expressive of repression and resentment, in the eyes of a settler in one of those islands that are ports of call for light-hearted tourists but refuges for those whose lives have been shipwrecked on the mainland.

Baker remarks shrewdly that 'from the outset Tiberius had an imaginary Capri in his mind.'[1] It is probable that the famous ship which the emperor built on Lake Nemi, a regular floating island, was not the outcome of a whim of extravagant luxury, to which his austerity did not lend itself, but represented yet another form of his instinct for isolation, for seclusion in an island world of his own.[2]

---

[1] Baker, 8.
[2] Concerning Tiberius's ship, see the monograph, rhetorical rather than erudite, by Maes, 59.

The Flight to Rhodes

In the course of his first journey to the east, when he was twenty-two, Tiberius stopped at Rhodes, and it had such an effect upon him that the memory of his impression remained on record in the chronicles.[1] Julius Cæsar had been there too, not to seek solitude, but to learn rhetoric from Apollonius Molo; for Rhodes was a land of great rhetoricians. But, as was to be expected, the island and rhetoric soon bored him.[2] Julius Cæsar was warm-hearted and frank, with a mind that belonged to the mainland, to cities. Incapable of resentment, he could never live anchored out at sea. Tiberius, on the contrary, could not forget Rhodes, and in the year 6 B.C. he made his first flight from Rome and shut himself up in that island, famous in the history of the Mediterranean world.

I have made several references to this event, one of the most commented upon in the reigns of Augustus and his stepson. At the time there was much debate about the reasons for this strange self-exile. These reasons, as I have already said, were doubtless diverse. Historians tend, for the most part, to seek a single cause for any event, as doctors seek a single cause for an illness. Often both of them are mistaken, because our actions, like our health, may spring from a complex combination of causes, and probably do more often than not.

We may take if for granted that Tiberius's journey to Rhodes sprang from two reasons at least: on the one hand, the misconduct of his second wife, Julia, and his more than probable sexual timidity; on the other hand, his spite against Augustus's favouritism towards the Cæsars, Caius and Lucius.[3] This spite Tiberius sought to disguise as dignity, by saying that he did not wish to stand in the way of the young princes' careers,[4] or, according to other authorities, by putting forward the pretext that he was tired.[5] That neither of these explanations was the true one is proved by the fact that Tiberius's departure was opposed by his mother and by Augustus: in Augustus's case with such insistence that, in

---

[1] Suetonius, *106, Tib.*, 11.
[2] Plutarch, *82, Cæsar*, 3.
[3] This is the opinion of Dion, *22,* XLV, 9.
[4] Suetonius, *106, Tib.*, 11.
[5] Velleius, *114,* II, 99.

order to obtain his consent, his stepson started a hunger-strike.[1]

Before all else his flight was undoubtedly the typical flight of a resentful man. Psychiatrists of today attribute it to a fit of melancholia; but the impulse was much more complex than any mere illness. In Rhodes Tiberius lived withdrawn from official circles, devoting himself to physical exercises and attending the frequent lectures and debates of professors and rhetoricians. But he soon tired of them. Rhodes did not assuage his thirst for solitude. It was too accessible to travellers going to and from the east, many of whom stopped there to see him, to find out what he was thinking, and perhaps to try to involve him in intrigues. He got bored, too, with the rhetoricians and sophists, who were pedantic or discourteous. Suetonius tells us that, when one disputant offended him in the course of a debate, he had him arrested and imprisoned, so great was his annoyance.[2]

In this disappointed frame of mind, he received the news that Augustus, finally aware of Julia's immorality, had exiled her and obtained his divorce from her. I have already commented on the relief which this news must have meant to him in respect of his sexual instinct, scared as he was of married life with this impetuous woman. Then, on the pretext that his term of office as tribune was over, he asked permission to return to Rome. But Augustus, who now had public grounds—those of his inexplicable flight—for giving expression to the dislike which he had always felt for him, sent him a disdainful order to stay where he was.

The second part of Tiberius's exile was, therefore, no longer voluntary, and this increased his misanthropy. He withdrew completely from all outside contacts, gave up riding and fencing, which he had practised assiduously, and refused to receive inquisitive travellers. It was then that he acquired his addiction to astrology, and, according to some accounts (which were certainly calumnies), it was at this time too that he made his first experiments in those dark vices which were to give him a reputation for lewdness in his old age.[3]

---

[1] Suetonius, *106, Tib.*, 10.   [2] Suetonius, *106, Tib.*, 11.
[3] Tacitus, *107*, IV, 57.

During this time he went to Samos to meet Caius, who was on his way to the east in surroundings of official pomp which must have wounded the exile deeply. Caius, at the instigation of Marcus Lollius, gave him a poor reception. His resentment must have increased still more when he finally received Augustus's order setting him at liberty, since this was due to the intervention of Caius himself; for nothing hurts a resentful man more than a favour at the hands of someone he dislikes. Caius's change of attitude towards him appears to have been associated with the disgrace of Lollius, who was a great enemy of Tiberius, and his replacement by Quirinus, who was closely associated with him.

Altogether Tiberius spent seven years in Rhodes. On his return to Italy, in A.D. 2, he retired to Mæcenas's estate, remote from Rome. There he spent two years more, and there he learnt of the death of the two Cæsars, Caius and Lucius, who had stood in the way of his career. Their death led to his reconciliation with Augustus, who, as we have already seen, adopted him, being forced to do so by the disappearance of his two favourite grandsons and by Livia's insistence.

'*Callipide*'

His retirement to Rhodes and its psychological significance are very important as explaining another, and a culminating, event in his life: his retirement to Capri. Both were manifestations of the same passion: flights due to resentment. Otherwise Tiberius was not addicted to travel. One of his chroniclers tells us that, during the first two years following his accession to the throne, he planned several expeditions; but, in the end, he never carried them out. When the imperial convoy was already waiting for him at the gates of the palace, ready to set off, he decided to postpone the start over and over again. For this reason he was nicknamed 'Callipide,' from a person in a Greek proverb who kept on running, but never made any headway. Only in A.D. 21 did he make a brief journey to the Campagna,[1] on the ground of having a rest and allowing his son, Drusus II, who shared the consulate with him, to exercise his powers alone and so train himself in the art of government.

[1] Suetonius, *106, Tib.*, 68.

The Flight to Capri

His habitual sedentariness gives all the more significance to his flights, above all his final one. This took place in A.D. 26, when he was sixty-seven. As in the case of his retirement to Rhodes, the reasons for his retirement to Capri have been much discussed. The one which found most credit at the time was that Sejanus, now in the full enjoyment of his influence over the emperor, persuaded him to retire in order to give freer play to his own omnipotence and sever Tiberius from his normal relationships.[1]

But Tacitus points out the improbability of this hypothesis, since the favourite was put to death shortly afterwards and nevertheless Tiberius continued his isolation in Capri until the end of his days. The shrewd historian and psychologist adds that 'the reasons were not to be sought outside himself'; in other words, that where they were to be sought was in his soul's inner need for isolating itself from others. But he did not isolate himself, as was said, to find full scope for his vices and his cruelty. What drove him to the island was unquestionably his resentment. It was also said at the time by some people that he had fled from his mother's imperious temperament, and, by others, that he fled because of the disgust which it aroused in him to let himself be seen as an old man with his face covered with plasters damp with pus. If so, these two causes worked together, since Livia and the ulcers on his flesh were two of the undoubted sources of his resentment.

The official pretext for his journey was to cross the Campagna in order to dedicate a temple to Jupiter in Capua and another to Augustus in Nola, where the great emperor had died. The people of his time believed this, just as people of today believe the official pretexts for the comings and goings of public personages. No one knew or even suspected the true object of his journey, still less that Tiberius would never return to Rome.

After performing the ceremonies which served him as a pretext, Tiberius went on to Capri. The island is such a wonderful place that his choice, as one of his apologists says, does credit to the emperor's good taste. Augustus himself had had an affection for

---

[1] Tacitus, *107*, IV, 57. It was said that Sejanus had been paving the way for the emperor's retirement for the past year (Tacitus, *107*, IV, 41).

the island, but on grounds other than those of Tiberius. It is said that, on a visit to the island, he saw an old holm oak, and, on his next visit, found its branches revived as though filled with fresh sap. As he believed implicitly in omens, he exchanged the island of Ænaria for Capri, which was owned by the city of Naples. But Augustus, like Julius Cæsar, was no islander, and he returned to Capri only for four days.[1]

Tiberius did not choose Capri by way of a pastime, nor was he influenced by any omen. He was taken there only by his resentment. It was his new Rhodes. But it was nearer Rome, of which the emperor could not entirely lose sight. Besides, the access to Capri was steep, and with its high cliffs falling sheer into the sea it suited his misanthropic soul. Finally, there were no importunate sophists and rhetoricians there, as there had been in Rhodes, but only solitude and a few friends whom he chose to keep him company without disturbing it.

Abnormality and Madness

What did Tiberius do in Capri during these last eleven years of his life? Let me repeat here my agreement with those who believe the story of his repulsive vices, which Suetonius describes in such detail and with almost ingenuous shamelessness, together with the story of his refined cruelties, to be a mere legend. Tiberius retired to the island sick of the whole of humanity, concentrated upon himself, fleeing into himself, to the point of anguish; irremediably isolated, not only from his living environment, but also from his memories and his hopes; by now without a past and without a future. With a mind in such a state, a body is in no mood for orgies.

It was said, even at that time, that Tiberius had lost his reason, and some modern commentators repeat this.[2] But, in the data which his contemporaries have handed down to us, there are no grounds for making an exact psychiatric diagnosis of the emperor,

[1] Suetonius, *106*, *Aug.*, 92 and 98. Dion says that the island, when Augustus took possession of it, produced nothing. Its fame began with the legend of Tiberius (Dion, *22*, LII, 43).
[2] Tacitus, *107*, VI, 38. See especially the study by Henting, *39*, according to whom Tiberius was a schizophrenic, and in the end suffered from senile dementia.

even taking into account the suspicion that he may have been syphilitic. Tiberius was—so much is certain—a schizoid; but he was not mad. The terrible anguish of his resentment gave the last years of his life the accent of abnormality, which is not madness, though it may be confused with it. His flight from Rome was not the act of a madman, but it was the act of an abnormal man. So was his refusal to return for eleven years, despite all the advantages of doing so. Abnormal, above all, were his tragic attempts to approach the city, with which I shall deal in a moment. He was not, in short, a sadistic madman.

Equally inadmissible, however, is the picture which some simplifying historians paint for us of an almost patriarchal old man, seeking rest after a long, sad life, and relief for his senses and his soul by plunging them in the incomparable sunsets of the Bay of Naples. Tiberius was simply a man whom the passion of resentment had made abnormal.

The most conclusive proof that he was merely abnormal is provided by the legend about him. Abnormality is not madness; but, precisely because of its element of ambiguity, and because it does not produce the definite attitudes of vigilance or pity which madness brings into play, those who are simply abnormal in mind often perturb homes or nations much more frequently and much more gravely than downright madmen. Legends do not grow around a madman. Madness is, in itself, a legend for the multitude; but the great legends grow around the abnormal man whose conduct, with its chiaroscuro, we cannot understand.

Around this man, who was not mad and yet was not entirely in his right mind; who kept on leaving Capri and coming back without apparent reason, always shutting himself up again in his inaccessible island mansions; who passed along the paths surrounded by soldiers who drove the curious away with blows; who was a rational and at the same time an incomprehensible ruler; who implacably carried on his life despite the death of his nearest relatives; who cast his favourite, within a few hours, from absolute power to destruction; who persecuted Agrippina's and Sejanus's friends with a cruelty disguised as strict legality; who saw his best friend deliberately commit suicide beside him; who was the prudent governor of a people ruled with shrewdness and at the same time terrorized by informing—around such an indecisive personality, complex and mysterious, legends were bound to grow.

So grew the legend of his cruelty in Capri, full of nice refinements, obviously invented by the populace. There was, for example, the story of the fisherman who startled the emperor by suddenly approaching him and offering him a fish. Tiberius had his face fiercely rubbed with it. When the poor fellow, who, like his emperor, was a humorist, congratulated himself, amid groans of pain, that he had not offered him a lobster, Tiberius, by way of capping the joke, sent for a lobster, and continued the cruel rubbing with its scaly shell.

The legend of such subtle cruelty created in turn the legend of his sexual vices and aberrations. The public's sense of sadism is always on the watch. To associate sexual pleasure with pain is instinctive in people at times of collective depravity or political terrorism. During the recent Spanish revolution, the legend that grew up around the unquestionable fact of cruelty became immediately associated with a complicated series of sexual aberrations, which people hitherto truthful declared they had witnessed and doubtless believed that they had. It was with the same dubious brand of truth that gossipers in Rome related stories about erotic mysteries in the grottoes of Capri. In all periods of social disturbance there are similar stories; and I am convinced that in every case they should be accepted with the same reserve.

Similarly legend must have exaggerated the fear which Tiberius undoubtedly displayed during his latter years; for the fact that he displayed it is unquestionable. Some authors, such as Ramsay,[1] suggest that it reached the point of regular persecution mania; and doubtless it sometimes looked like it. An imperial edict forbade anyone to approach the emperor along the paths, even at a distance; soldiers in his confidence escorted him everywhere; and even his letters to the Senate betray the fear in which he continually lived, suspecting ambushes and conspiracies all

[1] Ramsay, *82*, VI, 15, note.

round him.¹ But this was worry rather than real fear: the worry of old age, which increased his inborn timidity.

An infinite anguish marked the last phase of his life and his reign. It was the anguish of a resentful man who could find no relief either in revenge or in pardon, because the thorn of his anguish was in the essence of his own soul, incapable of generosity. He fled the world only to find himself in solitude; and solitude terrified him, because it was too close to his despair. It was an ambivalence of wanting and not wanting, of being able and being unable, which lived in his soul like two brothers, at one and the same time twins and deadly enemies.

The Tragic Round

We have often witnessed this same spectacle in outlaws or in historical personages. But in the case of Tiberius his anguish attained the dimensions of tragedy: a dreadful tragedy of sheer horror, such as has never yet been adequately described. He was the emperor of the world; and the whole world meant, to his uneasy spirit, what the cramped space of his cell means to an unhappy prisoner. He went from Capri to Rome and returned to Capri without entering the city, which attracted him and repelled him with one and the same force. 'He circled around Rome,' Tacitus tells us, 'almost always by lonely roads, seeming at once to seek it and to flee from it.'²

Twice he all but managed to touch its immemorial walls with his hands tremulous with terror and old age. On one occasion, on board a trireme, he ascended the Tiber to the naumachy which lay off his gardens; and then, for no known reason, he suddenly turned his back on that city peopled with ghosts and returned to Capri.³ On the other occasion, travelling by land, he got as far as the Appian Way. There he encamped, replied to letters from the consuls, and surveyed the trembling city, crushed by informing and executions.⁴ He sought to overcome his fear and approach it

---

[1] Suetonius, *106, Tib.*, 40. Tacitus, *107*, IV, 67 and 70. These last data, based upon the Senatorial documents of which Tacitus made so much use in compiling his *Annals*, are of unquestionable authenticity.
[2] Tacitus, *107*, VI, 15.
[3] Tacitus, *107*, VI, 1; and Suetonius, *106, Tib.*, 72.
[4] Tacitus, *107*, VI, 39.

more closely. But one morning he found in his own hand the corpse of a snake, a festering feast for ants: a bad omen which meant the hatred of the people towards him; and he returned trembling to his exile.[1] On both occasions, as usual, soldiers drove away the crowds from the banks of the river and the sides of the road. Only from a distance could his silent people catch a glimpse of him and furtively point out to their children the tall, bent figure of the sinister Cæsar.

Rarely has history given us a picture of superhuman anguish such as that of this emperor, prowling like a criminal around the scene of his crimes, without realizing that it was to be found, not in Rome, but in his own lost soul.

There are two sayings of his which depict his infinite spiritual solitude, without anchorage in the past or in the future. Seneca tells us about both of them. On one occasion, someone approached Tiberius and started speaking to him, asking: 'Do you remember, Cæsar? . . .' Tiberius cut him short. 'No,' he replied, sombrely, 'I remember nothing about what I have been.'[2] The other saying was a Greek verse. Tiberius repeated it often. It meant his renunciation of all hope. 'After me, let fire destroy the earth!'[3]

Such was Tiberius.

[1] Suetonius, *106, Tib.*, 72. [2] Seneca, *100*, V, 25.
[3] Seneca, *101*, 5. Dion (*22*, LVIII, 23) tells us that this was Tiberius's favourite saying. Nero repeated it too, perhaps having heard it from Seneca (Suetonius, *106, Nero*, 38).

Epilogue

DEATH OF THE PHŒNIX

THE passion of resentment which I have studied in this book explains the dual personality of Tiberius in the eyes of history, and his final outburst of cruelty, perhaps surpassed by other tyrants, but rarely more odious than in his case. Tiberius was a man of passion. This passion—resentment—was what gave the accent of abnormality to his life, and was the origin of his legend. The legend was deserved, and therefore in itself belongs to history too.

But passion alone does not explain, in all its distressing magnitude, the anguish which issues from his life and from the whole period of his reign. Everything in his time was impregnated with a superhuman uneasiness which hovered in the air of Rome, and of which the emperor was, so to speak, the tragic incarnation.

This magnificent civilization, from which present-day civilization still draws its nourishment, was rotten at its roots; and the confused consciousness of the multitude had a feeling—as perhaps it has today—that material splendour lacked a stable ethical basis. Behind the story of glorious achievements we can catch a glimpse of the fact that the men of that time realized with surprise and anxiety, that something, more important than the political structure of the empire which still stood firm, was going to pieces beneath their feet.

Men's souls were athirst for a fresh fountain; but no one knew where it was to be found. Sometimes a flash foretold the light, still distant. Seneca spoke in accents which seemed to foresee a world of souls new-born. Many men, touched by some strange influence, came to feel that the spirit had immortal rights beyond the all-embracing power of the emperors; that bodily pain might be a glory, poverty a privilege, and death a liberation. But the new doctrine, which gradually filtered into the most inaccessible souls—with that unexpected sensitivity to contagion which marks days when history is about to change course completely—lacked something that no one could define. What it lacked was the statement of something elementary: simply that all men are equal, that all men are brethren.

Behind the omnipotent empire men caught a glimpse of a void. Through the chinks of that Roman system of ethics, which was thought to be an unsurpassable model, began to seep, despite its coating of whitewash, the stench of corruption.

Tacitus, the mouthpiece of this period, and therefore of its distress, tells us that under the consulate of Paulus Fabius and Lucius Vitellius there took place the most extraordinary event of the century. Historians have scarcely considered why this event should have been not a battle but a prodigy. But prodigies are history too, and often they are the correctors of history.

In matchless prose Tacitus relates the story of this prodigy. He tells us that, after a lapse of centuries, the Phœnix had again appeared in Egypt. A profound gravity is to be observed in the passage in which the great historian describes this miraculous bird. It was not like any other bird, either in its shape or in its plumage. It lived for many centuries. When it was about to die, it laid a fertile germ in its nest; and from this germ, without the impure intervention of physical coupling, was born its successor. From its first flutterings this successor was infused with prudence. Its sole care was to honour the glory of its father. Laden with myrrh, it essayed long flights until it was sure of its strength; and then it took the remains of its father upon its back, flew with them through space to the sun, and burnt them on its altar. 'There is much that is uncertain in these stories,' Tacitus ends. 'They are vague stories and augmented with the fabulous; but no one doubts that this bird is sometimes seen in Egypt.'

However, the Phœnix never appeared again after this year, which was precisely the thirty-fourth year after the birth of Christ.

The Phœnix was not, strictly speaking, a fable, but the fabulous form which, in the minds of pre-Christian men, was assumed by their eternal thirst for immortality. About this year, the civilized world felt confusedly that this thirst was so great that it had become a dire distress. The multitude did not know what had happened; but they did not doubt that something miraculous had come to pass. The learned talked about the Phœnix. Tiberius, the sceptic, did not believe in myths. Perhaps, like a distant light in the darkness of his soul, he heard the echo of a supernatural voice, different from the dreary pagan fables; but he did not know whence it came. He had heard talk about Christ, but His name was barely spoken before it was erased from his memory. He was closer to the truth than any other Roman, and he could not see it.

Perhaps, in the course of one of his prowls around Rome, he read carelessly the news sent him by his governor in Judæa that a man who called himself the Son of God had been condemned to death on the Cross. Just one more, the taciturn old man may have thought, of the innumerable crosses which were being erected all over the empire. Close to him, perhaps, still stood those which he had ordered to be erected when, a few years earlier, he put to death the priests of Isis.

Neither Tiberius nor anyone else in Rome realized, until long afterwards, that the Phœnix was dead for ever, but that the Cross of Judæa was immortal.

Appendices

GENEALOGICAL TABLES OF THE IMPERIAL FAMILIES

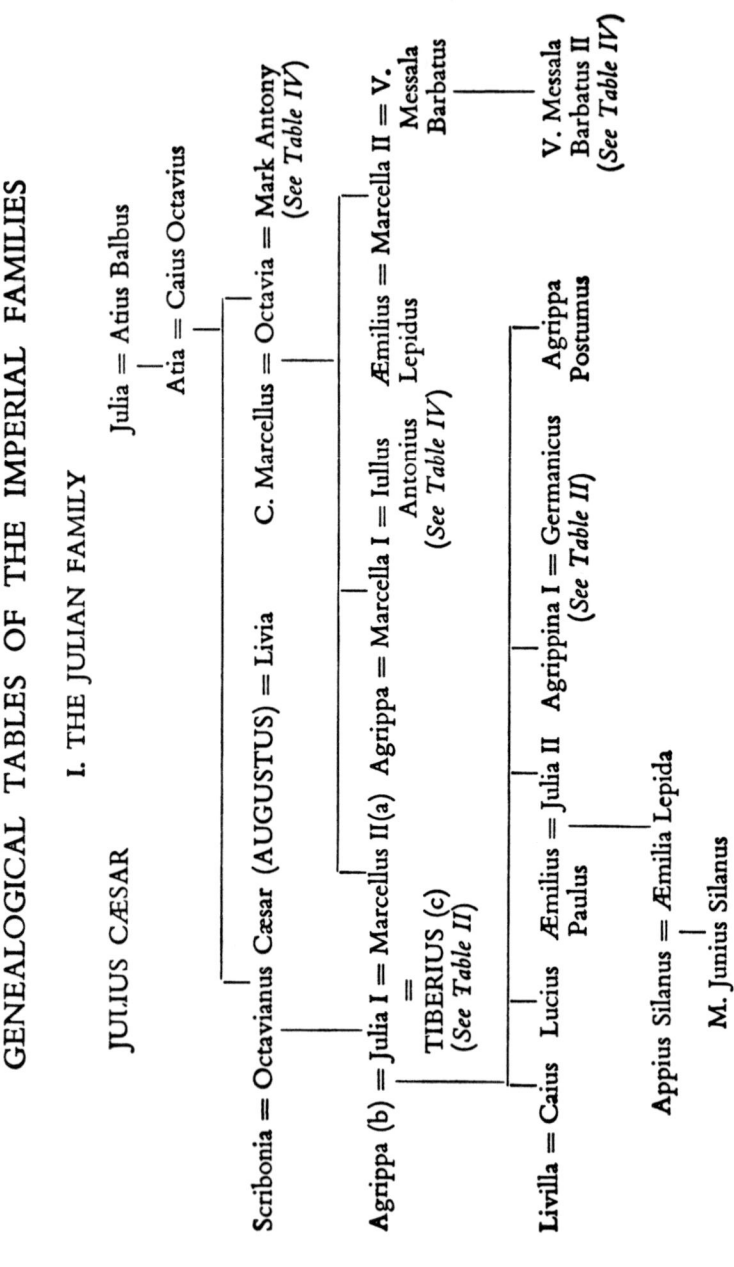

I. THE JULIAN FAMILY

JULIUS CÆSAR

Julia = Atius Balbus
|
Atia = Caius Octavius

C. Marcellus = Octavia = Mark Antony (*See Table IV*)

Scribonia = Octavianus Cæsar (AUGUSTUS) = Livia

Agrippa (b) = Julia I = Marcellus II(a)   Agrippa = Marcella I = Iullus Antonius (*See Table IV*)   Æmilius = Marcella II = V. Messala Barbatus
=
TIBERIUS (c)
(*See Table II*)

V. Messala Barbatus II (*See Table IV*)

Livilla = Caius   Lucius   Æmilius = Julia II   Agrippina I = Germanicus (*See Table II*)   Agrippa Postumus
Paulus

Appius Silanus = Æmilia Lepida
|
M. Junius Silanus

II. THE CLAUDIAN FAMILY

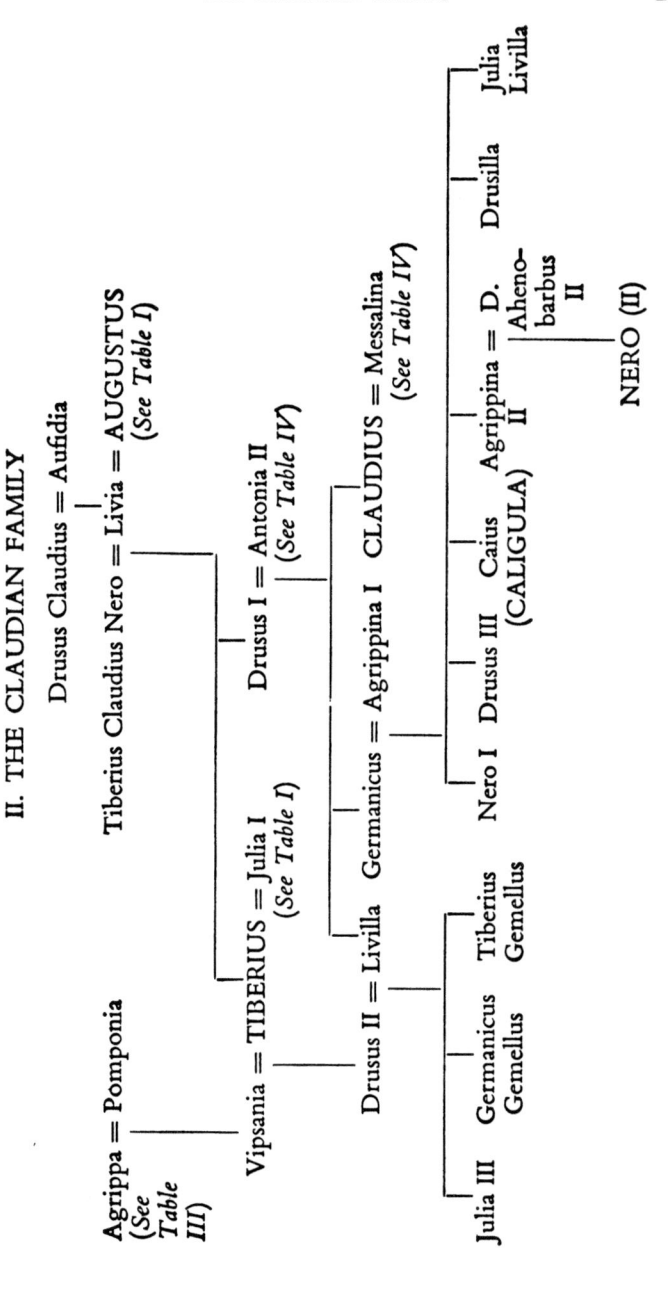

Drusus Claudius = Aufidia
|
Tiberius Claudius Nero = Livia = AUGUSTUS
                                 (See Table I)

Children of Tiberius Claudius Nero and Livia:
- Vipsania = TIBERIUS = Julia I *(See Table I)*
- Drusus I = Antonia II *(See Table IV)*

Agrippa = Pomponia *(See Table III)*

Children of Vipsania and Tiberius:
- Drusus II = Livilla
  - Julia III
  - Germanicus Gemellus
  - Tiberius Gemellus

Children of Drusus I and Antonia II:
- Germanicus = Agrippina I
- CLAUDIUS = Messalina *(See Table IV)*

Children of Germanicus and Agrippina I:
- Nero I
- Drusus III
- Caius (CALIGULA)
- Agrippina II = D. Ahenobarbus II
  - NERO (II)
- Drusilla
- Julia Livilla

III. AGRIPPA

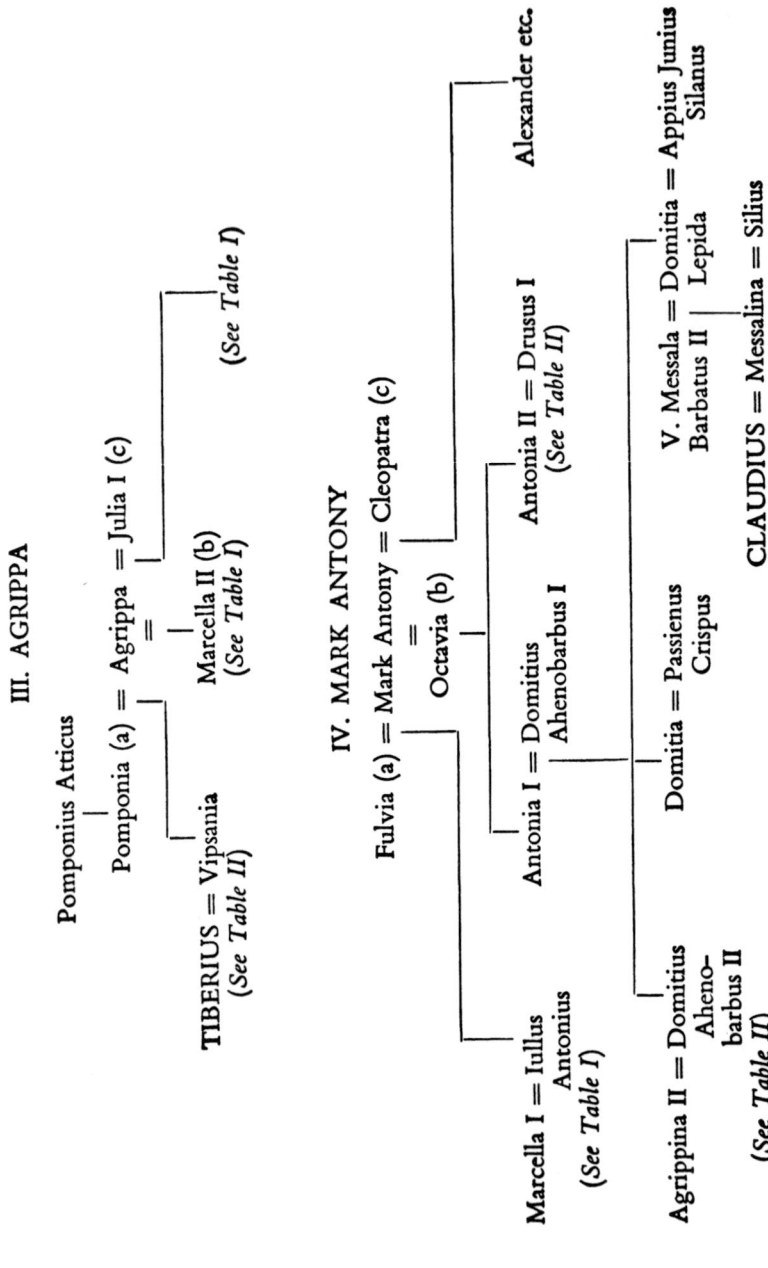

```
                    Pomponius Atticus
                           |
        Pomponia (a) = Agrippa = Julia I (c)
               |           ‖
               |       Marcella II (b)
               |       (See Table I)
               |
               |                              (See Table I)
    TIBERIUS = Vipsania
    (See Table II)
```

IV. MARK ANTONY

```
        Fulvia (a) = Mark Antony = Cleopatra (c)
                          ‖
                      Octavia (b)
    ┌─────────────────────┼──────────────────────┐
 Antonia I = Domitius              Antonia II = Drusus I         Alexander etc.
           Ahenobarbus I                (See Table II)
    ┌──────┴──────┐
 Domitia = Passienus
           Crispus

 Marcella I = Iullus
              Antonius
            (See Table I)

 Agrippina II = Domitius
                Aheno-
                barbus II
              (See Table II)

           V. Messala = Domitia = Appius Junius
                       Barbatus II |   Silanus
                                 Lepida

                CLAUDIUS = Messalina = Silius
```

CHRONOLOGICAL SUMMARY OF TIBERIUS'S LIFE[1]

B.C.
43: Marriage of Tiberius's parents (Claudius Nero and Livia).
42: Birth of Tiberius. First battle of Philippi. Birth of Marcellus II, son of Octavia.
41: Civil war in Italy.
40: Tiberius's parents flee with him from Italy. Marriage of Octavian (Augustus) and Scribonia.
39: Birth of Julia I, daughter of Octavian and Scribonia. Divorce between Octavian and Scribonia.
38: Divorce between Livia and Claudius Nero. Marriage of Livia and Octavian. Birth of Drusus I, son of Livia and Claudius Nero (? or of Octavian).
33: Death of Claudius Nero, father of Tiberius. Tiberius delivers his funeral oration.
31: Battle of Actium.
29: Illness of Octavian. His triumphal entry into Rome.
27: Octavian receives the title of Augustus.
26: Journey of Augustus and Tiberius to Spain.
25: Augustus returns to Rome. Wedding of Marcellus II and Julia I.
24: Illness of Augustus. Tiberius declared of age to receive honours.
23: Relapse of Augustus: he is saved by his doctor, Musa. Death of Marcellus II. Tiberius is appointed quæstor and entrusted with combating the famine in Rome.
21: Journey of Augustus to the east. Marriage of Agrippa and Julia I.
20: Journey of Tiberius to the east: he stops at Rhodes. Birth of Caius, son of Agrippa and Julia I.
19: Tiberius is appointed prætor. Birth of Julia II, daughter of Agrippa and Julia I. Marriage of Tiberius and Vipsania (?). Marriage of Drusus I and Antonia II (?).
16: Journey of Augustus and Tiberius to Gaul and Spain.
15: Campaign of Tiberius and Drusus I in the Central Alps. Birth of Germanicus, son of Drusus I and Antonia II.

[1] These references are mainly to the events related in this book and not, strictly speaking, to formal history.

CHRONOLOGICAL SUMMARY OF TIBERIUS'S LIFE

B.C.

14: Birth of Agrippina I, daughter of Agrippa and Julia I. Birth of Livilla, daughter of Drusus I and Antonia II.

13: Tiberius becomes consul for the first time.

12: Death of Agrippa. Divorce between Tiberius and Vipsania. Birth of Agrippa Postumus, son of Agrippa and Julia I. Marriage of Tiberius and Julia I. Campaign on the Danube by Tiberius and Drusus I.

11: Birth of Drusus II, son of Tiberius and Vipsania. Death of Octavia, sister of Augustus.

10: Birth of stillborn son of Tiberius and Julia I. Birth of Claudius, son of Drusus I and Antonia II.

9: Death of Drusus I. Campaign of Tiberius in Germany (until 6 B.C.).

8: Death of Mæcenas.

7: Tiberius consul for the second time.

6: Tiberius granted tribunician power. He retires to Rhodes.

5: Caius Cæsar becomes consul.

4: Conspiracy of Cornelius Cinna. Marriage of Julia II and Æmilius Paulus.

3: Birth of Æmilia Lepida, daughter of Æmilius Paulus and Julia II.

2: Julia I exiled for adultery.

1: Marriage of Caius Cæsar and Livilla. Expedition of Caius Cæsar to the east.

A.D.

1: Caius continues his journey in the east.

2: Return of Tiberius to Italy. Death of Lucius Cæsar.

3: Tiberius lives in retirement in Rome.

4: Death of Caius Cæsar. Augustus adopts Tiberius and Agrippa Postumus. Tiberius adopts Germanicus. Tiberius appointed tribune for ten years.

5: Tiberius wages war in Germany (until A.D. 9). Marriage of Germanicus and Agrippina I.

6: Famine in Rome. Birth of Nero I, son of Germanicus and Agrippina I.

7: Exile of Agrippa Postumus. Germanicus wages war in Pannonia and Dalmatia.

8: Exile of Julia II for adultery. Exile of Ovid. Birth of Drusus III, son of Germanicus and Agrippina I.

A.D.
9: Rout of Varus in Germany. Tiberius returns to Rome and postpones his triumph on account of Varus's defeat.
10: Tiberius wages war in Germany.
11: Return and triumph of Tiberius. He goes back to Germany (until A.D. 14).
12: Birth of Caius (Caligula), son of Germanicus and Agrippina I.
13: Augustus makes his will.
14: Return of Tiberius on account of Augustus's illness. Death of Augustus. Beginning of Sejanus's power. Tiberius proclaimed emperor in succession to Augustus. Assassination of Agrippa Postumus. Death of Julia I in exile. Mutiny of the legions in Germany and Pannonia. Drusus II and Germanicus quell this mutiny.
15: Further mutiny of the legions. Birth of Agrippina II, daughter of Germanicus and Agrippina I.
16: Death of Scribonia.
17: Return and triumph of Germanicus. Tiberius sends him to the east. Birth of Drusilla, daughter of Germanicus and Agrippina I. Tiberius consul for the third time.
18: Death of Ovid in exile.
19: Death of Germanicus in Syria. Tiberius persecutes foreign religions. Birth of Tiberius Gemellus and Germanicus Gemellus, sons of Drusus II and Livilla.
20: Agrippina arrives in Italy with Germanicus's ashes. Trial and execution of Piso, accused of assassinating Germanicus. Death of Vipsania.
21: Marriage of Nero I and Julia III. Tiberius consul for the fourth time. Rebellion in Gaul.
22: Dissension between Livia and Tiberius.
23: Death of Drusus II. Death of Germanicus Gemellus. Death of Lucilius Longus, friend of Tiberius.
24: Trial of Silius, whose wife was a friend of Agrippina I.
25: Sejanus asks Tiberius for Livilla's hand in marriage. Tiberius refuses consecration to him of a temple in Spain.
26: Tiberius retires to the Campagna and Capri. Rupture between Tiberius and Agrippina I.
27: Earthquake at Fidenoe and Monte Celio: Tiberius's generosity. Sabinus's plot in favour of Nero I.
28: Death of Julia II in exile. Marriage of Agrippina II and Domitius Ahenobarbus II.

A.D.
29: Death of Livia. Exile of Agrippina I and Nero I.
30: Trial of Asinius Gallus. Sejanus is appointed consul for A.D. 31.
31: Dismissal and execution of Sejanus. Apicata, Sejanus's widow, commits suicide and denounces Sejanus and Livia as Drusus II's assassins. Death of Livilla. Death of Nero I in exile.
32: Persecution and trial of Sejanus's friends.
33: Death of Drusus III by starvation. Marriages of Drusilla and Lucius Cassius, and Julia Livilla and Marcus Vinicius. Marriage of Caligula and Claudia. Death of Asinius Gallus.
34: Tiberius roams around Rome. Reported appearance of the Phœnix in Egypt.
35: Tiberius makes his will, naming Caligula and Tiberius Gemellus as his successors.
36: Suicide of Æmilia Lepida, accused of adultery. Reign of Terror. Tiberius again roams around Rome.
37: Illness and death of Tiberius.

BIBLIOGRAPHY

1. ÁLAMOS DE BARRIENTOS, *Tácito Español*; Madrid, 1614.
2. ALAMBERT, *Tacite. Morceaux Choisis*; Paris, 1784.
3. AMELOTE DE LA HOUSSAY, *Tibère. Discours politiques sur Tacite*; Amsterdam, 1683.
4. AMELOTE DE LA HOUSSAY, *La morale de Tacite. De la flaterie*; Paris, 1686.
5. AMELOTE DE LA HOUSSAY, *Tacite; avec des notes politiques et historiques*; Paris, 1690.
6. BABELON, *Tibère à Port-Mahon*; 'Anuario del Cuerpo Facultativo de Archiveros y Bibliotecarios,' Madrid, 1834, 2.
7. BACHA, *La gènie de Tacite*; Paris, 1906.
8. BAKER, *Tiberius Cæsar*; New York, 1928.
9. BARBAGALLO, *Tiberio*; Rome, 1922.
10. BARING-GOULD, *The Tragedy of the Cæsars*; London, 1892.
11. BEESLEY, *Catalina, Claudius and Tiberius*; London, 1878.
12. BERNOUILLI, *Römische Ikonographie*; Stuttgart, 1882.
13. BEYER G. GERH, *Römer in Germanien: Feldzüge römischer Heerführer z. Zeit. d. Augustus und Tiberius Kaiser Waren*; Schöning, 1935.
14. BOISSIER, *Tacite*; Paris, 1903.
15. BUCHAN, *Augustus*; London, 1937.
16. BUDÉ, *De l'institution du Prince*; Paris, 1547.
17. CIACERI, *Tiberio, Succesore di Augusto*; Milan, 1937.
18. COLUMBIA, *L'Impero Romano dal 44 a. C. al 395 d. C.*; Milan, 1906.
19. DEDERICH, *Die Feldzüge der Drusus und Tiberius*; Cologne, 1889.
20. DESSAU, *Geschichte der römischen Kaiserzeit*; Berlin, 1924-1930.
21. DI MARTINO FUSCO, *Tiberio a Capri seconde la tradizione storica*; 'Il Retaglio,' 1834, XIX, 1, 2.
22. DION CASSIUS, *History of Rome*.
23. DORATO, *Tiberio è la pretese orgia di Capri*; 'Il Messagero,' 7th October 1937.
24. DURUY, *Histoire des Romains*; Paris, 1879-1885.
25. FABIA, *Les sources de Tacite dans les histoires et les annales*; Paris, 1893.
26. FABIA, *L'événement officiel de Tibère*; 'Revue de Philologie,' 1909, 33, 28.
27. FERRERO, *Les femmes des Césares*; Paris, 1930.
28. FERRERO, *Nouvelle Histoire Romaine*; Paris, 1936.
29. PHILO, *Of Virtue*.
30. PHILO, *Caius's Embassy*.
31. FREITAG, *Tiberius und Tacitus*; Berlin, 1870.

BIBLIOGRAPHY

32. GARDTHAUSEN, *Augustus*; Leipzig, 1891–1904.
33. GENTILE, *Tiberio e la moderne critica storica*; Milan, 1885.
34. GERBER UND GREEF, *Lexicon Taciteum*; Leipzig, 1903.
35. GRAF, *Roma nella memoria e nella imaginazione del medioevo*; Turin, 1923.
36. GRAVES, *Claudius the God*; London, 1935.
37. GRAVES, *I, Claudius*; London, 1935.
38. GREGOROVIUS, *Wanderjhare in Italien*, I. Bd., *Figuren, Geschichte, Leeben und Scenaria aus Italia*; 4th Ed., Leipzig, 1874.
39. HENTING, *Über den Cesarenwahnsinnen, die Krankheit des Kaisers Tiberius*; Munich, 1934.
40. HOCHART, *De l'authenticité des annales et des histoires de Tacite*; Paris, 1890.
41. HOCHART, *Nouvelles considérations au sujet des annales et des histoires de Tacite*; Paris, 1894.
42. HOHL, *Wan hat Tiberius des Prinzipat übernommen*; 'Hermes,' 1933, LXVIII, 106.
43. HOMO, *Le Haut Empire*; Paris, 1933.
44. HOMO, *Auguste*; Paris, 1935.
45. HORACE, *Odes*.
46. IHNE, *Plea for the Emperor Tiberius*; Liverpool, 1875.
47. JOSEPHUS, *Jewish Antiquities*.
48. JULIAN THE APOSTATE, *Les Césares invités à la table des dieux*. French ed., de Lange. Paris, 1682.
49. JUVENAL, *Satires*.
50. KESSLER, *Die Tradition über Germanicus*; Berlin, 1905.
51. LA BLETERIE, *Traductions de quelques ouvrages de Tacite*; Paris, 1755.
52. LA BLETERIE, *Tibère ou les six premiers livres des annales de Tacite*; Paris, 1768.
53. LA HARPE, *Reflexions sur Tibère*; in his edition of *Les Douze Cèsares*; Paris, 1770.
54. LANG, *Beiträge zur Geschichte des Kaisers Tiberius*; Jena, 1911.
55. LEWIN, *Die Gifte in der Weltgeschichte*; Berlin, 1920.
56. LINGUET, *Histoire des Revolutions de l'Empire Romain*; Paris, 1766.
57. LINGUET, *Lettres sur la nouvelle traduction de Tacite*; Paris, 1768.
58. LIPSE (JUSTE), *Justi Lipsii Ad. Annales Corn. Taciti liber commentarius sive notae*; 1581.
59. MAES, *La Nave de Tiberio*; Rome, 1895.
60. MAIURI, *Breviario di Capri*; Naples, 1937.
61. MALCOVATI, *Imperatoris Cæsaris Augusti Operum fragmenta. Corpus Scriptorum Latinorum*. Paravianum No. 38; Turin, 1921.
62. MARAÑÓN, *La Evolución de la Sexualidad*; Madrid, 1930. Latest edition: *L'Evoluzione della Sessualità e gli stati intersessuali*; Bologna, 1934.
63. MARAÑÓN, *Amiel*; Paris, 1938.
64. MARAÑÓN, *Ginecología Endocrina*; Madrid, 1935.

65. MARAÑÓN, *El Conde-Duque de Olivares*. (*La Pasión de mandar*); Madrid, 1936.
66. MARAÑÓN, *Crónica y Gesto de la Libertad*; Buenos Ayres, 1938.
67. MARAÑÓN, *Vida e Historia*; Buenos Ayres, 1937.
68. MARTIAL, *Epigrams*.
69. MARSH, *The Reign of Tiberius*; Oxford, 1931.
70. MARX, *Des Tacitus Totengericht über Tiberius*; 'Humanist Gymnes,' 1933, XLIV, 73.
71. MERIVALE, *History of the Romans under the Empire*; London, 1865.
72. MOMMSEN, *Histoire des Romains*; French ed.; Paris, 1887.
73. MONTESQUIEU, *Œuvres Complètes*; Paris, 1888.
74. MUNTHE, *Le Livre de San Michel*; French ed.; Paris, 1935.
75. OVID, *Amores*.
76. OVID, *Tristes*.
77. OVID, *Consolation for Livia Augusta*.
78. PELLEGRINO, *In Difesa di Tiberio*; Padua, 1933.
PHILO, see Nos 29 and 30.
79. PLINY THE ELDER, *Natural History*.
80. PLINY THE YOUNGER, *Epistles*.
81. PLUTARCH, *Parallel Lives*.
82. RAMSAY, *The Annals of Tacitus*; London, 1904-1909.
83. REINACH, *Cultes, Mythes et Réligions, III*, 16; Paris, 1913.
84. REINACH, *Une Séance du Senat Romain sous Tibère*; 'Rev. Historique,' 1929, CLXII, 95.
85. RIVIÈRE, *Leggende e verita intorno a Tiberio*; 'Lavoro Fascista,' 15th July 1934.
86. RYCKIUS, *Theodori Rykii ad Cornel. Tacitum animadversiones*; Lugd. Batav., 1686.
87. ROSTOVTZEFF, *L'Empereur Tibère et le culte imperial*; 'Rev. Hist.' 1930, CLXIII, 1.
88. SAAVEDRA FAJARDO, *Empresas Politicas*.
89. SÁNCHEZ CANTÓN, *Correo erudito*; Madrid, 1940, 1.
90. SCHAEFER, *Tiberius und seine Zeit im Lichte der Tradition des Velleius Paterculus*; Inaug. Dissert.; Halle, 1912
91, 92. SCHILER, *Geschichte der römischen Kaiserzeit*; Gotha, 1883.
93. SCHOTT, *Die Kriminaljustiz unter dem Kaiser Tiberius*; Erlangen, 1883.
94. SANDELS, *Die Stellung der Kaiserlichen Frauen aus dem julisclaudischen Hause*; Darmstadt, 1912.
95. SENECA, *Fantasia on the death of Claudius*.
96. SENECA, *Constancy*.
97. SENECA, *Peace of mind*.
98. SENECA, *Consolation to Marcia*.
99. SENECA, *Consolation to Helvia*.

100. SENECA, *Beneficence.*
101. SENECA, *Clemency.*
102. SENECA, *Epistles.*
103. SIEVERS, *Tiberius und Tacitus*; Hamburg, 1850–1851.
104. SIEVERS, *Studien zur Geschichte der römischen Kaiser*; Berlin, 1870.
105. THAR, *Tiberius: Leben, Regierung, Charakter*; 2nd Ed., Berlin, 1873.
106. SUETONIUS, *The Twelve Cæsars.*
107. TACITUS, *Annals.*
108. TARVER, *Tiberius the Tyrant*; Westminster, 1902. French ed., *Tibère*; Paris, 1939.
109. THOMAS, *La critique de Tacite*; Paris, 1903.
110. TOFFANI, *Machiavelli e il Tacitismo*; Padua, 1921.
111. TUXEN, *Kaiser Tiberius*; Kobenhaun, 1896.
112. UGOLIN, *Rittrato di Tiberio trovato nella Villa Romana di Malta*; 'Bol. Comm. Archeol. Roma. Mus. Imp.' 1931, II, 21.
113. VALORI, *Tiberio*, 'Corriere della Sera,' 5th May 1935.
114. VELLEIUS PATERCULUS, *History of Rome.*
115. VIERTEL, *Tiberius und Germanicus: Eine historische Studie*; Göttingen, 1901.
116. VIRGIL, *Eclogues.*
117. VOLTAIRE, *Œuvres Complètes.* Edit. Condorcet, Paris, 1785–89.
118. WEICHARDT, *Le Palais de Tibère et autres edifices romains à Capri.* French ed., undated.
119. WEIGALL, *Nero*; French ed., Paris, 1931.
120. WILLENBÜCHER, *Tiberius und die Verschwörung des Sejan*; Gutersloh, 1896.
121. WILLRICH, *Livia*; Leipzig, 1911.

Printed in the United States
116813LV00003B/262/A